CONSPIRACY

CONSPIRACY

Why the
Rational
Believe the
Irrational

Michael Shermer

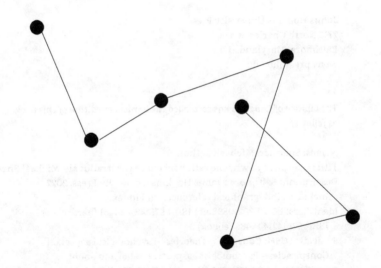

Johns Hopkins University Press | BALTIMORE

Johns Hopkins Paperback edition, 2024
9   8   7   6   5   4   3   2   1

Johns Hopkins University Press
2715 North Charles Street
Baltimore, Maryland 21218
www.press.jhu.edu

The Library of Congress has cataloged the hardcover edition of this book
as follows:

Names: Shermer, Michael, author.
Title: Conspiracy : why the rational believe the irrational / Michael Shermer.
Description: Baltimore : Johns Hopkins University Press, 2022. |
    Includes bibliographical references and index.
Identifiers: LCCN 2021053808 | ISBN 9781421444451 (hardcover) |
    ISBN 9781421444468 (ebook)
Subjects: LCSH: Conspiracy theories—Psychological aspects. |
    Conspiracies—Psychological aspects. | Belief and doubt.
Classification: LCC HV6275 .S54 2022 | DDC 001.9/8—dc23/eng/20220621
LC record available at https://lccn.loc.gov/2021053808

A catalog record for this book is available from the British Library.

ISBN 978-1-4214-4907-4 (paperback)

Special discounts are available for bulk purchases of this book. For more
information, please contact Special Sales at specialsales@jh.edu.

To Pat Linse

Cofounder of the Skeptics Society and *Skeptic* magazine, colleague, confidant, and friend, who embodied the maxim and mission of the Skeptics Society, adopted from the seventeenth-century Dutch philosopher Baruch Spinoza:

> "I have made a ceaseless effort
> not to ridicule,
> not to bewail,
> not to scorn human actions,
> but to understand them."

To understand is not to forgive. We can see why humans steer their reasoning toward conclusions that work to the advantage of themselves or their sects, and why they distinguish a reality in which ideas are true or false from a mythology in which ideas are entertaining or inspirational, without conceding that these are good things. They are not good things. Reality is that which, when you apply motivated or myside or mythological reasoning to it, does not go away. False beliefs about vaccines, public health measures, and climate change threaten the well-being of billions. Conspiracy theories incite terrorism, pogroms, wars, and genocide. A corrosion of standards of truth undermines democracy and clears the ground for tyranny. But for all the vulnerabilities of human reason, our picture of the future need not be a bot tweeting fake news forever. The arc of knowledge is a long one, and it bends toward rationality.

Steven Pinker, *Rationality: What It Is, Why It Seems Scarce, Why It Matters*, 2021

• Contents

• Apologia

My primary approach in this book is integrative in nature—that is, amalgamating research from multiple lines of inquiry into a readable, coherent narrative for both professional researchers and general readers, with the aim of solving a single problem—namely, *why people believe conspiracy theories, which ones are real, and what to do about them.* My model for this approach is what has come to be known as Third Culture books,[1] inspired by British scientist and novelist C. P. Snow's call for a third culture between the "two cultures" of science and the humanities (from his famous 1962 essay "The Two Cultures")[2] one that integrates ideas from all domains of knowledge—a consilience, or unity, of knowledge, in the phrasing of evolutionary biologist E. O. Wilson in his Third Culture book, *Consilience.*[3]

Other type specimens—determiners of the characteristics of a group—in the Third Culture genre include Jared Diamond's *Guns, Germs, and Steel,* a Pulitzer Prize–winning work that is a highly original assimilation of research from multiple fields, with the aim of solving one problem: why civilizations developed at different rates around the world over the past 13,000 years.[4] Another is Richard Dawkins's *The Selfish Gene*—which unified the research of evolutionary theorists Robert Trivers, William Hamilton, John Maynard Smith, and others into an consolidative whole—written for professionals and the public alike, in such style that it is considered not only a classic in science, but also a masterpiece of literature.[5] A third is Steven Pinker's *The Better Angels of Our Nature,* which also provides a model for how to deal with a complex human and social problem for which no single theory can possibly account.[6] Pinker detailed six historical trends, five historical forces, five inner demons, and four better angels as causal and interacting vectors to account for the decline of violence. Like Charles Darwin's *On the Origin of Species*, the above books are not popular versions of scholarly works. Instead, they are the only editions available, which can be read by everyone from professional scientists and scholars to airline passengers who pick up copies at an airport bookstall.

In trying to understand conspiracy theories and why people believe them, many different cognitive, social, political, economic, cultural, and historical factors are involved, so any explanation is necessarily going to be complex and possibly overdetermined. The prologue that follows outlines this volume in more detail, but allow me to briefly sketch my theoretical model of three overarching factors at work. They demonstrate why people believe conspiracy theories, with an aim toward illuminating what I am calling the conspiracy effect: *why smart people believe blatantly wrong things for apparently rational reasons*:

1. *Proxy conspiracism.* Many conspiracy theories are proxies for a different type of conspiracist truth—a deeper mythic, psychological, or lived-experience truth. As such, the details and verisimilitude of particular conspiracy theories are less important than the richer truths represented therein, which often contain self-identifying, existential, and moral meanings, frequently involving power—both for the conspiracist and for the perceived conspirators.
2. *Tribal conspiracism.* Many conspiracy theories harbor elements of other beliefs, dogmas, and adjacent or preceding conspiracy theories long believed and held as core elements of political, religious, social, or

tribal identity. As such, current conspiracy theories, like proxy truths, may serve as stand-ins for earlier ones having deep roots in history. This accounts for the cross-pollination of conspiracy theories and the propensity for people who believe in one to believe in many. An endorsement of these theories serves as a social signal of loyalty to the tribe that embraces them as part of that group's identity.

3. *Constructive conspiracism.* The assumption by most researchers of and commentators on conspiracy theories is that they represent false beliefs, which is why the term has become a pejorative descriptor. This is a mistake, because, historically speaking, enough of these theories represent actual conspiracies. Therefore, it pays to err on the side of belief, rather than disbelief, just in case. With a lot at stake, especially one's identity, livelihood, or even life—which was the case during the Paleolithic environment in which we evolved our conspiratorial cognition—it is often better to assume that a conspiracy theory is real when it is not (a false positive), instead of believing it is not real when it is (a false negative). The former just makes you paranoid, whereas the latter can make you dead.

Thus there is a mismatch between the rational conspiracism of our evolutionary ancestry and the modern world, filled as the latter is with a myriad of conspiracy theories so widespread and diverse that discerning truth from falsehood can be exceedingly difficult. To this end, I make a distinction between *paranoid conspiracy theories*, involving ultra-secret and über-powerful entities, for which there is little to no evidence and which are largely driven by paranoia, and *realistic conspiracy theories*, pertaining to normal political institutions and corporate entities that are conspiring to manipulate the system to gain an unfair, immoral, and sometimes illegal advantage over others. Because both history and current events are brimming with real conspiracies, I contend that conspiracism is a rational response to a dangerous world. Thus, in the common computer analog, it is a feature of—not a bug in—human cognition. The "apparently rational reasons" in my definition of the conspiracy effect are doing a lot of work. We will explore those reasons in depth in this book.

Layered on top of these three overarching factors are a number of additional psychological and sociological forces at work in reinforcing a belief in conspiracy theories. They include *motivated reasoning, cognitive dissonance, teleological thinking, transcendental thinking, locus of control, anxiety reduction, confirmation bias, attribution bias, hindsight bias, "myside" bias, oversimplification of complex problems, patternicity, agenticity,* and more. Think of these as proximate (or immediate) causes that reinforce conspiratorial beliefs already held, due to ultimate (or deeper) causal reasons, such as those overarching factors outlined above.

Finally, because so many conspiracy theories represent *real* conspiracies, the second part of the book is largely focused on determining their truth or falsity. As such, my more objective scholarly voice in the first half of the volume will be layered with that of my day job as head of an organization (the Skeptics Society) and publisher of a magazine (*Skeptic*) tasked with opining on the verisimilitude of the claims people make. That is, I am going to posit that there is a way to determine the "truth value" of most conspiracy theories, and I will offer my opinion on many of the most popular ones found both in history and today. My approach in this book, as it has been in most of my writing, is that of Charles Darwin, from a comment he made in a letter to a friend who had just informed him that critics had accused him of being too theoretical in his revolutionary 1859 book,

On the Origin of Species, and that he should have just "put his facts before us and let them rest." Darwin replied:

> About thirty years ago there was much talk that geologists ought only to observe and not theorize; and I well remember someone saying that at this rate a man might as well go into a gravel-pit and count the pebbles and describe the colours. How odd it is that anyone should not see that all observation must be for or against some view if it is to be of any service![7]

I call the final clause of this observation Darwin's Dictum,[8] and it bears repeating: *all observation must be for or against some view if it is to be of any service.*

CONSPIRACY

The Conspiracy Effect

Why Smart People Believe Blatantly Wrong Things
for Apparently Rational Reasons

"Have you ever wondered why we go to war? Or why you never
seem to be able to get out of debt? Why there is poverty, division,
and crime? What if I told you there was a reason for it all? What if I
told you it was done on purpose?"

Yes, as a matter of fact, I have wondered about such problems as war, poverty, divisiveness, and crime, as any thoughtful person might. There are entire fields composed of social scientists, historians, and policy analysts who study such problems and have constructed elaborate models with multi-factor analysis and regression equations to explain which of many causal vectors lead to armed conflict, crime and violence, poverty and debt, and political divisiveness. Each of these problems has sizable communities of experts—conducting thousands of studies published in hundreds of scholarly journals and books—to try to answer such important fundamental questions, which are vital for a functioning society to solve.

But what if, as conspiracists often believe, these conditions, and many more, are the result of a single factor that can be rooted out by the right person? That is the belief the author of the words in the epigram, a QAnon conspiracist nicknamed "Joe M." In his book on QAnon, *The Storm Is Upon Us*, investigative journalist Mike Rothschild describes it as "a cult, a popular movement, a puzzle, a community, a way to fight back against evil, a new religion, a wedge between countless loved ones, a domestic terrorism threat, and more than anything, a conspiracy theory of everything."[1] Joe M has one of the largest followings of any Q influencer on social media, and in a breathless "Plan to Save the World" video, he introduced viewers to the most seductive and dangerous conspiracy theory in years. According to Rothschild, "the 'Plan to Save the World' video that starts with that quote has been cited by a number of believers as their awakening to QAnon. Joe M was the Q guru behind the Grass Valley Charter School incident I wrote about in the book and had major pull in that world."[2]

QAnon followers and rigged-election conspiracists had gathered on the morning of January 6, 2021, to hear the man they believe is their unofficial leader, none other than then-president Donald J. Trump, who they thought would direct an apocalyptic event called "The Storm" to cleanse the world of the unspeakable evil of a Deep State, satanic, sex-trafficking cult, after which they and their followers would usher in utopia.[3] What does it feel like to be in possession of such secret knowledge? Here is how another QAnon YouTuber expressed it: "I'm excited. I'm happy! Once you know the information you are not in fear; you're, like, empowered! You are excited. You can't wait for justice to go down, you can't wait for the kids to be saved, you can't wait for the bad guys to be put in jail."[4]

These expressions of enthusiastic belief hint at one explanation for why people believe conspiracy theories: they provide all-encompassing explanations for myriad social problems. In a larger sense, the appeal of QAnon, which reduces complex problems like war, poverty, and crime to a single group of evildoers, is as old as conspiracism itself and includes such alleged cabals as the Bilderberger Group, the Council on Foreign Relations, the Freemasons, the Illuminati, the Knights Templar, the New World Order, the Priory of Zion, the Rothschilds, the Rockefellers, the Trilateral Commission, the British royals, and the Zionist Occupation Government taking orders from the Learned Elders of Zion.

The media and academia have long treated conspiracy theories as fringe beliefs, tantamount to UFOs, ESP, and other popular delusions of mad crowds. But conspiracism has been part of the fabric of society for centuries and, as I shall argue, is built into our nature as an evolved adaptation to detect external threats that take on the form of dangerous coalitions. When I saw the video of a middle-aged man walking across the rotunda in the Capitol Building dome on January 6, 2021, proudly waving a large Confederate flag, denoting the losing side in the Civil War—which was fought to end slavery—and representing bigotry and hate, I could not help but wonder, what was he thinking? He was later identified as Kevin Seefried. He was ultimately indicted on charges related to obstruction, entrance onto restricted property, and disorderly conduct, as was his son, who accompanied him. Kevin explained that he brought the flag from his home, where it was proudly displayed.[5] What went wrong with this man's beliefs? How can we reach him and the millions like him who embrace such conspiracies?

I was initially struck dumb that people who self-identify as conservative and Republican, and who claim to believe in law and order and the US Constitution, would take up arms against the very institutions that represent them and their beliefs. But then certain aspects about the nature of belief that I had been working on shed some light on this mystery of mysteries—what I am calling the *conspiracy effect*, or why smart people believe blatantly wrong things for apparently rational reasons. What are those, and what is the psychology behind them that leads otherwise rational people to think and behave so irrationally? As a preview of what is to come in the rest of this book, let's examine these factors in a little more detail, so we have a working theoretical model to hold the disparate factors together, using the QAnon conspiracy theory as a test case.

• - - • - - •

The QAnon conspiracy theory appears to have begun with an internet user called "Q Clearance Patriot," or "Q," who posted on internet message boards like 4chan and 8chan the evidence-free theory that inside the "Deep State" there is an "anonymous" source working against the Trump administration. "I can hint and point but cannot give too many highly classified data points," one Q conspiracist wrote, adding, "These are crumbs and you cannot imagine the full and complete picture."[6] As Mike Rothschild elaborated for me:

> The "I can hint . . ." and "these are crumbs . . ." quotes are directly from Q drops, which have become the scripture of a religion with Q and Trump at the top, and a layer of disciples who "interpret" the drops just below them. They were the early marching orders of a movement that's become enmeshed in American politics—all supposedly "leaked" by a military intelligence team using a rickety message board full of racism and pornography. They're also from right at the start of Q, when it was finding its footing and pulling in early evangelists.[7]

The "Qincidences" (spelled with a Q) include the recurrence of certain numbers, such as 17 (Q is the 17th letter) and 4, 10, and 20, corresponding to DJT, or Donald J. Trump. There are no coincidences in the mind of the conspiracist.

Another conspiratorial thread was the absurd 2016 "Qonspiracy theory" (also spelled with a Q) of "Pizzagate."[8] Promulgators of this version of the conspiracy theory asserted—without any evidence and utterly beyond rational belief—that a Hillary Clinton–led pedophilia ring was operating out of the basement of the Comet Ping Pong pizzeria in Washington, DC. Does anyone really believe this? One man did—Edgar Welch—and he had the courage of his convictions to go there with an AR-15-style rifle to break up the perceived perversion. "I can't let you grow up in a world that's so corrupt by evil," he told his two young daughters as he tucked them into bed before setting out on his crusade, "without at least standing up for you and for other children just like you."[9] Imagine Welch's surprise to discover that Comet Ping Pong doesn't have a basement, much less a satanic cult operating within it. As he told the judge in his case, "I came to DC with the intent of helping people I believed were in dire need of assistance. It was never my intention to harm or frighten innocent lives, but I realize now just how foolish and reckless my decision was." It was fortunate no one was hurt in that incident, but others were not so lucky, as we saw elsewhere with the storming of the US Capitol Building, which left four dead and many injured.

How blatantly wrong is the QAnon conspiracy theory? In the words of physicist Wolfgang Pauli, who was known for colorfully critiquing careless thinking and far-out theories, "it's not even wrong," because it cannot be proven wrong.

Consider again what is being proposed here. QAnon conspiracists contend that Hillary Clinton, Barack Obama, Beyoncé, Lady Gaga, Tom Hanks, and others are involved in a global satanic sex cult and pedophile ring operating out of a pizzeria. In my three decades of studying and debunking all manner of fringe beliefs and weird things, never did I imagine that such marginal convictions would find their way into the center of political power in the United States of America in the twenty-first century. But we saw it happen in Congress, as well as in the forces of the US military, where ranking members of the House of Representatives— and soldiers with guns—were proclaiming not only that the 2020 election was rigged and fraudulent, but that Sandy Hook was a false-flag operation, that the Clintons had John F. Kennedy Jr. murdered, that the 9/11 attack was an inside job by the George W. Bush administration, and that the Pentagon was hit by a cruise missile, not an airliner, on September 11, 2001.

The lunacy behind such illogicality is not a twenty-something, unemployed, tinfoil hat–wearing wingnut blogging from his parents' basement, but that of political figures like Congresswoman Marjorie Taylor Greene, elected by the people of Georgia to represent them. Greene's response to her conspiratorial skeptics was as defiant as it was revealing: "Every attack. Every lie. Every smear strengthens my base of support at home and across the country because people know the truth and are fed up with the lies."[10] The initial response from her Republican colleagues—who were called on by Democrats to censure Greene—was to refuse to do so. And Greene's rejoinder to those in her party who dared to consider censuring her was as combative as it was defensive: "The real cancer for the Republican Party is weak Republicans who only know how to lose gracefully," adding that she would "never back down."

That Greene ultimately did back down after she was removed from congressional committees of responsibility does not gainsay the fact that she was but one of 147 Republicans who voted in favor of objections to the results of the 2020 election, based on the QAnon-adjacent conspiracy theory that rigged ballot machines flipped votes from Republican to Democrat in the presidential race,[11] but, apparently, failed to do so for the 15 Democratic seats nabbed by the GOP.[12]

If observers thought the January 20, 2021, inauguration of Joe Biden as the forty-sixth president of the United States would put an end to such conspiratorial inanity, when winter morphed into spring and summer, conspiracy-fueled headline stories still appeared regularly in the media, while families were torn apart when one member embraced QAnon, to the consternation of the rest. For example, one woman recounted how conspiracism led directly to the dissolution of her marriage, starting with 9/11 conspiracy theories, "especially the videos that claimed it was a setup, and that the towers and buildings nearby were purposely demolished."[13] From there, her husband started listening to Alex Jones's conspiracy-mongering "Infowars" internet radio show and went down the rabbit hole. "He believed the numerous school shootings and the Boston [Marathon] bombing were faked, pulled off by crisis actors," she recalled. By the time her spouse embraced QAnon on the 4chan web community, their marriage was unraveling. "I was coming home from work and I was so stressed when I was walking in the door that I didn't want to be there, and I'd linger at work longer, just so I could have some peace and not have to go home. Just something to get my head together again, so I can go home and be like, 'OK, I'm strong. I can face this.'" Ultimately, she couldn't face her conspiracist husband's delusions. Her failed marriage reflects the fate of many other families torn asunder by the conspiracy effect, such as that of a survivor of the Parkland school shooting, whose own father became convinced by QAnon that it was all a hoax.[14]

QAnon conspiracism has also infiltrated the world of spiritualism, spreading through yoga, meditation, and various wellness circles that include New Age yogis, energy healers, sound bathers, crystal practitioners, and psychics, all primed for conspiracism by their extreme openness to any and all fringe ideas. The now-famous "QAnon Shaman"—Jake

Angeli—whose face and body paint and horned headgear at the Capitol insurrection gave him his 15 minutes of fame (and a trip to jail), along with ponytailed former police chief Alan Hostetter, both have ties to yoga and spirituality communities that are now splintering along conspiratorial lines. These groups also traffic in anti-vaccination conspiracy theories, such as Bill Gates plotting to depopulate the world through deadly vaccines, the Rothschilds controlling the world's banks, and the coming "storm" when Donald Trump exposes and arrests the global ring of satanic pedophiles. Yoga teacher Laura Schwartz coined an apt descriptor of this movement—"Woo-Anon"—after one of her acquaintances in the yoga community ranted on Instagram that the COVID-19 vaccine contains elements of aborted fetuses. "People aren't taking QAnon as seriously as they should," she said, "given how pervasive it is in these worlds—evangelical Christians, yogis—that otherwise have very little in common. They're creating a world where truth is whatever you feel like it is."[15]

That is the power the conspiracy effect holds over many millions of people, and the problem hasn't gone away with the exit of the forty-fifth president of the United States from office on January 20, 2021. As cognitive dissonance theory predicts, true believers doubled down on their belief, as has happened historically when facts failed to support a conspiracy theory. Although Facebook restricted over 10,000 pages, groups, and Instagram accounts associated with QAnon and US militia groups,[16] deep into 2021, polls suggested that tens of millions of Americans still expressed positions consistent with QAnon. For example, a May 2021 Public Religion Research Institute survey found that around 15 percent of Americans said they believe that "the government, media, and financial worlds in the U.S. are controlled by a group of Satan-worshipping pedophiles who run a global child sex trafficking operation," with Republicans

(23 percent) more likely than independents (14 percent) and Democrats (8 percent) to agree.[17] One in five Americans (20 percent) said they concur with the statement that "there is a storm coming soon that will sweep away the elites in power and restore the rightful leaders," with, again, more Republicans (28 percent) than independents (18 percent) and Democrats (14 percent) so believing.

On June 22, 2021, Trump issued a bizarre rant against "Fake News" and the "Lamestream Media," reminding his base that "I got 75 million votes (the most of any sitting President) despite all of that, together with a very Fraudulent Election." He signed off with "2024 or before!," presumably in reference to the coming "storm" of his return.[18] That same week, at a right-wing rally in Tampa, Florida, QAnon conspiracist speakers repeated lies about COVID-19 and the "rigged" election, capped off with a keynote presentation by unhinged MyPillow CEO Mike Lindell, who promised the gathering that an epic event was coming soon, which would include "cyber guys" plus "senators, governors, legislatures, secretary of states, and every single government official that wants to be there," so that "those Supreme Court justices are going to look at it then, and they're going to go 9-0 that this country was attacked. The election is gonna come down. Donald Trump will be in office by this fall, for sure!"[19]

Again, these are not just the delusional rantings of lone wingnuts. Sizable percentages of people are prepared to accept individual QAnon claims. For example, 18 percent of respondents in one survey agreed that it is "probably or definitely true" that Trump is secretly preparing for a "mass arrest of government officials and celebrities."[20] In another survey, this one conducted by the American Enterprise Institute in February 2021, almost 60 percent of Republicans said they agreed with the statement that "a group of unelected government officials in Washington, DC, referred to as the 'Deep State,' had been working to undermine the

Trump administration," while 30 percent said they believe that "Donald Trump has been secretly fighting a group of child sex traffickers that include prominent Democrats and Hollywood elites."[21] My own survey on the conspiracy beliefs of over 3,000 Americans, undertaken during summer 2021, found that a little over one in four people agreed (slightly, moderately, or strongly) that "the actions of the US government are not determined by elected officials, but by an unelected secret group of business and cultural elites known as the Deep State," with another 25 percent being uncertain (see the coda for more on this survey).

Trump himself equivocates when queried about QAnon. He once described the conspiracists as "people that love our country" and who "like me very much, which I appreciate." At a pre-election televised town hall interview, Trump was asked by the moderator, NBC's Savannah Guthrie, if he would denounce the conspiracy claim that "Democrats are a satanic pedophile ring, and that you are the savior." He refused, so Guthrie pressed the case, asking him to admit that his political opponents aren't devil-worshipping child molesters. Trump's response only fueled QAnoners and their conspiratorial mindset: "I don't know that, and neither do you know that."[22]

Actually, we do know that. So does Trump, and, I suspect, on some level so do his followers. If you sat down one on one with a QAnon/Deep State conspiracy believer or, more poignantly, with an elected official like Ted Cruz, Josh Hawley, or Marjorie Taylor Greene—all of whom have hinted at believing some form of this statement and the rigged-election conspiracy theory—and asked them, point blank, "Do you really believe that there is a satanic cult of pedophiles secretly trafficking children through a Washington, DC, pizzeria, led by Hillary Clinton and Tom Hanks?," I strongly suspect that the answer would be "No," and maybe even "Of course not." A person could be forgiven for thinking that anyone who truly believes this QAnon conspiracy theory is either dumb or delusional, and there is no way that a third of all Republicans can be either. It simply defies common sense and the demographics of the distribution of intelligence. What, then, is going on here?

• - - • - - •

I contend that such beliefs have less to do with a specific conspiracy theory and more to do with general beliefs and truths. Recall the three overarching factors at work to explain why people believe conspiracy theories, which I briefly outlined in the apologia: *proxy conspiracism* (where specific conspiracy theories are often proxies for something else, either another type of truth, perhaps a mythic truth, a historical truth, or a lived-experience truth); *tribal conspiracism* (where conspiracy theories harbor elements of other beliefs, dogmas, and adjacent or preceding conspiracy theories, long believed and held as core elements of, religious, social, political, or ideological tribal identity); and *constructive conspiracism* (where it is often better to assume that a conspiracy theory is real when it is not, rather than to assume it is not real when it is). Let's look at these a little deeper here, as a prelude to the chapter-length analyses to come.

Proxy Conspiracism

Consider the O.J. Simpson murder trial as a type specimen. Anyone who paid attention to the gripping day-by-day testimonies of evidence in that case could not help but conclude that O.J. killed his ex-wife Nicole Brown Simpson and her friend Ronald Goldman. The evidence was so overwhelming that this should have been one of the most straightforward and clear-cut murder cases in history.[23] And yet the jury voted to acquit. Why? The answer, I contend, was that it was because Simpson's defense team floated a convincing conspiracy theory: the police planted the evidence against their client. Even though no such police tampering in this case was ever proven, it was apparent that some (or at least one) of the cops was probably racist and, more importantly, the history of encounters between the African American community in Los Angeles and the L.A.P.D. over the previous half century reveals that a great many cops truly were racist and some really did plant evidence to frame Blacks. One rationale goes something like this: "We know this guy did it, but we may not be able to prove it in court, so let's plant some evidence against him, just in case; otherwise he might go free and offend again."[24]

Thus the O.J. Simpson defense team's conspiracy theory of racist cops planting evidence against their client was a type of mythic or historical or lived-experience truth for enough members of the jury that they acquitted Simpson. As journalist Sam Smith noted in his coverage of the trial and this conspiracy theory defense, "Everything is true except the names, times and places."[25] I strongly suspect the jury—along with most of the African American community—knew that Simpson was guilty, but the "police planted the evidence" conspiracy theory was generally truer than the specific case at hand. In other words, the truth of the deeper *underlying* conspiracy theory trumped the countervailing facts of the obviously false *proximate* conspiracy theory.

People who say they believe such conspiracy theories often haven't carefully thought through the evidence in each case, but instead allow it to stand in for something else that concerns them, such as the power of governments, corporations, and institutions, or, in this case, the police. African Americans don't trust the police. Anti-vaxxers don't trust Big Pharma. Anti-GMOers don't trust big corporations. Anti-nuclear activists don't trust big regulators. John F.

Kennedy assassination conspiracists don't trust big committees, like the Warren Commission. The 9/11 Truthers don't trust big government. And QAnoners don't trust the Deep State. Here, mythic truth overrides empirical truth, and specific conspiracy theories are proxies for larger ones involving power brokers.

Tribal Conspiracism

QAnon is the incarnation of earlier conspiracy theories with deep roots in tribal history, reaching back to the "inside job" conspiracy theory following 9/11 in the 2000s, the "satanic panic" conspiracy theory of the 1990s, the New World Order conspiracy theory of the 1980s, the "false-flag" conspiracy theories of the 1970s and 1960s, the Vatican conspiracy theory of the 1950s, the white nationalism conspiracy theories of the 1930s and 1940s, the "stab-in-the-back" conspiracy theory that Hitler embraced in the 1920s, and the anti-Semitic conspiracy theory of *The Protocols of the Learned Elders of Zion* in the 1900s and 1910s. They even go back centuries, to the "blood libel" conspiracy theory that Jews ritually murdered Christian children and drank their blood, a false belief that led to sporadic pogroms of Europe's Jews. So QAnon is not only a proxy truth, but it also represents earlier conspiracy theories that reflect fears and anxieties of the past.

Publicly stating one's belief in QAnon acts as a social signal to one's fellow tribe members—sometimes called "virtue signaling"—that loyalty to the group supersedes the immediate truth or falsity of the specific conspiracy theory.[26] Here is how I explained it to a *Washington Post* journalist who asked me to help readers understand the pull of such seemingly delusional conspiracy theories as QAnon: "It's tribal loyalty—a statement that I am so loyal that I am willing to signal my belief in this crazy idea. They are doubling down on their beliefs . . . as a way of social signaling that they are devotees of the cause."[27]

Constructive Conspiracism

Our third global factor in understanding why people believe conspiracy theories is that enough of them are true, so it pays to err on the side of belief rather than skepticism. For example, the assassinations of Julius Caesar and Abraham Lincoln indeed were conspiracies, as were Watergate and Iran-Contra. The Pentagon Papers and Wikileaks have revealed many more conspiracies contrived by the US government, and who knows what cabals are forming behind closed doors even as you read these words. Such genuine conspiracies are frequent enough that we tend to believe a great many more theories that are not real. The rigged-election conspiracy theory surrounding the 2020 presidential election did not pan out, but suffice it to note that there have been election irregularities in American history, and rigged elections are not that uncommon throughout the globe. Does anyone think Russia's Vladimir Putin and China's Xi Jinping have been legally reelected for life? Or, for that matter, that three generations of the Kim family have won elections in the oxymoronic Democratic People's Republic of Korea?

Constructive conspiracism derives from a game-theoretic model for why making a *Type I error* in assuming something is real when it is not (a *false positive*) is better than making a *Type II error* in assuming something is not real when it is (a *false negative*). In our evolutionary past, it was better to assume that a rustle in the grass was a dangerous predator when it turned out to be the wind (a Type I, false positive error) than it was to assume the rustle was just the wind when actually was a ravening beast (a Type II, false negative error). The latter could result in you being the predator's next meal. We don't always assume the worst, but if enough information points in the direction of conspiracy, or trusted sources of information assert that a conspiracy is afoot, we're more likely to believe it, just in case—better to be safe than sorry. In several chapters to follow, we will explore the psychology behind constructive conspiracism (particularly the negativity bias and why "bad" is stronger than "good"), along with a reminder of just how many conspiracy theories turned out to be true. A detailed look at some of them reveals how conspiracies actually work in the real world, in contrast to how we think they work in our imaginations.

• - - • - - •

These three overarching causal factors are intended to be ultimate (deep) causes, on top of which are a number of proximate (immediate) psychological and sociological forces that are interwoven throughout the three larger and often overlapping factors, all of which reinforce belief in particular conspiracy theories. These include *motivated reasoning, cognitive dissonance, teleological thinking, transcendental thinking, locus of control, anxiety reduction, confirmation bias, attribution bias, hindsight bias, myside bias, oversimplification of complex problems, patternicity, agenticity,* and more. Personality characteristics and demographic factors can drive conspiracism by operating in conjunction with these larger forces. Moreover, specific variables, along with situational conditions—such as uncertainty, anxiety, and a loss of power or control—further feed the acceptance of conspiracy theories as true. So my approach in this book will be to move from ultimate causes to proximate causes, from underlying factors to immediate causes, from the general to the specific. In so doing I am, in part, countering the common narrative that conspiracists are simply unintelligent, uneducated, and irrational in giving credence to conspiracies. Instead, I argue, many of their conspiratorial beliefs are rational when viewed through these larger factors. In this sense, they may have what political scientist Russell Hardin called a "crippled epistemology" (which Hardin applied to political extremists of all kinds, especially terrorists).[28] They just don't know how to reason about claims and instead use their evolved heuristic of constructive conspiracism to assume the worst, based on limited knowledge— knowledge typically gleaned from other people in an echo chamber of self-reinforcing beliefs. This forms the core of part I of the book.

In part II we will consider how to determine which conspiracy theories are likely to be true, are probably false, or are indeterminate. After building a model for testing the verisimilitude of conspiracy theories, we will look in detail at a number of the most popular ones, including and especially the 9/11 Truthers, the Obama Birthers, and the assassination of John F. Kennedy. This will be followed by an overview of real conspiracies throughout history, most especially those of the twentieth century, and then a deep dive into the deadliest conspiracy in history—the assassination of Archduke Franz Ferdinand of Austria by a cabal of Serbian nationalists, which launched the First World War and resulted in the deaths of tens of millions of people.

Part III presents practical and actionable implications of conspiracy theories in two realms: the personal and the public. I will outline how to talk to conspiracy theorists, using the best tools available for rational and thoughtful conversations, in circumstances ranging from family dinners to formal debates. For example, what should you say at a gathering of colleagues around the water cooler, or a table full of family members at the next holiday dinner, when someone blurts out that global warming is a Chinese hoax, or that Sandy Hook was a false-flag operation, or that Barack Obama wasn't born in the United States, or that Donald Trump will be back in the White House any day now? I have devoted 30 years of my career not only to understanding why people believe weird things (the title of my first book[29]), but also to talking to believers in all domains, with the aim of giving them the tools of skepticism and the ability to think like a scientist.[30]

In the final chapter, we will consider the foundations of truth in our society and ways to reestablish trust in its institutions, which has eroded dramatically in the twenty-first century. As former president Barack Obama noted in a November 15, 2020, interview in The Atlantic, "If we do not have the capacity to distinguish what's true from what's false, then by definition the marketplace of ideas doesn't work. And by definition our democracy doesn't work. We are entering into an epistemological crisis."[31] In an earlier period of political upheaval, political philosopher Hannah Arendt made a similar point in her 1951 book, The Origins of Totalitarianism: "The ideal subject of totalitarian rule is not the convinced Nazi or the convinced communist, but people for whom the distinction between fact and fiction (i.e., the reality of experience) and the distinction between true and false (i.e., the standards of thought) no longer exist."[32]

The problem of today's conspiracism is urgent—arguably more pressing than at any time in our history. We need a model to explain who believes in conspiracy theories, and why; what evolutionary, psychological, social, cultural, political, and economic conditions fuel them; ways to classify and systematize conspiracy theories, in order to tease apart their different causes; and means to determine which conspiracy theories might be true, inasmuch as some do turn out to be so. To that end, you might say that we're all conspiracy theorists now. In what follows, I present an overarching theory of conspiracism, thus enabling us not only to explain the conspiracy effect—why smart people believe blatantly wrong things for apparently rational reasons—but also to undo false conspiracy theories, in order to remediate their deleterious effects on the fabric of trust that binds us together a pluralistic democracy.

PART I

Why People Believe Conspiracy Theories

Conspiracism is a stubborn creed because humans are pattern-seeking animals. Show us a sky full of stars, and we'll arrange them into animals and giant spoons. Show us a world full of random misery, and we'll use the same trick to connect the dots into secret conspiracies. For most of us, our desire to impose an artificial pattern on world events is held in check by our rational sense, which tells us that life often is cruel and unpredictable. Or we find compartmentalized, socially accepted outlets to give expression to our pattern-seeking—such as astrology or mainstream religion. Conspiracism takes root when . . . our pattern-seeking appetite overwhelms these containment mechanisms.

JONATHAN KAY, *Among the Truthers: A Journey through America's Growing Conspiracist Underground*, 2011

CHAPTER 1

Conspiracies and Conspiracy Theories

The Difference in Thinking and the Difference It Makes

On Wednesday, May 16, 2012, I spent several hours on a hot bus, in a neon desert called Las Vegas, with a merry band of British conspiracists during their journey around the southwestern United States in search of UFOs, aliens, Area 51, and government cover-ups, all for a BBC documentary. One woman regaled me with a tale about orange balls of energy hovering around her car on the I-405 Freeway in Los Angeles, which were subsequently chased away by black ops helicopters. A man tasked me to explain the source of a green laser beam that followed him around the British countryside one evening.[1]

Conspiracy theories are a perennial favorite for television producers, because there is always a receptive audience for a wide swath of cabals. For example, a Canadian Broadcasting Company (CBC) documentary I participated in, called *Conspiracy Rising*, featured conspiracy theories behind UFOs, Area 51, 9/11, and the deaths of John F. Kennedy and Princess Diana, presented as though there was a common thread running through all of them. According to the notorious conspiracy monger Alex Jones, also featured in the film, "the military-industrial complex killed John F. Kennedy"; and "I can prove that there's a private banking cartel setting up a world government, because they admit they are"; and "no matter how you look at 9/11, there was no Islamic terrorist connection—the hijackers were clearly US government assets who were set up as patsies, like Lee Harvey Oswald."[2]

Alex Jones has spun countless conspiracy theories like these on his "Infowars" website, as well as in his many appearances on Joe Rogan's wildly popular podcast, with its tens of millions of viewers.[3] To his credit, Joe has also had me on his podcast many times, to present a skeptical perspective on these and other conspiracy theories.[4] Joe has pointedly asked Jones for evidence for such claims, but to date, none have been provided. After Jones promoted the conspiracy theory that the massacre at the Sandy Hook elementary school was a false-flag operation by the Obama administration, in order to pass draconian gun control laws, his deranged followers harassed the broken-hearted parents of those slain children. As a result, Jones was sued by one of them and subsequently defenestrated from YouTube, Twitter, Facebook, Spotify, Instagram, and PayPal.[5] Nevertheless, Jones's conspiracism lives on in the darker regions of the internet, and he apparently now supports himself by hawking dietary supplements on Amazon.[6]

• - - • - - •

One question among many that arose in 2020 about QAnon was, What type of conspiracy theory is it, exactly? Political? Economic? Satanic? Secret society? Answering this question offers us a doorway into the world of classifying conspiracy theories and characterizing their believers. In order to understand, explain, and, where appropriate, counter false conspiracy theories, we need to know what we're talking about. Social scientists call this process an "operational definition"—namely, stating clearly what it is you are studying by defining it precisely and explaining how you would measure it operationally. Let's begin by distinguishing between a *conspiracy* and a *conspiracy theory*.

> A conspiracy is two or more people, or a group, plotting or acting in secret to gain an advantage or harm others immorally or illegally.
> A conspiracy theory is a structured belief about a conspiracy, whether or not it is real.
> A conspiracy theorist, or conspiracist, is someone who holds a conspiracy theory about a possible conspiracy, whether or not it is real.

The scientific literature on conspiracy theories is rich.[7] For example, political scientists Joseph Uscinski and Joseph Parent proposed four elements that must be in place for there to be a conspiracy: (1) "a group, (2) acting in secret, (3) to alter institutions, usurp power, hide truth, or gain utility, (4) at the expense of the common good."[8] Conspiracy researchers Jan-Willem van Prooijen and Mark van Vugt suggested that a conspiracy theory contains at least five critical elements: (1) "an assumption of how people, objects, or events are causally interconnected" into a meaningful pattern; (2) "the plans of alleged conspirators are deliberate" and therefore imply agency; (3) "a coalition, or group, of actors working in conjunction"; (4) "an element of threat"; and (5) "an element of secrecy"—in short, patterns, agency, coalitions, threats, and secrecy.[9]

Whatever elements one includes in one's definition, it is important to distinguish conspiracies themselves from the theories about them. Following my definition of a

conspiracy—two or more people, or a group, plotting or acting in secret to gain an advantage or harm others immorally or illegally—even a Wikipedia-level understanding
of history reveals that conspiracies are common at every
level, in all human communities and societies, throughout history, enough to make constructive conspiracism (i.e.,
better to assume that a conspiracy theory is real when it is
not, rather than to assume it is not real when it is) an adaptive feature in human cognition. But the theories about
conspiracies—and which ones are probably true, most likely
false, or indeterminate—is a separate matter from the conspiracies themselves. So many conspiracy theories exist
that we need a system to classify them, perhaps starting by
subject type:

- *Aliens*: UFOs, Men in Black, alien abductions, Area 51,
  Roswell, moon landing hoax, the Face on Mars, the
  Black Knight satellite.
- *Anti-Semitism*: *The Protocols of the Learned Elders of Zion*,
  the stab-in-the-back theory, Holocaust denial.
- *Aviation*: unidentified aerial phenomena (UAPs),
  black helicopters, mind control via chemtrails, the
  Denver Airport conspiracy, Korean Airlines flight
  007, TWA flight 800, Malaysia Airlines flight MH370.
- *Biblical*: anti-Christ, Jesus married and had children,
  anti-Catholicism.
- *Medicine*: water fluoridation, vaccinations, secret
  cancer cures, artificial diseases, Big Pharma, the
  invention and spread of AIDS.
- *Science and technology*: weather and earthquake
  control, global warming, RFID chips, Hollow Earth,
  Flat Earth, technology suppression, Nikola Tesla,
  Free Energy.
- *Suspicious deaths*: who really killed John F. Kennedy,
  Robert F. Kennedy, Martin Luther King Jr., Jimmy

Hoffa, Princess Diana, Kurt Cobain, and so on, as well as the suspicious deaths of Amelia Earhart, Elvis Presley, Marilyn Monroe, Tupac Shakur, and the Notorious B.I.G.

- *Government*: false-flag operations, Pearl Harbor, the Gulf of Tonkin incident, 9/11, FEMA prison camps, Sandy Hook, the Philadelphia Experiment, the Clintons, Project MKULTRA, the High-Frequency Active Auroral Research Program (HAARP), QAnon, the rigged election, and the Deep State.
- *Secret organizations*: the Bilderberg Group, the Council on Foreign Relations, the Freemasons, the Illuminati, the Knights Templar, the International Monetary Fund, the World Bank, the New World Order, the Priory of Zion, the Rockefellers, the Rothschilds, the Trilateral Commission, the Zionist Occupation Government, QAnon, and the Deep State.

QAnon and the corresponding Deep State conspiracy theory are firmly embedded in these last two types of conspiracy theories: government and secret organizations. As conspiracy researcher Mike Rothschild told me, "QAnon is definitely rooted in your last two categories of conspiracy theories," but added that it "touches on most of the others as well. It's hugely antisemitic, liberally quotes from the Bible in Q drops, talks quite a bit about secret technology and suppressed cures for diseases, and incorporates suspicious and/or unsolved deaths. Hence my calling it a conspiracy theory of everything—and the spillover between conspiracy types has only gotten worse with COVID."[10]

To wrap our minds around all of these conspiracy theories, researchers have tried cataloging them into conceptual types. For example, in *The United States of Paranoia*, journalist Jesse Walker identified four types of "enemy" conspiracy theories:[11]

1. The "Enemy Outside" refers to theories based on figures alleged to be scheming against a community from without.
2. The "Enemy Within" finds conspirators lurking inside the nation, indistinguishable from ordinary citizens.
3. The "Enemy Above" involves powerful people manipulating events for their own gain.
4. The "Enemy Below" features the lower classes working to overturn the social order.

In A Culture of Conspiracy, political scientist Michael Barkun classified conspiracy theories into three all-encompassing types:[12]

1. Event conspiracy theories, such as the JFK assassination, 9/11, the rigged election.
2. Systemic conspiracy theories, such as those involving social control, political power, and even world domination.
3. Superconspiracy theories, such as those involving a single individual or force that controls everything, ranging from a politician to an alien force to Satan himself.

In these classificatory schemes, QAnon is an "enemy within" conspiracy theory, as well as a combination of systemic and superconspiracy theories.

For believers, conspiracy theories like QAnon appear to explain what normal historical and political forces cannot, as well as to make sense of a world that otherwise seems nonsensical. Such theories also reduce the complexity of the world into a simple Manichean battle between the forces of good and the forces of evil. In the mind of conspiracists, the theories elevate adherents to a higher status than perhaps they would otherwise enjoy by believing that they are in on a secret that the brainwashed gullible masses (the "sheeple") have missed.

In *Conspiracies Declassified*, investigative journalist Brian Dunning cataloged no less than 50 conspiracy theories, and even that's a restricted list, as he insisted on two requirements to qualify them:[13]

1. *They must be specific enough to be falsifiable.* "Too often, proposed conspiracy theories are so uselessly vague that they are always going to be true."
2. *They must be known by the conspiracy theorist before being revealed by the media or law enforcement.* "Many times, conspiracy theorists will look back on historical conspiracies and claim they are examples of conspiracy theories proven true," Dunning observed, identifying hindsight bias in conspiratorial thinking, which we will explore in a later chapter.

QAnon certainly meets these requirements, inasmuch as it has been falsified—over and over again—and the conspiracists who believe in it are most certainly known by the media and law enforcement, especially after their assault on the US Capitol Building on January 6, 2021.

Dunning's 50 conspiracies only partially overlap with the 1994 book by Jonathan Vankin and John Whalen, *The Fifty Greatest Conspiracies of All Time*, a title I have in my personal library from decades ago, which was subsequently updated as *The 60 Greatest Conspiracies of All Time* and *The 80 Greatest Conspiracies of All Time*, as the genre grows by the decade.[14] A quick Amazon search generates many such works. To name but a few: *The Greatest Conspiracy of All Time*; *History's Greatest Conspiracies*; *The World's Greatest Alien Conspiracy Theories*; *The Mammoth Book of Cover-Ups: The 100 Most Terrifying Conspiracies of All Time*; *Hidden History: An Expose of Modern Crimes*; *Conspiracies and Cover-Ups in American Politics*; and *Conspiracy Theories and Secret Societies for Dummies*. Another volume from my bookshelves that piqued my interest as a curious teenager, *None Dare Call It Conspiracy*, is advertised as "a primer for anyone who wishes to understand the basic workings of the global network of Insiders that is determined to wield power over all of mankind in the coming New World Order."[15] The list could go on for pages, depending on which key words one uses to search.

The Manichean simplicity and the Machiavellian morality of most conspiracy theories is part of their appeal. It's hard to wrap our minds around the matrix of causal variables that factor into explaining historical, political, and economic events. Indeed, social scientists have developed sophisticated statistical techniques and computer models to tease apart the many variables that go into explaining any human behavior or social phenomenon. "Things seem a whole lot simpler in the world according to conspiracy theories," psychologist Rob Brotherton explained in *Suspicious Minds: Why We Believe Conspiracy Theories*.[16] "The prototypical conspiracy theory is an unanswered question; it assumes nothing is as it seems; it portrays the conspirators as preternaturally competent; and as unusually evil."

• - - • - - •

I would add another distinction to these classificatory schemes: that between *paranoid conspiracy theories*, involving ultra-secret entities for which there is little to no evidence and are largely driven by paranoia, and *realistic conspiracy theories*, involving normal political institutions and corporate entities conspiring to manipulate the system to gain an unfair, immoral, and sometimes illegal advantage over others.

Paranoid conspiracy theories may include aliens, evil forces, world-domination schemes, control of entire races or nations of people, or cabals so numerous and plots so complicated that they could never be pulled off. Examples include the Bildebergers, Rockefellers, or Rothschilds running the world's economies, the Illuminati or the Deep State determining political elections and power relations, and even 9/11 when seen as an inside job. Historian Richard Hofstadter, in his classic essay, "The Paranoid Style in American Politics," gave less extreme examples, but still in the paranoid style.[17] He used that phrase as a pejorative, because "the paranoid style has a greater affinity for bad causes than good." What Hofstadter, a lifelong liberal, had in mind with "paranoid style" was conservatism in the Barry Goldwater fashion. When Hofstadter wrote his famous essay in *Harper's* magazine in 1964, this form of conservatism had arisen from the more extreme factions of the Right a decade earlier, most notably from Senator Joseph McCarthy and his belief in a Communist conspiracy "on a scale so immense as to dwarf any previous such venture in the history of man." To his credit, however, Hofstadter also chronicled the paranoid style of "the anti-Masonic movement, the nativist and anti-Catholic movement, in certain spokesmen for abolitionism who regarded the United States as being in the grip of a slaveholders' conspiracy, in many writers alarmed by Mormonism, in some Greenback and Populist writers who constructed a great conspiracy of international bankers, in the exposure of a munitions makers' press," as well as "the contemporary American right wing."

Realistic conspiracy theories include government agencies and corporate entities engaged in power consolidation, personal profiteering, tax-cheating schemes, regulation-dodging activities, and any number of shenanigans that we see routinely on the nightly news. Watergate is an example from government, Volkswagen cheating on emission regulations is an example from industry, Wells Fargo opening fake bank accounts is an example from business, and the

usual insider trading and tax-avoidance rackets are examples from finance. Realistic conspiracy theories often involve power—or the lack of it. In historian Frank Mintz's
1985 book, *The Liberty Lobby and the American Right*, linking
"race, conspiracy and culture," he popularized the term
"conspiracism" to describe the beliefs of people without
power who were prone to viewing human history as being
primarily driven by people with power.[18] "Conspiracism
serves the needs of diverse political and social groups in
America and elsewhere," Mintz noted. "It identifies elites,
blames them for economic and social catastrophes, and assumes that things will be better once popular action can
remove them from positions of power."

Power as a central element in the structure of conspiracy
theories and the reasons why people believe them was affirmed by political scientists Joseph Uscinski and Joseph
Parent, who conducted a content analysis of over 100,000
letters sent to the *New York Times* over the course of 121
years, which they (and their graduate students) coded for
conspiracy-related themes.[19] Their analysis generated three
pages worth of conspirators, from Adolf Hitler and the African National Congress to the World Health Organization and
Zionist villagers, cataloged into seven types: Left, Right,
Communist, capitalist, government, media, and other
(which includes Freemasons, the American Medical Association, and even scientists).

For example, letter writers in the 1890s voiced suspicions
that Mormons had rigged elections in favor of Republicans,
and that Canada and England were conspiring to reclaim US
territory. In the early 1900s, correspondents were worried
about the role of financial interests in undermining democracy (a perennial paranoia, grounded in reality). This continued throughout the twentieth century, dispelling the myth
that conspiracism is a recent phenomenon. In fact, conspir-

acy theorists have been around since at least 64 AD, when the Great Fire in Rome left most of the city in smoldering ruins, leading some observers to suspect it was an inside job by the emperor, Nero, for his own (and other varied) motivations.

The common theme running throughout these letters was *power*. People writing to the *New York Times* editors expressed their concern that someone or something was engaged in getting or using illegitimate power to manipulate others, which, as we shall see later in this book, is not always an unwarranted worry.[20]

• - - • - - •

How many people really believe such conspiracy theories? In *Conspiracy Theories and the People Who Believe Them*, Uscinski and Parent compiled data from numerous polls and surveys, which revealed some disturbingly high numbers:[21]

- About a third of Americans believe the Birther conspiracy theory that Obama is a foreigner.
- About as many believe that 9/11 was an "inside job" by the George W. Bush administration.
- About 10 percent think that the chemtrail conspiracy theory is "completely true" and another 30 percent think it is "somewhat true," meaning that over 100 million Americans believe that the government and the airline companies are conspiring to poison or drug US citizens by spraying chemicals from airplanes.
- 4 percent believe that shape-shifting reptiles are secretly running the world.
- 7 percent believe that the moon landings were faked.
- 9 percent believe that the government adds fluoride to water not to fight tooth decay (which it does), but in order to control the lives of citizens.

- 21 percent believe that an alien spaceship crash landed in Roswell, New Mexico, in 1947; that the government is hiding the ship and its aliens in a secret warehouse, possibly in Area 51; and that we back-engineered computer technology from them.
- Since 1963, more than half of all Americans have believed that more than one person was responsible for the assassination of President John F. Kennedy, with a high of 81 percent in the 1970s and a low of 61 percent in the 2010s.

Conspiracy theories are not restricted to America and its paranoid style of politics. A 2016 YouGov survey among British citizens revealed the following:[22]

- 51 percent believe that despite being a democracy, "a few people will always run things in this country anyway."
- 41 percent believe that the government is "hiding the truth about how many immigrants really live in the country."
- 13 percent believe that "regardless of who is officially in charge, there is a single group of people who secretly control events and rule the world together."
- 9 percent believe that "the idea of man-made global warming is a hoax that was invented to deceive people."
- 4 percent believe that "the AIDS virus was created and spread around the world on purpose by a secret group or organization."
- 2 percent believe that "the official account of the Nazi Holocaust is a lie."

In 2016 my colleagues at Chapman University, where I teach, conducted a study on what Americans fear the most. The research team, led by Christopher Bader, found the following percentages of Americans who believe that the government is concealing what they know about various events:[23]

the 9/11 attacks (54.3 percent)
the JFK assassination (49.6 percent)
alien encounters (42.6 percent)
global warming (42.1 percent)
plans for a one-world government (32.9 percent)
Obama's birth certificate (30.2) percent
the origin of the AIDS virus (30.2) percent
the death of US Supreme Court Justice Antonin Scalia
    (27.8 percent)
the moon landing (24.2 percent)
the North Dakota crash (33 percent)

If you are not familiar with the conspiracy theory of the North Dakota crash, that's because Bader and his colleagues made it up, just to see if people would say they believe in this nonexistent event. A third of the respondents did so, indicating that there is something else going on here—namely, a deeper and more foundational distrust in authorities, in this case the US government. Ticking the box for believing in a nonexistent conspiracy that no one could possibly have heard of shows that such beliefs are proxies for something larger underlying the specific cases. A distrust of authorities is one such overarching reason.

The Chapman University researchers also measured the correlation between the number of conspiracies someone believes in and their fear that "the world will end in my lifetime." The results were revealing:

- 5.2 percent of those who don't believe in conspiracies still believe that the world will end in their lifetime, compared to
  o 6.4 percent of those who believe in 1–3 conspiracies,

- o 14.4 percent of those who believe in 4–7 conspiracies, and
- o 22.6 percent—almost one in four—of those who believe in 8–10 conspiracies.

The implications are clear. There is a relationship between believing in conspiracies and being fearful, although it isn't apparent which way the causal arrow points. Believing conspiracy theories possibly makes one fearful, but it is just as likely that fearful people are more likely to believe conspiracy theories.

Moreover, Bader and his colleagues found two measures indicating a correlation between the number of conspiracy beliefs held by people and their distrust of others: (1) fear that their significant other is cheating, and (2) fear that others are talking about them:

- For those with no conspiracy beliefs, these two fears were held by 6.6 percent and 4.4 percent, respectively.
- For those who believe in 1–3 conspiracies, the numbers were 7.4 percent and 6.6 percent.
- For those who believe in 4–7 conspiracies, the numbers were 11 percent and 6 percent.
- For those who believe in 8–10 conspiracies, the numbers were 17.6 percent and 11.3 percent.

Perhaps most disturbingly for the real world consequences of believing in conspiracies—as evidenced in the number of conspiracy theories associated with gun violence, such as the mass public shooting in two mosques in Christchurch, in New Zealand, in 2019—Bader and his colleagues found that the more conspiracies people believe in, the more likely they were to buy a gun:

- 7.1 percent of people with no conspiracy beliefs bought a gun out of fear, compared to

- o 10 percent for those believing in 1–3 conspiracies,
- o 15.7 percent for those believing in 4–7 conspiracies, and
- o 17.4 percent for those believing in 8–10 conspiracies.

In studying the people most likely to believe in conspiracies, the Chapman University researchers concluded that conspiracy theorists "tend to be more pessimistic about the near future, more fearful of government, less trusting of other people in their lives and more likely to engage in actions due to their fears, such as purchasing a gun."[24]

This research helps explain, in part, the actions of extremist groups like the Aryan Nations and the Ku Klux Klan, as well as terrorist organizations such as al-Qaeda and ISIS. People in these groups are more likely to embrace conspiracy theories out of fear, and they do so in predictable ways. The Aryan Nations and the KKK fear that Jews and other minorities are plotting to replace whites and destroy Western culture. The jihadists of al-Qaeda and ISIS fear that the United States is conspiring to occupy the Middle East and destroy Islamic culture, if not Islam itself, a conspiracy theory popularized by the intellectual founder of al-Qaeda, Abdullah Azzam, in *The Defense of Muslim Lands*.[25]

Political extremism on both the Left and the Right is also affiliated with conspiratorial cognition. As Dutch psychologist Jan-Willem van Prooijen reported in *The Psychology of Conspiracy Theories*, people on "the political extremes reported feeling more uncertain about their economic future than moderates were and, for instance, worried that there would be little pension for them when they were old, or that in the near future the Western world would be set back to a much lower level of prosperity."[26] Distressingly for social harmony, compared with moderates, people on the growing political extremes are less tolerant of people from groups that differ from them. On the Left, this includes bankers, millionaires, and soldiers; on the Right, Muslims, gays and lesbians, and scientists. Such individuals are also more likely to agree with statements like "people who think differently than me about political issues are of lesser value than I am." Studies on political extremism in the Left and the Right—for example, socialists on the populist Left and anti-immigrationists on the populist Right— find that adherents on both sides are more susceptible to believing conspiracy theories than are moderates.

In 2015, van Prooijen and his colleagues conducted a study of nationally representative samples of the Dutch voting population about a range of conspiracy theories—from politically neutral to politically slanted toward either the Left or the Right—as a function of their political extremism.[27] "Participants who placed themselves at either the extreme left or the extreme right were on average more likely to believe conspiracy theories than participants who placed themselves in the political center," van Prooijen reported. Other researchers found similar rates of conspiratorial belief among extremists in Germany, showing how party preference predicts what the researchers called a "conspiracy mentality," as measured by the tendency to agree with conspiratorial statements such as "there are secret organizations that have great influence on political decisions." Those most likely to concur came from both the German radical Socialist party and the German anti-immigration parties. Centrists scored lowest in their conspiracy mentality.

In 2016, van Prooijen and his colleagues conducted a study in the United States along the lines of the one they did in Holland and found similar beliefs among extremists about the financial crisis.[28] For example, people on the Far Left were more likely to believe that the Great Recession of 2009 was caused by a conspiracy of corrupt bankers and politicians, while people on the Far Right were more likely to believe that the financial meltdown was caused by a conspiracy of government agents. Given the fact that conspiracy theories were quite common in both far-left communist regimes and far-right fascist regimes throughout the twentieth century, this makes sense. The suppression of civil rights, civil liberties, and the free press by totalitarian regimes is almost always tethered to a conspiracy theory about a threat that must be met with extreme measures to take away these rights.

In the coda to this book, I will review the findings of my Skeptic Research Center study on conspiracy theories and why people believe them, which reinforce the revelations that there are often good reasons to be conspiratorial about those in power.

• - - • - - •

Findings such as these remind us of the multifarious nature of conspiracy theories and their verisimilitude. Totalitarian governments suppress the rights of their citizens in the interest of maintaining power, concocting conspiracy theories about threats to the nation that such authoritarian measures are implemented to combat. Citizens, in turn, must determine which conspiracy theories to believe—those related to real threats that governments are normally instituted to counter, such as foreign invaders or internal insurrectionists, or those made up by the government itself to conceal its own illegal or immoral actions. It can get confusing—all the more reason why we need a robust science of conspiracies and conspiracy theories.

Such conspiratorial machinations unfolded not only in European countries throughout much of the twentieth century—such as in Fascist Italy, Nazi Germany, and Soviet Russia in the 1930s and 1940s, as well as throughout countries controlled by the USSR during the Cold War—but also in the United States. For example, President Woodrow

Wilson and the US Supreme Court threatened the liberties of German Americans during World War I, President
Franklin D. Roosevelt forced Japanese Americans into
prison camps during World War II, and Senator Joseph
McCarthy blacklisted writers perceived to be Communists
in the 1950s. And lest we grow complacent with how much
the arc of the moral universe has bent toward justice in
the last half century, recall what the Pentagon Papers revealed about what the US government was doing in Vietnam without congressional approval (much less public
awareness); what the Wikileaks documents laid bare
about how both the George W. Bush and Obama administrations were surveiling American citizens; and what the
Afghanistan Papers exposed about America's longest war,
including that President Bush didn't know the name of his
Afghanistan war commander, Secretary of Defense Donald Rumsfeld admitted he had "no visibility into who the
bad guys are," and his successor, Robert Gates, confessed
that "we didn't know jack shit about al-Qaeda."[29]

As we shall see in more detail in later chapters, there are
good reasons to be constructively conspiratorial about the
goings-on of government. In *Real Enemies: Conspiracy Theories and American Democracy, World War I to 9/11*, historian
Kathryn S. Olmsted cataloged the many conspiracies and
cabals of the twentieth century, which are numerous.[30] She
wrote, "The institutionalized secrecy of the modern US government inspired a new type of conspiracy theories
[which] proposed that the federal government itself *was* the
conspirator." Olmsted outlined three good reasons why,
because of this history, Americans are prone to believing in
government conspiracies. These include (1) Watergate, the
Tuskegee syphilis experiment, Project MKULTRA, and
the CIA's collaboration with the Mafia to assassinate Fidel
Castro, as examples of "genuine government overreach
and secrecy during the Cold War"; (2) beliefs about Germans

infiltrating the United States during World War II and Saddam Hussein helping to orchestrate 9/11 and having weapons of mass destruction, as examples of "government-sanctioned conspiracy theories as propaganda in the form of misinformation"; and (3) the Sedition Act of 1918 and the numerous red scares in the 1950s and 1960s, most notably the McCarthy hearings, as examples of "the distrust fostered by the government's spying and harassment of dissenters."

Half a century later, we're experiencing the effects of such constructive conspiracism. In the next chapter, we will explore the mind of conspiracists, to better understand the psychology of conspiratorial belief.

CHAPTER 2

A Brief History of Conspiracy Theories and Conspiracists

Toward a Science of Conspiracism

On Friday, March 15, 2019, a 28-year-old Australian man wielding five firearms stormed two mosques in Christchurch, New Zealand, and opened fire, killing 50 people and wounding dozens more. It was the worst mass public shooting in the history of that country, prompting Prime Minister Jacinda Ardern to reflect, "While the nation grapples with a form of grief and anger that we have not experienced before, we are seeking answers."[1]

One answer may be found in the shooter's rambling 74-page manifesto, "The Great Replacement," inspired by a book of the same title published in 2012 by French author Renaud Camus.[2] "The Great Replacement" is a right-wing conspiracy theory that claims white Catholic French in particular, and white Christian Europeans in general, are being systematically replaced by people of non-European descent, most notably from North Africa, sub-Saharan

Africa, and the Arab Middle East, through immigration and demographic growth (i.e., higher birthrates).[3]

The New Zealand killer's name is Brenton Harrison Tarrant, and his manifesto is filled with white supremacist tropes focused on this conspiracy theory, starting with his opening sentence, "It's the birthrates," repeated three times.[4] "If there is one thing I want you to remember from these writings, it's that the birthrates must change. Even if we were to deport all Non-Europeans from our lands tomorrow, the European people would still be spiraling into decay and eventual death." Tarrant then cited the replacement fertility level of 2.06 births per woman, grumbling that "not a single Western country, not a single white nation," reaches this level. The result, he concluded, is "white genocide."[5]

This is classic nineteenth-century "blood-and-soil" romanticism.[6] Tarrant described himself as "an Ethno-nationalist Eco-fascist," saying he went on this murderous spree "to ensure the existence of our people and a future for white children, whilst preserving and exulting nature and the natural order." His screed goes on and on like this for dozens of pages, culminating in a photo collage of attractive white people and well-armed militiamen. It is reminiscent of the "Unite the Right" event in Charlottesville, Virginia, in August 2017, when white supremacists shouted slogans like "blood and soil" and "Jews will not replace us." Given that there are only about 15 million Jews in the world, Judaism employs no missionary effort at conversion, and birthrates among Jewish families are among the lowest in the world, why would any group worry about being "replaced" by Jews? They're not. They're reflecting the conspiracy theory that Jews control the media, politics, banking and finance, and even the world economy.

In his manifesto, Tarrant referenced the number 14, alluding to the 14-word slogan originally coined by white supremacist David Lane while in federal prison serving a

190-year sentence for his role in the 1984 murder of Jewish radio talk show host Alan Berg.[7] Here are those 14 words: "We must secure the existence of our people and a future for white children."[8] The number is sometimes rendered as 14/88, with the eights representing the 8th letter of the alphabet (H) and 88, or HH, standing for "Heil Hitler."[9] Lane was inspired by Adolf Hitler's conspiracy theory-laden book, Mein Kampf, in which the Nazi Führer growled:

> What we must fight for is to safeguard the existence and reproduction of our race and our people, the sustenance of our children and the purity of our blood, the freedom and independence of the fatherland, so that our people may mature for the fulfillment of the mission allotted it by the creator of the universe. Every thought and every idea, every doctrine and all knowledge, must serve this purpose. And everything must be examined from this point of view and used or rejected according to its utility.[10]

Hitler went on to identify the enemy of his mission—the Jews—which reflects another conspiracy theory, called the "stab-in-the-back," that was popular in Germany in the 1920s and 1930s. It claimed that the only reason the Germans lost World War I was that they were stabbed in the back by the "November Criminals" (the Armistice was signed on November 11, 1918), who, the Nazis insisted, were Jews, Marxists, and Bolsheviks.[11] And this stab-in-the-back conspiracy theory was, itself, part of an earlier and larger theory involving The Protocols of the Learned Elders of Zion, a hoaxed document purporting to be the proceedings of a secret meeting of Jews plotting global domination,[12] which a number of prominent people at the time believed, including American industrialist Henry Ford, who published his own conspiratorial tract titled The International Jew: The World's Foremost Problem.[13] He later withdrew the book from circulation when he found out that the conspiracy theory was a fake, but he never issued a genuine retraction for his broader anti-Semitism, most likely because he believed the underlying themes of such anti-Semitic conspiracism.[14]

Note that this particular 2019 conspiracy theory taps two of the overarching factors in conspiracism outlined above—proxy conspiracism and tribal conspiracism—along with the psychological power of conspiratorial belief to motivate a wide spectrum of people to act, including performing murderous actions that range from killing dozens in New Zealand to slaughtering millions in the Holocaust. To understand why, we begin with a brief history of conspiracy theories and conspiracists.

•--•--•

Recall from the previous chapter that I define a conspiracy as two or more people, or a group, plotting or acting in secret to gain an advantage or harm others immorally or illegally; I define a conspiracy theory as a structured belief about a conspiracy, whether or not it is real; and I define a conspiracy theorist, or conspiracist, as someone who holds a conspiracy theory about a possible conspiracy, again whether or not it is real. Although the terms "conspiracy theory," "conspiracy theorist," and "conspiracist" do sometimes carry pejorative connotations, meant to traduce someone or their beliefs—as in "that's just a crazy conspiracy theory" or "he's one of those wackadoodle conspiracists"—the terms have a rich history that is not meant to disparage.

Historian Andrew McKenzie-McHarg tracked the earliest use of the label "conspiracy theory" through, ironically enough, a conspiracy theory—specifically, 1967 CIA Dispatch 1035-906, a directive related to the growing skepticism surrounding the assassination of John F. Kennedy and meant to tar the *Warren Commission Report* with "the pejorative label of conspiracy theory."[15] From there, McKenzie-McHarg followed the thread back in time to the assassination of President James Garfield in 1881, notably to a press interview in which a reporter from the *Evening Star* (Washington DC) asked Attorney General William A. Cook what his "theory of the assassination" was. Cook's response distinguished facts from theories when he noted, "All theories should be temporarily entertained, so as to be considered in connection with all the facts that may be ultimately elicited."[16] Here, "theory" includes accusations at the time that the assassin—a mentally unstable man named Charles Guiteau (more about him in chapter 9)—had not acted alone but was, in fact, a patsy of a cabal, about which one could form a "conspiracy theory." For example, some speculated that "if Guiteau is insane there is 'method in his madness,' and that he was but a tool in the hands of others."[17] When an attempt was made on Guiteau's life a few days after his trial began, conjectures about conspiracy ran rampant, as one newspaper reported: "Mysterious hints have been thrown out from time to time since the beginning of the trial of the existence of a desperate band of conspirators who are bound by a terrible oath to risk their individual lives in turn until an end has been reached in Guiteau's death."[18]

Political scientist Lance deHaven-Smith referred to "today's blanket condemnation of conspiracy beliefs as ludicrous by definition," pinpointing it to the 1960s and the attempt to discredit skeptics of the *Warren Commission Report*.[19] With some hyperbole, deHaven-Smith asserted that "one of the most successful propaganda initiatives of all time" was orchestrated by none other than "CIA technocrats who are trained to break people psychologically, destroy relationships, tear apart governments, stir up old hatreds," stating that "the reach of these people should never be underestimated." Maybe so, especially if you live in a country whose policies and interests conflict with those of the United States, but neither should that reach be overestimated, as it can lead to false positive claims of conspiracy where none exist, a danger all its own, which we will explore later.

Historian Katharina Thalmann has written an entire book on "the stigmatization of conspiracy theory since the 1950s," which she described as "a plot to make us look foolish," a line from a 1955 editorial cartoon by the Washington Post's popular political cartoonist Herbert "Herblock" Block, inked after the nadir of the red scare, driven by the anti-communist conspiracy theories propagated by Senator Joseph McCarthy, which were rampant during that era of political paranoia.[20] The cartoon depicts members of the House Un-American Activities Committee (HUAC) and the Department of Justice upon hearing that one of their most prominent anti-communist informants, Harvey Matusow, was actually an FBI stooge. The anti-communists, dressed as jesters and clowns, deny the revelation by concocting their own conspiracy theory in the caption that reads, "Exactly! There's a plot to make us look foolish!" As Thalmann noted, "The cartoon, of course, implies the opposite: there is no plot to make the anti-communists look foolish; they have been foolish all along to believe in Matusow's testimony and the anti-communist conspiracy theories." The editorial cartoon, Thalmann said, represents a shift in the use of the term "conspiracy theories." "Throughout much of American history," she continued, "it had been considered foolish not to believe in the existence of conspiracies or not to heed warnings about perfidious plots, but starting in the mid-1950s, it was increasingly considered foolish and ridiculous to believe in or spread conspiracy theories."

My reading of the historical record aligns with Thalmann's. By invoking the three overarching factors I believe contribute to conspiracist belief psychology—proxy conspiracism, tribal conspiracism, and constructive conspiracism—I also concur with those in our historical memory who would think us foolish not to recognize the reality of conspiracies nor "heed warnings about perfidious plots," which are numerous in our past (discussed in part II). As Thalmann noted in her concluding remarks, what goes around comes around: "Indeed, the sudden reemergence of conspiracy theories on campaign trails and in public speeches and the improbable ascendance of a conspiracy theorist to the White House, offers a different perspective on the status of conspiracy theory than the one I have adopted throughout this book. . . . It appears that conspiracy theories have returned into serious, political discourse as a perfectly acceptable rhetoric."[21] Indeed they have, a lacuna filled with both rational and paranoid conspiracy theories.

In his 2018 book, *Escaping the Rabbit Hole*, science writer and conspiracy investigator Mick West traced the history of the term "conspiracy theory" back to 1870, in "a theory about a conspiracy to physically abuse the criminally insane in mental asylums. The term took hold in the United States as a description for a particular theory about the secession of the South from the Union and appears in several books around 1895."[22]

According to West, long before the *Warren Commission Report* popularized the term, "conspiracy theory" was used "as a descriptor for largely unfounded theories that seek to explain events with a nefarious conspiracy. At that time one of the main sources of such theories was the 'Radical Right'—extreme-right religious and nationalist organizations like the Ku Klux Klan and the John Birch Society."[23] Searching the Newspaper Archive database to tally the total employment of the term "conspiracy theory" in newspapers between 1960 and 2011, West found spikes in usage in association with the JFK assassination in 1963, Watergate in 1972–1974, the House Select Committee on Assassinations's report in 1978, the Iran-Contra scandal in 1988, and especially the films *Conspiracy Theory* and *Men in Black* in 1997, both of which present conspiracy theories as true (after initially being perceived as bonkers).[24] To these I would add the wildly popular television series *X-Files*, which featured a conspiracy believer and a skeptic in tension over nearly every conspiracy theory imaginable, with the now-iconic "cigarette-smoking man" lurking in the shadows behind them all.

For the 2000s, West turned to Google Trends data to reveal three spikes in the use of the term "conspiracy theory" (in 2009, 2010, and 2012), all associated with the popular television series *Conspiracy Theory with Jesse Ventura*, in which the former wrestler, actor, and governor of Minnesota portrayed nearly every conspiracy theory he encountered as true, meeting clandestine operatives in underground parking garages who whispered to him in hushed voices about what was "really" going on.[25]

• • • • • •

Who believes in such conspiracies? The idea that conspiratorial beliefs are held just by a bunch of nerdy, middle-aged, overweight white guys living in their parents' basements is a myth. In research reported in *American Conspiracy Theories*, political scientists Joseph Uscinski and Joseph Parent found that conspiracists "cut across gender, age, race, income, political affiliation, educational level, and occupational status."[26] Take political affiliation. Liberals are more likely to be conspiracists when conservatives are in power, and vice versa. Which specific conspiracy theories are believed also vary by party affiliation. For example, GMO conspiracy theories are embraced primarily by those on the Left (who accuse Monsanto of conspiring to destroy small farmers), while climate change conspiracy theories are endorsed primarily by those on the Right (who incriminate academic climate scientists for manipulating data to destroy the American economy and indict capitalism itself).[27]

There are other factors at work, as well. For example, race is not a strong predictor of overall conspiracism, but it does partially determine which conspiracy theories are likely to be embraced. For example, African Americans are more inclined to believe that the federal government invented AIDS to kill Blacks and that the CIA planted crack cocaine in inner-city neighborhoods to ruin them. By contrast, white Americans are more likely to suspect the feds are conspiring to abolish the Second Amendment and convert the nation into a socialist commune.[28]

Education appears to attenuate conspiracism, with 42 percent of those without a high school diploma scoring highly in having conspiratorial predispositions, compared with those holding postgraduate degrees, who come in at 22 percent.[29] Nevertheless, over one in five Americans with MAs or PhDs believe in conspiracies, which tells us something else is going on here.

That "something else" includes personality traits influencing conspiratorial cognition, which psychologists Joshua Hart and Molly Graether explored in an article titled "Something's Going on Here: Psychological Predictors of Belief in Conspiracy Theories."[30] Subjects were exposed to some of the more paranoid conspiracy theories, such as chemtrails (chemicals purportedly released in the contrails of jets to gain mind control over citizens), and Sandy Hook as a false-flag operation by the US government (in order to pass draconian gun control laws, if not confiscate Americans' guns altogether). Administering a battery of questions about such conspiracies to over 1,200 American adults in two different studies, Hart and Graether then measured their personality traits and cognitive styles, concluding that conspiracy believers "are relatively untrusting, ideologically eccentric, concerned about personal safety, and prone to perceiving agency in actions." Conspiricists also scored higher in dangerous-world beliefs (beliefs that life is a fiercely competitive and violent struggle and that others are constantly threatening harm), agency detection (the belief that there are hidden intentional agents controlling events), and schizotypal personality ("a constellation of tendencies including interpersonal suspiciousness, social anxiety and isolation, and eccentric ideas and perceptions"). This combination of traits and styles appears to attenuate anxiety over the uncertainty of a dangerous world that is controlled by nefarious agents. As Hart and Graether put it, "There is some measure of comfort to be drawn from the notion that life's ills are (at least sometimes) attributable to hostile agents working in secret, because in that event, at least there is 'theoretically' a solution to one's suffering." Revealingly, Hart and Graether also found a negative correlation between science-mindedness and conspiratorial thinking. That is, the more one identifies with a scientific worldview, the less likely one is to believe in conspiracies. I suspect that this is because the scientific mind is alert to the role of ineptitude and randomness in the unfolding of events, thereby expanding on Hanlon's razor: "never attribute to malice that which is adequately explained by stupidity."[31] When this is applied to conspiracy theories, it might be called the *conspiracism principle*: never attribute to malice what can be explained by incompetence or chance.

In a study of the relationship between loss of control and illusory pattern detection, psychologists Jennifer Whitson and Adam Galinsky explored how people have a difficult time recognizing randomness and instead attribute agency to the patterns they perceive.[32] Whitson and Galinsky sat subjects down in front of a computer screen, telling them that they would be presented with a series of images for which they were to determine the underlying concept. For example, they might see a capital A and a lowercase *a*, one or both of which could be colored, underlined, or surrounded by a circle or square. Subjects were then tasked with generating an underlying concept, such as all capital As are red or are surrounded by a circle. There was no actual underlying concept—the computer randomly combined characteristics and was programmed to frequently tell the subjects that they were either "correct" or "incorrect." Consequently, the ones hearing that they were often wrong developed a sense of lacking control. The subjects were then shown 24 "snowy" photographs, half of which contained hidden images—such as a hand, horses, a chair, or the planet Saturn—whereas the other half just saw photographs consisting of random grainy dots (figure 2.1). Although nearly everyone saw the actual hidden figures, subjects in the lack-of-control group saw more figures in the photographs that had no embedded images.

In a second experiment, Whitson and Galinsky had the participants vividly recall an experience in which they either had full control or lacked control over a situation. The subjects then read scenarios in which a character's success or failure was preceded by unconnected and superstitious behaviors, such as foot stomping before a meeting where the character wanted to have certain ideas approved.

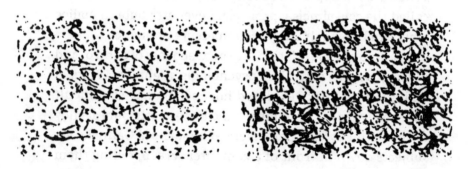

Figure 2.1. "Snowy" photographs containing (left) a hidden figure of the planet Saturn and (right) random grainy dots. Used with permission from Jennifer Whitson.

Participants were then asked whether they thought a character's behavior was related to the outcome. Those who had brought to mind an experience in which they lacked control were significantly more likely to perceive a greater connection between the two unrelated events than those who recalled controlling a situation. Tellingly, the low-control subjects who read a story about an employee who failed to receive a promotion tended to believe that a behind-the-scenes conspiracy was the cause.

This finding confirms research by field workers who have found that conspiratorial speculation runs higher after natural disasters like fires, floods, and earthquakes, or when people fear that they may lose their job.[33] Propinquity also matters. For example, a content analysis of Twitter postings found that people were more likely to tweet about the Fukushima nuclear power plant disaster in Japan the closer they were to it.[34]

Defining "illusory pattern perception" (what I call *patternicity*) as "the identification of a coherent and meaningful interrelationship among a set of random or unrelated stimuli (such as the tendency to perceive false correlations, see imaginary figures, form superstitious rituals, and embrace conspiracy beliefs, among others)," Whitson and Galinsky's thesis was confirmed: "when individuals are unable to gain a sense of control objectively, they will try to gain it perceptually."[35] I asked Whitson about the implications of her findings. She told me, "Feelings of control are essential for our well-being. We think clearer and make better decisions when we feel we are in control. Lacking control is highly aversive, so we instinctively seek out patterns to regain control—even if those patterns are illusory." I then asked her about conspiracy theories and what her research said about conspiratorial thinking. She responded, "Consider 9/11. There we saw an unstable environment caused by the terrorists attacks that led directly and almost instantly to the generation of hidden conspiracy theories." But 9/11 *was* a conspiracy, I reminded her, only it was a conspiracy by 19 members of al-Qaeda to fly planes into buildings, not an "inside job" by the George W. Bush administration. What's the difference between these two conspiracies? She replied, "It may be that even though we were told immediately that it was al-Qaeda, there was a terrible uncertainty about the future, a sense of loss of control, leading to the search for hidden patterns, which the 9/11 Truthers think they found."[36] Of note, Whitson confessed to me that she originally devised this research protocol when she was going through a particularly stressful time in her life and feeling rather out of control.

What can we do about illusory correlations and the broader problem of illusory pattern detection? In their final experiment, Whitson and Galinsky gave one group of subjects a sense of control by asking them to contemplate and affirm their most important values in life, which is a proven technique for reducing learned helplessness, dissonance, and other aversive psychological states. (Another group ruminated about the least important values in their lives, while a baseline group affirmed nothing at all.) The researchers then presented participants with the same snowy pictures used in the previous experiment, finding that the subjects in the lack-of-control condition, with no opportunity for self-affirmation, saw more nonexistent patterns than did those in the self-affirmation condition.[37]

Since Whitson and Galinsky's paper was published, much debate has followed about the extent to which anxiety and loss of control effect conspiratorial cognition. For example, a 2020 meta-analysis on lack of control and conspiracy beliefs by Ana Stojanov and Jamin Halberstadt found a small overall effect, but it was not statistically significant. Nevertheless, these authors concluded that "the predicted effect of control was more likely to be observed when beliefs were measured in terms of specific conspiracy theories, rather than as general or abstract claims."[38] So, in the way I am interpreting the findings from Whitson and Galinsky here, the effect still remains. When I queried conspiracy researcher Jan-Willem van Prooijen on this issue, he replied, "If you look more closely at the results of Stojanov and Halberstadt, you'll see that they actually *do* find the effect for specific conspiracy theories, just not for more general conspiracy beliefs (e.g., conspiracy mentality, a generalized predisposition to attribute events in the world to conspiracies)."[39]

Additional research has corroborated the findings that anxiety, alienation, and feelings of rejection or loss of control are factors in conspiracism. For example, the participants in a Princeton University study wrote a brief description of themselves, which they then shared with two other people in their small group, after being informed that the latter would judge the description. The subjects who were told that what they wrote was rejected were more inclined to believe in conspiracy-related scenarios.[40] Another study by Whitson, with her colleagues Mark Landau and Aaron Kay, considered how people compensate for a perceived loss of control with three primary strategies for restoring control—"bolstering personal agency, affiliating with external systems perceived to be acting on the self's behalf, and affirming clear contingencies between actions and outcomes"—to which the researchers proposed a fourth strategy, "seeking out and preferring simple, clear, and consistent interpretations of the social and physical environments."[41] Their meta-analysis of 55 prior studies "revealed that control reduction predicts nonspecific structure affirmation," which is a fancy way of saying that people prefer physical and social environments that are simple rather than complex, clear and discernable rather than hidden or obscure, and consistent and stable rather than erratic and disordered. Conspiracy theories are a compensating strategy, inasmuch as they are simple, clear, discernable, and stable when compared with the messiness, complexity, and (often) obscurity of the real world—and, I might add, real conspiracies. As the authors noted, "Conspiracy theories boil down the welter of information about the social world to the systematic machinations of a few malevolent agents."

Cultural anxiety may also lead to conspiracy thinking. For example, a 2018 survey of over 3,000 Americans found that those who reported feeling that American values were eroding were more likely to agree with conspiratorial statements such as "many major events have behind them the actions of a small group of influential people."[42] The feeling of being in control reduces anxiety, but the opposite—concern about what may be out of your control—can increase anxiety and conspiratorial paranoia about things that could go wrong. For example, in a 2015 study conducted in the Netherlands, researchers divided the subjects into three groups: (1) those primed to feel powerless and out of control, (2) those primed to feel in control and powerful, and (3) a control group not primed for anything. The participants were then told about a construction project undergoing problems that could be related to a conspiracy by the city council to steal money from the project's budget. Subjects primed to feel powerless and out of control were more likely to believe the conspiracy theory.[43]

A final factor in the appeal of conspiracy theories is their entertainment value, not unlike science fiction, fantasy, horror, detective, and adventure novels and films that titillate readers and viewers with fantastic Manichaean stories of good and evil forces and people plotting to assassinate a foreign leader, overthrow a political regime, conquer an evil empire, or even rule the world. Literary scholars and social scientists have explored the apparent paradox of the appeal of anxiety-producing and tension-generating novels and films in which people pay to be scared, anxious, frightened, or even horrified.[44] Like play, sports, and recreation, which often mimic real-world challenges and thus can serve as a proxy for actions that bring existential meaning to having conquered many of life's challenges without the risk of death (with the exception of actual death-defying sports), such emotion-arousing fictional stories are a relatively risk-free way to consider and play out how real-world forces and people operate in the world. "Much like a scary movie or detective novel, conspiracy theories typically involve spectacular narratives that include mystery, suspected danger, and unknown forces that one does not fully comprehend," Jan-Willem van Prooijen and his colleagues wrote in their paper reporting the results of their research on this factor.[45] "Jointly, these features can make learning about a conspiracy theory a fascinating and emotion-arousing experience," because "many conspiracy theories have potential entertainment value, which we define as the extent to which people appraise a particular narrative as interesting, exciting, and attention-grabbing." To test this hypothesis, the researchers exposed subjects to either a conspiratorial text (the death of Jeffrey Epstein) or a non-conspiratorial text (the Notre Dame cathedral fire) and found that the former elicited stronger entertainment appraisals and intense emotions than the latter. Additional studies found that the more entertaining the way the account of the conspiracy theory was presented, the more likely subjects were to believe it. These findings affirm my experiences interacting with conspiracy theorists who, when recounting what they think "really" happened on 9/11, or with JFK, or the moon landing, or Pearl Harbor, and so on, become noticeably emotionally engaged, evincing literal wide-eyed enthusiasm and even agitation. And I have to admit that in the course of reading thousands of books, essays, and documents purporting to reveal a true conspiracy—especially when watching films, both documentary and, allegedly, dramas like Oliver Stone's JFK—I find myself emotionally absorbed, unlike any other field I have engaged in over a long career spanning a wide diversity of fringe and extraordinary claims. It is entertaining to take these accounts seriously, even if skeptically!

• - - • - - •

To return to where we began this chapter, people often act on their beliefs, and when those beliefs contain conspiracy theories about nefarious goings-on, those acts can turn deadly, as happened at the Tree of Life synagogue in Pittsburgh on October 27, 2018, when an assailant, armed with guns and one of the oldest conspiracy theories about the Jews running the world, murdered eleven congregants before he was captured. "I just want to kill Jews," he announced.[46] Consuming content on the online social network Gab, the conspiracist grew paranoid about the Hebrew Immigrant Aid Society (HIAS), which the Tree of Life synagogue helped support. On Gab, the conspiracist read that HIAS provided aid to migrant caravans moving north from Central America toward the United States' southern border. "HIAS likes to bring invaders in that kill our people," the assassin posted on Gab just before he committed the mass murder, adding, "I can't sit by and watch my people get slaughtered. Screw your optics, I'm going in."

This brings us back to the mass murder in New Zealand which began the chapter. These are just two of countless conspiracy theories with real-world consequences, mostly negative. As we analyze examples like these in the chapters ahead, an implication emerges that the subject of this book—conspiracy theories and why people believe them—may well be one of the most important topics in need of explanation, as well as crucial problems in need of solutions.

CHAPTER 3

Proxy and Tribal Conspiracism

How Conspiratorial Beliefs Are Reinforced as Truths

I have been studying conspiracies and conspiracy theories for my entire career. I once met a politician who told me that he believed the fluoridation of water has been the greatest scam ever perpetrated on the public, because it not only poisoned citizens, but it also profited major corporations. I have been confronted by 9/11 Truthers who have insisted the al-Qaeda attack was actually an "inside job" by the George W. Bush administration. Others have regaled me for hours with their breathless tales of who really killed John F. Kennedy, Robert F. Kennedy, Martin Luther King Jr., Jimmy Hoffa, and Princess Diana, along with the nefarious goings-on of the Federal Reserve, the New World Order, the Trilateral Commission, the Council on Foreign Relations, the Committee of 300, the Knights Templar, the Freemasons, the Illuminati, the Bilderberg Group, the Rothschilds, the Rockefellers, and the Zionist Occupation Government (ZOG) that secretly runs the United States. It would take

Madison Square Garden to hold all the conspiracists plotting world domination.

The mystery I am trying to solve in this book is why people believe conspiracy theories, not just those with some degree of plausibility—corrupt politicians or corporations conspiring to gain an immoral or illegal advantage over others are obvious examples—but those with little to no evidentiary support, such as grand schemes for global domination through political or economic plots, or control of the world's population through vaccinations or 5G internet towers. I am especially interested in why smart people believe blatantly wrong things for apparently rational reasons—in other words, the conspiracy effect. In this chapter I will make the case that such obviously false beliefs are true in the minds of believers, not necessarily in the specifics of a theory, but in the more general truths for which it stands—proxy truths and tribal truths.

In the second half of this book, I will deal with and debunk several popular conspiracy theories, most notably the JFK assassination industry, the 9/11 Truther movement, and the Obama Birther lobby. Even as I do so, however, I recognize that believers in such conspiracy theories may not abandon their beliefs for lack of evidence, or even in the teeth of contradictory evidence, because these beliefs are proxies for something deeper troubling the conspiracists—such as mistrust in government agencies, commissions, and politicians—especially as perceived from a tribal perspective.

For example, to many Trump supporters, the tsunami of documented lies he told (numbering over 30,000 by some accounts[1])—from the size of his inauguration crowd in 2016 to the rigged election claims of 2020—are irrelevant because, to them, he spoke a different type of truth: a mythic truth about the Deep State he would combat, or a political truth about the Far Left he would stand up to. As another example, 9/11 Truthers traffic in the minutia of how and why burning buildings collapse and the temperature at which steel melts, but explaining those details with an aim to understand what, exactly, happened on 9/11 is not what their movement is really about, which is that governments cannot be trusted, politicians look for excuses to take their nations into wars for political and economic gain, and citizens have far less say in liberal democracies than we think we do.

• - - • - - •

In *The Believing Brain*, I made the case for what I call *belief-dependent realism*.[2] I argued that our beliefs arise from a variety of subjective, personal, emotional, and psychological reasons, in environments created by family, friends, colleagues, culture, and society at large. We then defend, justify, and rationalize them with a host of intellectual reasons, cogent arguments, and logical explanations. Beliefs come first, followed later by explanations for those beliefs.

Once beliefs are formed, the brain begins to look for and find confirming evidence in support of them, while ignoring or rationalizing away disconfirming evidence—the larger cognitive process is called *motivated reasoning*—and this reinforces those beliefs with an emotional boost from the thought that one is correct. Frequently, we feel not just right, but morally superior. That is, we often tend to place a value judgment on our beliefs, because our evolved tribal tendencies lead us to form coalitions with like-minded members of our group and demonize others who hold differing ones. Thus when we hear about contrary beliefs, we are naturally inclined to dismiss or dismantle them as nonsense or evil, or both.[3]

Belief-dependent realism means that we cannot escape this epistemological trap. We can, however, employ the tools of science and rationality, which are designed to test whether a particular model or belief about reality matches observations made not just by ourselves, but, more importantly, by others as well. A key point of this book is that some conspiracy theories represent models of the world that are true, while others represent models that are false. In most cases we can discern the true from the false, but only if we understand what the beliefs actually represent— actual truths, or proxy or tribal truths? Psychologist Steven Pinker, in his book *Rationality*, drew a distinction between the reality mindset and the mythology mindset.[4] He noted how "people divide their worlds into two zones. One consists of the physical objects around them, the other people they deal with face to face, the memory of their interactions, and the rules and norms that regulate their lives." People are reasonably rational in this zone, Pinker noted, because they have to be: "That's the only way to keep gas in the car, money in the bank, and the kids clothed and fed. Call it the reality mindset." The other zone, however, is beyond the reach of most people—for example, "the remote past, the unknowable future, faraway peoples and places, remote corridors of power, the microscopic, the cosmic, the counterfactual, the metaphysical." As Pinker explained:

> People may entertain notions about what happens in these zones, but they have no way of finding out, and anyway it makes no discernible difference to their lives. Beliefs in these zones are narratives, which may be entertaining or inspiring or morally edifying. Whether they are 'true' or 'false' is the wrong question. The function of these beliefs is to construct a social reality that binds the tribe or sect and gives it a moral purpose. Call it the mythology mindset.[5]

Here is how Daniel Loxton, an editor and a regular contributor to *Skeptic* magazine, put it in an email to Steven Pinker and me in a discussion of this problem of identifying the correct form of belief or truth or mindset:

It's hard to know what people mean when they affirm a belief—and that uncertainty varies by claim. For example, surveys of Icelandic belief in little people dramatically exaggerate actual serious belief, but no one knows how much. Icelanders have a cultural norm of winking 'belief' in fairies. Sincere believers surely exist, but it's hard to know how many. Flat Earth surveys are similarly tricky because of trolling.[6]

The latter example here is especially poignant, inasmuch as proponents of the Flat Earth idea are themselves conspiracy theorists who counter arguments against their belief—for example, photographs from space of a round, rotating Earth—by asserting that NASA faked all those photos in a grand conspiracy to cover up the fact that they never sent astronauts into space (which then overlaps with the conspiracy theory that the moon landings were faked in a Hollywood film studio). Such "winking beliefs" are a nod to what sort of truth is being represented here: a mythic or political truth about illimitable government power. "The brazen lies and conspiracies of Trumpian post-truth can be seen as an attempt to claim political discourse for the land of mythology rather than the land of reality," Pinker noted. "Like the content of legends, scripture, and dramas, they are a kind of theater; whether they are true or false is beside the point."[7]

In an article for *Skeptic* titled "The Fringe Is Mainstream," Loxton elaborated on the different domains of truth at stake when we're traveling through the conspiracy landscape.[8] "Humans have always known that there are events and forces beyond our control, such as earthquakes, weather, or the changing of the seasons. We have tended to intuit these as the domain of the gods. We may accept these forces as inevitable, or we may beseech the gods—but we do not expect to command these forces ourselves, using our own power."

This is in contrast to the practical realms, where "we have agency to bring about change. We can seek knowledge, solve mysteries, take action, counter threats, design solutions." Loxton's third realm is that "which is considered beyond the ordinary, but not necessarily beyond reach. This is the subject matter for 'skeptics' under the tradition of 'scientific skepticism.' And yet, we do not have a good umbrella term for this domain."

This third domain is often characterized as "fringe," where we put things like Bigfoot or ESP, but these are not strictly the same, inasmuch as finding another bipedal primate wandering about in the hinterlands of Canada or the Himalayas would not upturn biology, whereas the discovery of ESP would be likely to upset an aspect of physics, in that—as it is presented—it would require a heretofore undiscovered force of nature (which, very probably, would have been discovered by now, were it true). "The claims in this X-Files domain have some 'thisness' in common, but it's hard to specify exactly what that is," Loxton continued, providing a list to "differentiate the rationalist domain from its spookier mirror image by loose contrast." We can classify conspiracy theories in this larger framework:

ordinary / extraordinary
mundane / mystical
knowledge / intuition
science / pseudoscience
natural / magical
explained / mysterious
visible / hidden
history / conspiracy

Although most scientists and rationalists promote the rationalist/reality mindset as the best approach toward a worldview of what Pinker called "universal realism"—with which I agree and have devoted my career to promoting—

for the vast sweep of human history, there were no tools for determining the difference between mythological claims and reality, between objective truths and subjective truths, between empirical truths and mythic truths. So our default position is to believe whatever it is that reinforces our preferred preferences—that is, our subjective internal truths. This is what the belief-dependent realism model predicts. Thus the many cognitive biases we are all susceptible to in our motivated reasoning toward what we want to be true—confirmation bias, hindsight bias, myside bias, status quo bias, and many more—mean that we reason more like lawyers defending a client (our beliefs, in this metaphor), rather than reasoning like scientists trying to determine what is *actually* true and real, regardless of what we *want* to be true and real.

· – – · – – ·

In December 1954, psychologist Leon Festinger noticed a newspaper headline that read, "Prophecy from Planet Clarion Call to City: Flee that Flood." The article revealed that a Chicago housewife, Marion Keech, had been receiving messages from aliens from the planet Clarion, who told her that the world would end in a great flood sometime before dawn on December 21 of that year. On the evening of December 20, Keech and her followers gathered together at midnight to await the mother ship carrying the Guardians who, they were confident, would arrive just in time to whisk them away to safety.

Festinger saw this as an opportunity to study the phenomenon of mental tension created when someone holds two conflicting thoughts simultaneously.[9] Many of Mrs. Keech's followers had made a strong behavioral commitment to the UFO conspiracy by quitting their jobs, leaving their spouses, and giving away their possessions, so Festinger predicted that they would be the *least* likely to admit their error when the prophecy failed (admitting that one made a mistake increases anxiety) and instead rationalize a positive outcome. That is precisely what happened.

As midnight approached, Keech's group grew jittery with excitement. As instructed by the aliens (channeled by Marion, of course), the members eschewed all metallic items and other objects that they believed would interfere with the operation of the spaceship. When one member's watch read 12:05 AM on December 21, nervous glances and anxious squirming were attenuated when someone declared that it was actually only 11:55 PM on another person's watch. At 12:10 AM, the slower watch finally reached midnight as the group apprehensively awaited their salvation. As the minutes and hours ticked by, Mrs. Keech's clique grew more restless. At 4:00 AM, Keech began to cry in despair, but at 4:45 AM she recovered, claiming to have received another message from the Guardians of Clarion, instructing her that Earth would be spared because of the group's stalwart efforts and unwavering devotion. "By dawn on the 21st, however, this semblance of organization had vanished as the members of the group sought frantically to convince the world of their beliefs," Festinger narrated. "In succeeding days, they also made a series of desperate attempts to erase their rankling dissonance by making prediction after prediction in the hope that one would come true, and they conducted a vain search for guidance from the Guardians."

In the coming weeks and months, Marion Keech and her most devoted followers redoubled their efforts at recruitment, noting that the prophecy had actually been fulfilled with an opposite outcome, due to their staunch faith. Festinger concluded that the dissonance Keech's assemblage experienced was cognitively reduced by reconfiguring the perceived results into a favorable outcome, reinforced by converting others to the cause. Festinger called this psychological process *cognitive dissonance* and explained it this way:

Suppose an individual believes something with his whole heart; suppose further that he has a commitment to this belief, that he has taken irrevocable actions because of it; finally, suppose that he is presented with evidence, unequivocal and undeniable evidence, that his belief is wrong: what will happen? The individual will frequently emerge, not only unshaken, but even more convinced of the truth of his beliefs than ever before. Indeed, he may even show a new fervor about convincing and converting other people to his view.[10]

Doomsday conspiracies are especially vulnerable to cognitive dissonance, particularly when they make specific end-of-the-world predictions that can be checked against reality. What typically happens is that the faithful spin-doctor the nonevent with such rationalizations as the date was a miscalculation; the date was a loose prediction, not a specific prophecy; the date was a warning, not a prophecy; God changed his mind; predictions were just a test of members' faith; the prophecy was fulfilled physically, but not as expected; and the prophecy was fulfilled spiritually.[11]

The result of Festinger's research was an aptly titled book, *When Prophecy Fails*, and it has become a classic in psychology literature on the power of belief. It introduced a new theoretical construct to the field: cognitive dissonance.[12] Cognitive dissonance is also created when there is an imbalance or mismatch between the size or importance of an event and that of its purported cause. Call it the *proportionality problem*. For comparison, take the Holocaust as an example of the opposite. The Holocaust is one of the worst crimes against humanity in history, perpetrated by one of the most evil regimes. This creates a sense of *cognitive harmony*, or a balance between two ideas—in this case, cause and effect. By contrast, the assassination of John F. Kennedy by a lone assassin named Lee Harvey Oswald is out of proportion. The handsome and articulate leader of the free world, the most powerful person on the planet, is taken out by a lone nut like Lee Harvey Oswald? Impossible! That imbalance engenders cognitive dissonance. To create cognitive harmony, conspiracists insert additional operatives to balance the cognitive proportional scale, such as the FBI, the CIA, the KGB, the Cubans, the Mafia, the military-industrial complex, and even Vice President Lyndon Johnson.

Or take the case of Princess Diana's death. Here is one of the most famous and glamorous people on the planet—a princess, no less—whose cause of death was a combination of drunk driving, speeding, and no seatbelt.[13] That feels like a lack of balance between cause and effect. Even though tens of thousands of people die every year from these same causes, they are ordinary people.[14] Princess Di was extraordinary, so the cause of her death must be proportionally so. This mismatch creates cognitive dissonance. To create cognitive harmony, conspiracists concoct additional agents at work to even out the cognitive proportions, such as the driver of the car, her bodyguards, the driver of a mysterious white Fiat Uno automobile that her car collided with in the accident, the MI6 intelligence agency, and even the royal family (ranging from Prince Charles wanting her out of the way so he could marry Camilla Parker-Bowles to the royals' fear it would come out that Diana was a direct descendant of Jesus and Mary Magdalene).[15]

As a final example, 9/11 generated the ultimate in cognitive dissonance over the disproportion between cause and effect. As 9/11 Truthers like to snarl, "Are you telling me that 19 guys with box cutters could so easily defeat the United States?" To create proportional harmony, there must have been other forces at work to balance the cognitive scale, such as the George W. Bush administration orchestrating a false-flag operation involving hundreds if not thousands of secret agents covertly conspiring to attack our nation.

• - - • - - •

In addition to cognitive dissonance and the proportionality problem, there is another phenomenon I've noticed in my many years on the conspiracy beat: people who believe in one conspiracy theory tend to give credence to many other equally improbable and sometimes even contradictory cabals. For example, people who believe that the moon landings were faked are also more likely to accept that alien structures were discovered on the back side of the moon. Or those who are convinced that John F. Kennedy was assassinated by a conspiracy are more likely to believe that a cabal of assassins also murdered Robert F. Kennedy, Martin Luther King Jr., and Princess Diana.

There is a reason for this consistency in conspiratorial thinking, which was explored by psychologists Michael Wood, Karen Douglas, and Robbie Sutton in a paper aptly titled "Dead and Alive: Beliefs in Contradictory Conspiracy Theories."[16] The authors began by noting that once someone believes "one massive, sinister conspiracy could be successfully executed in near-perfect secrecy suggests that many such plots are possible." With this cabalistic paradigm in place, conspiracies can become "the default explanation for any given event—a unitary, closed-off worldview in which beliefs come together in a mutually supportive network known as a monological belief system."

This monological—or unitary, or all encompassing—belief system explains the significant correlations these psychologists found between different conspiracy theories in their study. For example, "a belief that a rogue cell of MI6 was responsible for [Princess] Diana's death was correlated with belief in theories that HIV was created in a laboratory, that the moon landings were a hoax, and that governments are covering up the existence of aliens." The effect continues even when the conspiracies contradict one another. In another example, participants from their study who said they believed Diana faked her own death were also more likely to say they believed she was murdered. The same was true for Osama bin Laden, in which people who believed he was already dead when US special forces attacked his compound in Pakistan were also more likely to believe he was still alive somewhere. How anyone can hold both of those ideas at the same time initially appears baffling, but it's proxy conspiracism at work, in which both contradictory conspiracy theories (alive *and* dead) stand in for a deeper distrust of social institutions and government authorities. As the researchers noted, there is a higher-order process at work, called "global coherence," that overrules local contradictions. "Someone who believes in a significant number of conspiracy theories would naturally begin to see authorities as fundamentally deceptive, and new conspiracy theories would seem more plausible in light of that belief." Thus "conspiracy advocates' distrust of official narratives may be so strong that many alternative theories are simultaneously endorsed in spite of any contractions between them." For example, "the more that participants believe that a person at the centre of a death-related conspiracy theory, such as Princess Diana or Osama Bin Laden, is still alive, the more they also tend to believe that the same person was killed, so long as the alleged manner of death involves deception by officialdom."

In a follow-up study, Robbie Sutton and Karen Douglas cautioned that no single variable—such as monological thinking—explains all conspiratorial cognition, noting that many beliefs in conspiracy theories "are associated with similar personality variables, beliefs about the self, and beliefs about the world."[17] The correlation of beliefs between conspiracy theories, or even within a single conspiracy theory with contradictory tenets (e.g., that Princess Diana both was murdered and faked her death), the researchers noted, "may be best viewed not as separate psychological variables but as facets of an underlying variable." In another study on "The Psychology of Conspiracy Theories," Sutton, Douglas, and their colleague Aleksandra Cichocka found that conspiratorial belief is primarily driven by three motives: (1) epistemic (understanding one's environment), (2) existential (being safe and in control of one's environment), and (3) social (maintaining a positive image of the self and the social group).[18]

Epistemic motives involve finding causal explanations that create a "stable, accurate, and internally consistent understanding of the world." That is, a conspiracy theory is an explanation of the world that makes sense, is relatively simple, and accounts for a great many goings on in the world that, at first glance, may seem chaotic, random, and inexplicable. For instance, the economy is not this crazy patchwork of supply and demand laws, market forces, interest rate changes, tax policies, business cycles, boom-and-bust fluctuations, recessions and upswings, bull and bear markets, and the like. Instead, it is a conspiracy of a handful of powerful people variously identified as the Illuminati, the Bilderberger group, the Council on Foreign Relations, the Trilateral Commission, the Rockefellers and Rothschilds—or, more recently, the one-percenters—somehow determining economic outcomes.

Existential motives involve finding causal explanations that "serve the need for people to feel safe and secure in their environment and to exert control over the environment." Thus politics is not this messy process of campaigns, primaries, the general election, the electoral college, district gerrymandering, lobbying, voting, and the like. It's all run by a secret cabal of cigarette-smoking, backroom-dealing, shady characters being bribed by corporate interests and other forces that determine the outcome of elections.

Social motives involve "the desire to belong and to maintain a positive image of the self and the in-group." Within our group, we can see how the world really works, in all its messiness and chanciness, but other groups—particularly those we fear are out to harm us—are well-orchestrated cabals driven by a secret mission to gain power immorally or illegally. This is one of the particularly odious aspects of conspiracism: the demonizing of other groups as evil and on the wrong side of history, in contrast with our group, which is good and on the side of the angels.

A concept related to the idea of global coherence is teleological thinking, defined by psychologist Pascal Wagner-Egger and his colleagues, in a paper they wrote to explain both creationism and conspiracism, as "the attribution of purpose and a final cause to natural events and entities."[19] They defined the latter as "the proneness to explain socio-historical events in terms of secret and malevolent conspiracies." Think of it this way: creationists believe that the complex and messy world of living organisms can all be explained by a single creator and creation event at the beginning of time, leaving nothing to chance and explaining everything by this final telos, or purpose of life. In an analogous manner, conspiracists believe that the complex and messy world of politics, economics, and culture can all be explained by a single conspiracy and conspiratorial event that downplays chance and attributes everything to this final end of history. "Conspiricism," the psychologists concluded, is "a type of creationist belief targeting socio-historic events (e.g., specific events have been purposefully created by an all-powerful agency)." In other words, "everything happens for a reason" and "it was meant to be" infuse both creationist and conspiratorial cognition, because of this teleological thinking.

Everything *does* happen for a reason, and that is what science is all about—trying to determine why things happen, or causality. With the exception of some quantum effects at the subatomic level, effects do have causes, and we want to comprehend what they are by understanding the laws of nature and the principles operating at all levels of analysis: physical, biological, psychological, and social. To this end, I make a distinction between *transcendentalists*, who tend to believe that everything is interconnected and all events occur for a reason that operates on a supernatural or conspiratorial level, and *empiricists*, who seek natural causes for natural events. Empiricists tend to think that randomness and coincidence interact with the causal net of our world, as well as that belief should depend on evidence for each individual claim. Transcendentalists discount the role of chance and weave all strands of conspiracies together into one tapestry of meaning. I am definitely an empiricist, but the problem for conspiracy thinking is that transcendentalism is intuitive, and empiricism is not.

This interpretation is reinforced by a study on conspiracies by cognitive scientist Stephan Lewandowsky and his colleagues in a paper cheekily titled "NASA Fakes the Moon Landing—therefore (Climate) Science Is a Hoax."[20] The authors noted, "People can assume that if these bad guys weren't there, then everything would be fine. Whereas if you don't believe in a conspiracy theory, then you just have to say terrible things happen randomly." To the conspiratorial mind, history is not the result of the crooked timber of humanity, as philosopher Immanuel Kant poetically opined, or the herky-jerky, contingent pathway buffeted by a complex array of social, economic, and political forces operating in a matrix of causes. Instead, history is predetermined by a secret plan, where its chronological unfolding was laid out from the beginning. Thus we are all just flotsam and jetsam on the surface of a massive current flow-ing from the beginning to the end of time.

• - - • - - •

Once a conspiracy theory is in place, it is easy to find evi-dence to support it. This step involves another process in our cognition that I mentioned earlier: *confirmation bias*. It is the tendency to seek and find confirming evidence in sup-port of already existing beliefs and to ignore or reinterpret disconfirming evidence. This falls under the umbrella phenomenon of motivated reasoning. Its meaning is self-evident, and experimental examples abound. For example, a study by psychologists Bonnie Sherman and Ziva Kunda pre-sented a group of subjects with evidence that contradicted a belief they held deeply, along with other evidence that sup-ported those same beliefs.[21] The results showed that the sub-jects recognized the validity of the confirming evidence but were skeptical of the value of the disconfirming evidence. In a study by psychologist Deanna Kuhn, when children and young adults were exposed to evidence inconsistent with a theory they preferred, they failed to notice the contra-dictory evidence, or, if they did acknowledge its existence, they tended to reinterpret it to favor their preconceived be-liefs.[22] In a related study, Kuhn exposed subjects to an audio recording of an actual murder trial and discovered that in-stead of evaluating the evidence first and then coming to a conclusion, most subjects concocted a narrative in their mind about what happened, made a decision of guilt or in-nocence, then riffled through the evidence and picked out what most closely fit their story.[23]

Conspiracism confirmation bias comes in many forms. Once the mind is focused on finding a conspiracy behind a momentous event, mundane occurrences may be elevated to significance, a point well made by Arthur Goldwag in *Cults, Conspiracies, and Secret Societies*, which covers everything from the Freemasons, the Illuminati, and the Bilderberg Group to black helicopters and the New World Order. He cited the assassination of President John F. Kennedy as a prime example:

> When something momentous happens, everything leading up to and away from the event seems momentous too. Even the most trivial detail seems to glow with significance. Knowing what we know now (and knowing how many things there are that we still *don't* know), film footage of Dealey Plaza from November 22, 1963, seems pregnant with enigmas and ironies—from the oddly expectant expressions on the faces of the onlookers on the grassy knoll in the instants before the shots were fired ("What were they thinking?"), to the play of shadows in the background ("Could that flash up there on the overpass have been a gun barrel gleaming in the sun?"). Each odd excrescence, every random lump in the visual texture seems suspicious. Why is that man carrying an umbrella on a sunny day? Who is that woman in the babushka? That lady in the bright red dress?[24]

Another cognitive bias at work in conspiracy cognition is *hindsight bias*, or the tendency to reconstruct the past to fit present knowledge.[25] Once an event has occurred, we look back and reconstruct how it happened, why it had to occur that way and not in some other manner, and why we should have seen it coming all along. Such Monday-morning quarterbacking is not only on display after Sunday football games, but it is also more seriously evident after a major disaster, when everyone thinks they know how and why it happened, and why our experts and leaders should have seen it coming. For example, after the space shuttle Challenger exploded during launch, pundits and politicians said NASA engineers should have known that the O-rings on the solid rocket booster joints would fail in freezing temperatures, leading to a massive explosion, but that conclusion was not understood until an investigation was conducted, months later.[26] That's hindsight bias, which was also at play after the space shuttle Columbia disaster, in which a small piece of foam striking the leading edge of the wing during launch resulted in the shuttle's destruction upon re-entry.[27] Such highly improbable and unpredictable events become not only probable, but also practically certain, *after they happen*. The hand-wringing and finger-pointing by the members of NASA's investigative commissions tasked with determining the causes of the two space shuttle disasters were case studies in hindsight bias. Had such certainty really existed before the fact, then different actions would have been taken.

Hindsight bias is equally evident in times of war, which are major generators of conspiracy theories. For example, almost immediately after the Japanese attack on Pearl Harbor on December 7, 1941, conspiracy theorists went to work to prove that President Franklin D. Roosevelt must have known it was coming, because of the so-called bomb plot message that was intercepted in October 1941 by US intelligence.[28] In it, a Japanese agent in Hawaii was instructed by his superiors in Japan to monitor warship movements in and around the naval base at Pearl Harbor. That sounds fairly damning, and there were eight such messages dealing with Hawaii as a possible target that were intercepted and decrypted by US intelligence before December 7. How could our leaders not have seen it coming? They must have, and therefore they let it happen for nefarious and Machiavellian reasons.

In conspiracy circles this is known LIHOP (let it happen on purpose), in contrast to MIHOP (made it happen on purpose).[29] With hindsight bias in full operation, conspiracists have concocted theories ranging from President Roosevelt letting it happen on purpose to those who think he made it happen on purpose. Before December 7, 1941, however, and in the larger context of all information available to the experts at the time (who did not benefit from our hindsight), between May and December of that year, there were no less than 58 intercepted messages regarding Japanese ship movements that indicated an attack on the Philippines, 21 messages that involved an attack on Panama, 7 messages affiliated with attacks in Southeast Asia and the Netherlands East Indies, and even 7 messages connected to the United States' West Coast. There were so many intercepted messages that Army intelligence stopped sending memos to the White House, out of concern that there might be a breach in security, leading to the Japanese realization that we had broken their codes and were reading their mail. As Roberta Wohlstetter noted in her thoughtful analysis in *Pearl Harbor: Warning and Decision*:

> The record is full of references to supposedly unambiguous indications of the Japanese plan. The MAGIC message "East Wind Rain" is one of the most famous. But, in fact, the signal picture in the limited locale of Honolulu is amazingly complex, and the mass of signals grows increasingly dense and freighted with ambiguities as we move to the larger assemblage of agencies in Washington. In both places signals announcing the Pearl Harbor attack were always accompanied by competing or contradictory signals, by all sorts of information useless for anticipating this particular disaster. We refer to these competing signals as "noise." To understand the fact of surprise it is necessary to examine the characteristics of the noise as well as the signals that after the event are clearly seen to herald the attack.[30]

President George W. Bush was subject to the same type of conspiratorial hindsight bias after 9/11, when a memo dated August 6, 2001, surfaced, entitled "Bin Laden Determined to Strike in US."[31] Reading the memo in hindsight is eerie, with references to hijacked planes, the bombing of the World Trade Center, and attacks on Washington, DC, and the Los Angeles International Airport.[32] The only question for conspiracists was, Did President Bush let it happen on purpose (LIHOP), or did he make it happen on purpose (MIHOP)? If you read this message in a pre-9/11 mindset, however, and put it in the context of the hundreds of intelligence memos tracking the various comings and goings and potential targets of al-Qaeda—an international organization operating in dozens of countries and targeting numerous American embassies, military bases, naval ships, and the like—it is not at all clear when, where, or if such attacks might happen.[33] Think about hindsight bias in today's context, in which we know with near certainty that al-Qaeda or ISIS or some new terrorist cell will strike again, but we lack the information to pinpoint where and when and how they will attack, leading us to defend against what happened in the last attack.

•--•--•

Earlier, we noted the role of *power* in conspiratorial thinking: those who don't have it tend to believe those who do therefore conspired to get it. Feeling like you have power, or that you don't have power, is related to a psychological phenomenon called *locus of control*. People who rate high on an *internal* locus of control tend to believe that they make things happen and are in control of their circumstances, whereas people who score high on an *external* locus of control tend to think that circumstances are beyond their control, so things just happen to them.[34] The perception here is that having a high internal locus of control leads you to be more confident in your personal judgment, more skeptical of outside authorities and sources of information, and less likely to believe in conspiracy theories. People having a high external locus of control tend to believe conspiracy theories, because they place too much emphasis on what is happening to them or what others are doing to them.[35] My favorite observation of this effect comes from Alan Moore, author of the graphic novels *Watchmen* and *V for Vendetta*, after conducting his own investigation into the world of conspiracies:

> The main thing that I learned about conspiracy theories is that conspiracy theorists believe in a conspiracy because that is more comforting. The truth of the world is that it is actually chaotic. The truth is, that it is not the Jewish banking conspiracy, or the Gray aliens, or the 12-foot reptiloids from another dimension that is in control. The truth is far more frightening. Nobody is in control. The world is rudderless.[36]

Locus of control also comes into play in conspiratorial cognition. Michael Wood and Karen Douglas, the psychologists we met earlier who discovered that people who believe in one type of conspiracy are more likely to believe in other conspiracy theories—even when they contradict each other—noted that "a die-hard skeptic might see conspiracy theories as the mark of someone who is paranoid and suspicious by nature. Likewise, for the more conspiracy-minded, it is tempting to think that conspiracy skeptics are naïve and gullible. Because of the fundamental attribution error, these sorts of explanations are simply the first things that come to mind."[37]

• - - • - - •

Such cognitive biases in conspiracism leads us into personality psychology and the search for individual differences in assessing who is more or less likely to believe in conspiracy theories. Early research found that conspiracy believers were less trusting of others than conspiracy skeptics, and the former's distrust encompassed friends, neighbors, and coworkers, not just the government and the media. In which direction the causal arrow points, however, is unclear. Do distrustful people gravitate toward conspiracy theories, or does believing in conspiracies make people distrustful, or is there some third factor leading to both distrustfulness and conspiracism? We don't know. I suspect the first possibility—distrustful people self-select for conspiracy theories that match their personal paranoias—but further research is needed.

This qualification applies to many of the studies discussed in this chapter. Researchers exploring these and additional cognitive, attitudinal, social, political, and other factors in conspiracy cognition often contradict one another. It isn't always clear which factors are the strongest and to what extent they interact. For example, Adam Enders and Steven Smallpage, in a paper titled "Who Are Conspiracy Theorists?," concluded that "the psychological antecedents of conspiracy beliefs used to explain those beliefs vary considerably by the stimuli or events at the center of a given conspiracy theory. Therefore, disproportionately favoring one type of conspiracy theory on one's survey may result in inferences about conspiracy theorists that do not translate across studies." They added, "Though we are not yet capable of fully determining who conspiracy theorists are, conspiratorial thinking, paranormal beliefs, and political orientations are more predictive of particular conspiracy beliefs than other attitudes, predispositions, and orientations."[38]

There are also individual differences in how skeptical various people are, although this may depend on the target of their skepticism. For example, there are 9/11 skeptics—those who doubt the government's explanation that al-Qaeda orchestrated the attack—and there are skeptics of the 9/11 skeptics, of whom I am one, who doubt that the 9/11 Truthers have made their case for an alternative explanation (regardless of the government's account). Wood and Douglas conducted an analysis of online arguments about 9/11 and found that "people advocating conspiracy theories more often argued against the mainstream explanation ('the official story is impossible') than for their own ('this is evidence that 9/11 was a conspiracy'). People arguing in favor of the mainstream account of 9/11 did the opposite."[39]

Thus skepticism, as a disbelief or distrust of mainstream authority, can be found in most of the popular conspiracy theories, and this is a two-edged sword. If you believe that JFK was murdered by a conspiracy of assassins, the moon landings were faked, and chemtrails are poisonous vapors being sprayed into the atmosphere for nefarious reasons, you are more likely to also believe that the fluoridation of water is a government conspiracy to harm citizens, and 9/11 was an inside job by the George W. Bush administration. Again, it's the deeper elements of proxy and tribal conspiracism at work.

On the negative side of the skeptical ledger, however, conspiracy skeptics are more likely to make a Type II error—a false negative—and miss real conspiracies, such as Project MKULTRA, in which the CIA conducted mind control and brainwashing experiments on American citizens during the Cold War, dramatized by Errol Morris in the Netflix documentary series *Wormwood*, starring Peter Sarsgaard as Dr. Frank Olson, a biological warfare scientist and CIA operative who committed suicide by jumping out of a 10-story hotel window shortly after he was dosed with LSD by his CIA supervisor.[40] I discuss this in more detail in chapter 9, covering real conspiracies.

For psychologist Rob Brotherton, it is the simplicity of most conspiracy theories that makes them appealing.[41] "The prototypical conspiracy theory is an unanswered question," he wrote. It's hard to wrap our minds around the matrix of causal variables that factor into explaining social, political, or economic events. Indeed, social scientists have developed sophisticated statistical techniques and computer models to tease apart the many variables that go into explaining any human behavior or social phenomenon. But that takes time and training and does not come naturally to the mind. Instead, as Brotherton noted, a conspiracy theory "assumes nothing is as it seems; it portrays the conspirators as preternaturally competent; and as unusually evil."

But the effects of belief in such simple conspiracies alter people's behavior, as evidenced by a 1995 study conducted by Stanford University psychologists Lisa Butler and colleagues of people who had just seen Oliver Stone's 1991 film JFK, which presents most of the JFK assassination conspiracy theories in one dramatic narrative arc.[42] Viewers of the film, compared with those who had not seen it, said they were less likely to donate to or volunteer for a political campaign, or to vote in an upcoming election. "Merely watching the movie eroded, at least temporarily, a little of the viewer's sense of civic engagement," Brotherton stated.[43] This effect of conspiracism was also found with other conspiracy theories. For example, subjects in an experiment who were exposed to climate change conspiracy theories said they were less likely to try to reduce their carbon footprint. People who believe that vaccinations are a conspiracy by either the government or the medical establishment (or both) said they were less likely to seek vaccinations. And African-Americans who believe the conspiracy theory that HIV was a government plot against their community said they were less likely to use protection against STDs.[44]

Finally, and to the core of tribal conspiracism, is an underlying motive identified as *myside bias* by cognitive psychologist Keith Stanovich in his aptly titled book, *The Bias that Divides Us*.[45] Stanovich characterized this cognitive propensity, which has become a modern scourge of cultural divisiveness, as follows:

Myside bias occurs across a wide variety of judgment domains. It is displayed by people in all demographic groups, and it is exhibited even by expert reasoners, the highly educated, and the highly intelligent. It has been demonstrated in research studies across a variety of disciplines, including: cognitive psychology, political science, behavioral economics, legal studies, cognitive neuroscience, and in the informal reasoning literature. Myside bias has been found to occur in every stage of information processing. That is, studies have shown a tendency toward biased search for evidence, biased evaluation of evidence, biased assimilation of evidence, biased memory of outcomes, and biased evidence generation.[46]

We tend to characterize those who disagree with us as unreasonable, uneducated, or ignorant, but note Stanovich's lumping of expert reasoners, highly educated, and highly intelligent as susceptible to the bias. I would go even further, as I did in my book *Why People Believe Weird Things*, in noting that the problem is especially prevalent among highly educated and highly intelligent people who are even better at rationalizing and justifying beliefs that they hold for non-smart reasons.[47] As Stanovich documents, you might be subject to the myside bias if you evaluate acts more favorably when they support your group, apply logical rules better when logical conclusions support your strongly held beliefs, you search or select information sources that are likely to support your position, you de-emphasize the costs of your moral commitments, you distort the perception of risk and reward in the direction of your personal preferences, you selective use moral principles, you selectively learn facts favorable to your political party, you resist evidence when it leads to unwanted social changes, you interpret facts favorable to your preferred group, you selectively question the scientific status of evidence.[48]

• - - • - - •

Beliefs matter, because people act on them, and belief in conspiracy theories very much matter on both a national and a personal level. In the next chapter, we will consider why conspiracy theories have such a negative emotional valence to them.

CHAPTER 4

Constructive Conspiracism

Paranoia, Pessimism, and the Evolutionary
Origins of Conspiracy Cognition

Ever since the 2016 and 2020 presidential elections, much
has been made over the conspiracy theory that the Russians
meddled in American politics, ranging from manipulating
social media with fake accounts operated by bots to backroom deals between Russian operatives and members of
President Donald Trump's family or inner circle. At least
that's the conspiracy theory promulgated by Democrats
who, when they were confident Hillary Clinton would win
in 2016, defended the electoral process against Trump's
fears that it was already rigged against him. After Trump
won, Democrats decided that the election was rigged after
all, but the results of the Mueller investigation into the
matter of Russian collusion did not pan out as they had
expected.[1]

Not that Republicans are off the conspiratorial hook.
During the 2016 campaign, they cooked up a number of
doozies, including the following:[2]

- Hillary Clinton had epilepsy or heart problems, as evidenced by a video clip of her stumbling as she got into her car after a campaign speech.
- The Mueller investigation of the 2016 election was rigged (before the results came out in their favor, after which it was a fair and balanced investigation).
- President Obama wiretapped Trump Tower during the campaign.
- Hillary and the FBI conspired against Trump's campaign.
- The Deep State arranged for Hillary to escape prosecution (despite "lock her up!" chants) for her mishandling of classified emails.
- Conspirator-in-Chief Trump famously blamed the Chinese for creating a global warming hoax; before that, he spent years accusing his presidential predecessor Barack Hussein Obama—emphasis on the middle name—of being foreign born.

Alleged conspirators can even swap sides. Democrats initially accused FBI Director James Comey of conspiring with Russia to prejudice the 2016 election against Hillary Clinton after he announced that he was launching an investigation into her emails, but when Trump fired the FBI director after the election, Democrats exonerated Comey and turned to Trump's son-in-law, Jared Kushner, as the conspirator du jour.[3]

You can set your watch by these political conspiracy theories. If you think the 2016 and 2020 elections were contentious and divisive, then your long-term memory needs refreshing. Harken back to the 2000 election, when Al Gore lost to George W. Bush by the width of a hanging chad on a Florida ballot. Democratic conspiracists pounced, with opinion polls showing that almost half believed that election was rigged.[4] Or recall the 2004 election, when

Bush won a second term and Democrats concocted a conspiracy theory that the election was stolen in the pivotal state of Ohio, investigations of which proved false.[5]

When liberals occupied the White House between 2008 and 2016 under President Obama, Democratic conspiracists were quiescent, while Republican conspiracists dialed up their conspiracy meter, believing the following:[6]

- The community activist group Acorn, with which Obama was associated, had engaged in illegal voter registration practices, even though there was no evidence of this.
- Obamacare was said to contain "death panels" that would determine who would live and die under the Affordable Care Act.
- Obama was bringing 100 million Muslims to America.
- Obama was influenced or controlled by the Muslim Brotherhood.
- Obama redecorated the Oval Office in Middle Eastern style.
- Obama was funded by a Saudi prince.
- Obama's birth certificate showing he was born in Hawaii was fake, and he was actually born in Kenya.

By the end of his second term, Obama himself admitted that if he watched only Fox News, where such conspiracy theories about Democrats are routinely promoted, he wouldn't vote for himself.[7]

You'll notice something common among all these conspiracy theories: they have a negative emotional valence to them. That is, rarely do people believe there's a conspiracy afoot to make the world a better or safer place. Conspiracy theories nearly always involve nefarious agents conspiring to do bad things. Indeed, it is the very definition of a conspiracy theory that we've adapted for this book, and it is what most people think regarding conspiracies. Even the flip side to this negativity gradient—namely, that conspiracy theorists believe that in uncovering and exposing an evil cabal, they are doing the world a positive service—still necessitates a negative threat that must be countered. "Many conspiracy theories actually assume a hidden struggle between 'good' and 'evil' conspiracies," conspiracy researcher Jan-Willem van Prooijen noted, citing QAnon as a type specimen.[8] "Surely this is about an evil, satanic 'deep state' of Democratic elites. But part of the theory also is that the Trump administration is fighting a secret war against this deep state. So here we have a secret, 'benevolent' conspiracy trying to make the world a better place by fighting an evil conspiracy as part of the narrative."

In this chapter, I want to consider the deeper psychological reasons for conspiratorial thinking, starting with the observation that conspiracy theories are slanted toward the negative. There are good evolutionary reasons for such pessimism.

• – – • – – •

My friend and colleague Jared Diamond, a Pulitzer Prize–winning author who spends every summer in Papua New Guinea with the indigenous peoples there, identified what he has called "constructive paranoia," or "the importance of being attentive to hazards that carry a low risk each time but are encountered frequently.[9] One night when out in the rain forest with his native colleagues, Diamond proposed they pitch their tents under a big tree. "To my surprise," he recalled, "my New Guinea friends absolutely refused. They explained that the tree was dead and might fall on us." At first, Diamond thought them overly paranoid. Over the years, however, he formed a different opinion with some back-of-the-envelope calculations: "I came to realize that every night that I camped in a New Guinea forest, I heard a tree falling. And when I did a frequency/risk calculation, I understood their point of view." If the odds of a tree falling on you any given night are only 1 in 1,000, but you sleep under trees every night, "you'll be dead within a few years." Diamond's "constructive paranoia" is an insight we can apply to conspiracism. Call it *constructive conspiracism*—the tendency to assume conspiracy theories are true, just in case.

Psychologist Steven Pinker also invoked an anthropological example to make the point that there are good evolutionary reasons why constructive conspiracism may be hardwired into our nature.[10] "Conspiracy theories, for their part, flourish because people have always been vulnerable to real conspiracies. Foraging people can't be too careful. The deadliest form of warfare among tribal peoples is not the pitched battle but the stealthy ambush and the predawn raid." It's what the Yanomamö of Amazonia call *nomohori*, which anthropologist Napoleon Chagnon translated as "dastardly trick," such as when one tribe invites another for a feast and then ambushes them when they're most vulnerable. Here's an account of one such *nomohori* that Chagnon gleaned from a missionary:

> The headman of the group organized a raiding party to abduct women from a distant group. They went there and told these people that they had machetes and cooking pots from the foreigners, who prayed to a spirit that gave such items in answer to the prayers. They then volunteered to teach these people how to pray. When the men knelt down and bowed their heads, the raiders attacked them with their machetes and killed them. They captured their women and fled.[11]

In his ethnography on the Yanomamö, *Into the Heart*, anthropologist Kenneth Good recounted what life was like for these prehistoric people who, in serving as an analog of our Paleolithic ancestors, would have had to develop a constructive conspiracism about other people, both in their own group and especially in other tribes. In an interview for a story I did on the "anthropology wars" of the 1990s over the characteristics of human nature, Good offered this explanation:

> Fidelity in Yanomami land is not considered a standard of any sort, let alone a moral principle. Here it is every man for himself. Stealing, rape, even killing—these acts aren't measured by some moral standard. They aren't thought of in terms of proper or improper social behavior. Here everyone does what he can and everyone defends his own rights. A man gets up and screams and berates someone for stealing plantains from his section of the garden, then he'll go and do exactly the same thing. I protect myself, you protect yourself. You try something and I catch you, I'll stop you.[12]

Many antisocial behaviors in Yanomami land, such as theft, are kept at a minimum through such social constraints as shunning, or through personal constraints, such as fear of violence and retaliation. In this context, constructive conspiracism emerges as a rational strategy, which is backed by game-theoretic logic. Here's how Pinker explained it:

> The only safeguard against this cloak-and-dagger subterfuge is to outthink them preemptively, which can lead to convoluted trains of conjecture and a refusal to take obvious facts at face value. In signal detection terms, the cost of missing a real conspiracy is higher than that of false-alarming to a suspected one. This calls for setting our bias toward the trigger-happy rather than the gun-shy end of the scale, adapting us to try to get wind of possible conspiracies even on tenuous evidence.[13]

From his extensive studies on conflict and violence in hunter-gatherer bands, anthropologist Lawrence Keeley showed just how common and dangerous coalitional con-spiracies probably were for our ancestors: "The most ele-mentary form of warfare is a raid (or type of raid) in which a small group of men endeavour to enter enemy territory undetected in order to ambush and kill an unsuspecting iso-lated individual, and to then withdraw rapidly without suffering any casualties."[14] That's a conspiracy, so the pro-pensity to believe conspiracy theories about behind-the-scenes, backstabbing conspirators has an evolutionary basis.

That is also the finding of conspiracy researchers Jan-Willem van Prooijen and Mark van Vugt in their analysis contrasting *proximate* (immediate) mechanisms underlying conspiracy beliefs, such as pattern recognition, agency de-tection, threat management, and alliance detection, and *ul-timate* (evolutionary) mechanisms, such as "a functionally integrated mental system to detect conspiracies that in all likelihood has been shaped in an ancestral human environ-ment in which hostile coalitions—that is, conspiracies that truly existed—were a frequent cause of misery, death, and reproductive loss."[15]

The problem is that there is often an evolutionary mis-match between traits that were adaptive for survival in our Paleolithic environment but are not necessarily functional in modern settings. Being constructively conspiratorial in an ancient hunter-gatherer milieu may not be especially beneficial today, especially if one acts on one's conspirato-rial beliefs, from barging into a Washington, DC, pizzeria to storming the US Capitol.

• - - • - - •

Such paranoia about bad things that can happen hints at a deeper psychological reason for conspiracy beliefs, called *negativity bias*, or, in the title of a paper by psychologist Roy Baumeister and his colleagues, "Bad Is Stronger Than

Good."[16] There are many examples. For instance, in investing, behavioral economists have identified a phenomenon called loss *aversion* to explain why investors tend to be risk averse: losses hurt twice as much as gains feel good.[17] To get people to gamble on an investment, the potential payoff must be twice what the potential loss might be. Nor does this occur just in finance. Tennis superstar Jimmy Connors once said, "I hate losing more than I love winning."[18] Cycling champion Lance Armstrong echoed this sentiment when explaining to filmmaker Alex Gibney why he was more motivated to not let cancer—and, subsequently, other cyclists—defeat him, than he was by the pull of the positive payoffs of winning: "I like to win, but more than anything, I can't stand this idea of losing. Because to me, losing means death."[19]

Pessimism and negativity bias are ubiquitous in life. Psychologists consistently find that criticism and negative feedback hurt more than praise and positive feedback feel good.[20] Losing money and friends has a greater impact on people than gaining these objectives.[21] Bad impressions and negative stereotypes form faster and are more resistant to change than positive ones.[22] A study of the emotional content of diaries found that bad events negatively influenced both good and bad moods, whereas good events were limited to affecting only good moods.[23] Bad everyday occurrences also have a greater impact than good ones. For example, having a good day does not necessarily lead to a good mood the next day, whereas a bad day often does carry its consequences over into the next day.[24] Traumatic events leave traces in mood and memory longer than good things that happen. For example, a single childhood traumatic event, like sexual molestation, can erase years of positive experiences.[25] Morally bad actions weigh far more in the moral evaluation of a person by others than morally good actions.[26] In an analysis of over 17,000 psychological research papers, 69 percent of them dealt with negative issues, compared with only 31 percent for positive ones.[27] This probably is because bad things have a greater impact on human thought and behavior than good ones do, so research on negative life events is more likely to get funded and be published.

In a long review paper covering hundreds of such studies, Baumeister and his colleagues not only consistently found that in all domains of life, bad is stronger than good, but they were also unable to find a *single* counterinstance in which good outdid bad—and it wasn't for lack of trying.[28] "We had hoped to identify several contrary patterns, which would have permitted us to develop an elaborate, complex, and nuanced theory about when bad is stronger versus when good is stronger," they stated. Instead, bad always triumphed. "It is found in both cognition and motivation; in both inner, intrapsychic processes and in interpersonal ones; in connection with decisions about the future and to a limited extent with memories of the past; and in animal learning, complex human information processing, and emotional responses."

Psychologists Paul Rozin and Edward Royzman were the first to call this effect *negativity bias*, in which "negative events are more salient, potent, dominant in combinations, and generally efficacious than positive events."[29] In the numerous examples above of how pessimism triumphs over optimism, Rozin and Royzman noted that negative events lead us to seek their causes more readily than positive events do. For example, wars generate endless analyses in books and articles, whereas peace literature is paltry by comparison. Everyone asks, "Why is there war?" Almost no one asks, "Why is there peace?" Moreover, negative stimuli command more attention than positive stimuli. For example, in rats, negative tastes elicit stronger responses than positive ones. In taste-aversion experiments, a single exposure to a noxious food or drink can cause lasting avoidance of that item, but there is no corresponding parallel with good-tasting food or drink.[30] Tellingly, we have more words to describe the qualities of physical pain (deep, intense, dull, sharp, aching, burning, cutting, pinching, piercing, tearing, twitching, shooting, stabbing, thrusting, throbbing, penetrating, lingering, radiating, etc.) than we have to describe physical pleasure (intense, delicious, exquisite, breathtaking, sumptuous, sweet, etc.).[31]

Not only that, but there are more cognitive categories for and descriptive terms of negative emotions than positive ones.[32] As Leo Tolstoy famously observed in 1875, and since then became elevated into the Anna Karenina principle: "Happy families are all alike; every unhappy family is unhappy in its own way."[33] In addition, evil contaminates good more than good purifies evil. As an old Russian proverb says, "A spoonful of tar can spoil a barrel of honey, but a spoonful of honey does nothing for a barrel of tar." In India, members of the higher castes may be thought to be contaminated by eating food prepared by members of the lower castes, but those in the lower castes do not receive an equivalent rise upward in purity status by eating food prepared by their higher-caste counterparts.[34] Related to these effects, an evolutionary component of negativity bias may be seen in the emotion of disgust, which evolved to drive organisms away from noxious stimuli, because noxiousness is an informational cue that such stimuli could kill you through poison (e.g., food substances) or disease (e.g., fecal matter, vomit, and other bodily effluvia). This explains why negative events are more contagious than positive ones. Germs are the basic biological model for a contagion, for which there is no positive parallel.[35]

There's a good reason for this cognitive asymmetry between good and bad. Progress is mostly made incrementally and in small steps, whereas regress can easily come about in one colossal calamity. For example, in a complex machine or body, all the parts must consistently work to keep the thing going, but if one part or system fails, it can be catastrophic to all the rest. This can spell the end of the machine or organism. Stability of the overall body must be maintained, requiring the brain, which runs the body, to devote the most attention to threats that could terminate the organism. And in life, there are more ways to fail than there are to succeed. It is difficult to attain success, and the paths to it are few, but there are many ways to fail to achieve success, and the paths away from it are many.

• - - • - - •

Let's dig even deeper into our evolved psychology to understand the logic behind negativity bias. Steven Pinker argued that in our evolutionary past, there was an asymmetry of payoffs in which the fitness cost of overreacting to a threat was less than the fitness cost of underreacting, so we err on the side of overreaction—in other words, we assume the worst.[36] Why? Because the world was more dangerous in our evolutionary past, so it paid to be risk averse and highly sensitive to threats. If things were good, then taking a gamble to improve them a little bit more was not perceived to be worth the risk of things becoming worse.

Pinker placed the blame for our evolved constructive paranoia squarely on the shoulders of the second law of thermodynamics, or entropy. Entropy is a fundamental physical rule that closed systems (those not taking in energy) move from order to disorder, from organization to disorganization, from structured to unstructured, and from warm to cold. Although entropy can be temporarily reversed in an open system with an outside source of energy, such as heating cold food in a microwave, isolated systems decay as entropy increases. Without an outside source (like the sun), energy dissipates; systems run down; warm things turn cold; metal rusts; wood rots; weeds overwhelm gardens; bedrooms get cluttered; and social, political, and economic systems fall apart if not maintained. In our world—particularly the world in which our ancestors evolved the cognition and emotions that we inherited—entropy dictates that there are more ways for things to go bad than to turn out well, so our modern psychology is attuned to a world that was more dangerous in our evolutionary past than it is today. Thus, as I concluded in an essay on the meaning and purpose of life, the second law of thermodynamics is also the first law of life.[37] By doing nothing, entropy pushes you toward greater disorder and then death. Life's basic purpose is to combat entropy by doing something extropic—expending energy to survive and flourish.

The ne plus ultra explanation for entropy can be found on the bumper sticker "SHIT HAPPENS." As such, so-called misfortunes like accidents, plagues, famine, and disease have no purposeful agency behind them—no gods, demons, witches, or conspiracists intending evil—just entropy taking its course. Because we tend to find meaningful patterns and intentional agents in random events, we attribute many of life's outcomes to conspiracies. And because of negativity bias, in which bad is stronger than good, a belief in negative conspiracy theories is a feature, not a bug, in our cognition.

• - • - - •

The two main aspects of our cognition that lead to conspiracy thinking in this regard are what I briefly mentioned earlier: patternicity and agenticity. I would like to return to these and develop them in more detail, to better understand the logic behind constructive conspiracism.

Recall that patternicity is the tendency to find meaningful patterns in both meaningful and meaningless noise.[38]

To explain why we evolved this feature in our thinking, let's start with a thought experiment. Imagine you lived three million years ago on the plains of Africa as a small-brained bipedal primate, highly vulnerable to predators. You hear a rustle in the grass. Is it just the wind, or is it a dangerous predator? If you assume the rustle in the grass is a dangerous predator, but it turns out to be just the wind, you have made a *Type I error*, or a *false positive*—believing something is real when it isn't. You connected A (the rustle in the grass) to B (a dangerous predator), but in this case A is not linked with B. No harm occurs. You move away from the rustling sound and become more alert and cautious.

But if you assume the rustle in the grass is just the wind, and it turns out to be a dangerous predator, you have made a *Type II error* in cognition, or a *false negative*—believing something is not real when it is. You failed to connect A (the rustle in the grass) to B (a dangerous predator), and in this case A is tied to B. Harm is likely, and you could be the predator's next meal. The problem is that assessing the difference between a Type I and a Type II error is highly problematic—especially in the split-second, life-and-death decisions in our ancestral environments—so the default position is to assume that all patterns are real—that is, assume all rustles in the grass are made by dangerous predators, not the wind. We are the descendants of those who were most successful at finding such patterns.

I call this constructive conspiracism, and my interpretation is supported by what van Prooijen and Van Vugt called "adaptive conspiracism," where "conspiracy theories uniquely helped ancestral humans to navigate their social world better and anticipate and overcome imminent dangers in their environment."[39] They termed the threat coalitional violence, or "violence committed by actual conspirators occurring both within and between groups," and they noted that our psychology would have evolved to be attentive to this as an adaptation for survival. Similar to my analysis above of the relative risks of making Type I versus Type II errors and of erring on the side of assuming the worst—in this case, that the conspiracy theory is true—they invoked error-management theory, which came from evolutionary psychology. This theory was first developed by Martie Haselton and David Buss to explain the massive male and female differences in sexual behavior and preferences that lead women to be far more cautious and choosy than men when it comes to sex, because they have so much more to lose (ranging from pregnancy to physical violence).[40] Thus, van Prooijen and Van Vugt concluded, "error-management theory would predict that underrecognizing conspiracies becomes more costly (and overrecognizing conspiracies less costly) to the extent that the dangers of real conspiracies increase."[41]

The evidence that we evolved conspiracy detection cognition comes from having met the requirements for all psychological adaptations—that is, complexity, universality, domain specificity, interactivity, efficiency, and functionality.[42] Conspiracy theories contain complex predispositions, such as pattern and agency detection, alliance detection, and threat management; are universal; are specific to domains of human life and thought; interact with other cognitive domains; trigger detection cues quickly and efficiently; and are functional, in that they "lead people to display emotions and behaviors designed either to avoid the suspected conspiracy (e.g., fear and avoidance) or to actively confront it (e.g., anger and aggression)." Van Prooijen and Van Vugt presented substantial evidence that all of these domains are tapped by conspiracism.[43] Thus, by implication, constructive conspiracism most likely is an evolved adaptation.

Colloquially, we might think of constructive conspiracism as the default position when living in a dangerous world. If it turns out that there is no danger, no harm is done, and not much energy is expended in being a little paranoid. Instead, if it turns out that there is danger, being constructively paranoid pays off. In other words, *assume the worst!* In this model, constructive conspiracism is a type of pattern, a belief about the world in which our ancestors benefited from focusing more on the negative than the positive. Thus it offers an evolutionary explanation for a worldview in which bad is stronger than good. Finding conspiracies where none exist is a lower-cost error than not finding conspiracies when they are present, especially if someone or something is conspiring to harm you.

Therefore, constructive conspiracism has a deep evolutionary foundation in the brain—in the form of patternicity—but there's more. Conspiracy theories usually involve other people conspiring to do something nefarious, so we need to add the concept of agenticity—the tendency to infuse patterns with meaning, intention, and agency—to our explanatory model. Agenticity is directly related to patternicity, inasmuch as we tend to instill the patterns we find with intentional agents. Returning to my thought experiment with the hominid on the plains of Africa who hears a rustle in the grass, and the crucial matter of whether the sound represents a dangerous predator or just the wind—what's the difference between the wind and a dangerous predator? "Wind" is an inanimate force, whereas "dangerous predator" signals an intentional agent—that is, someone or something out there that plans to make me its next meal. That is, we often impart agency and intention to the patterns we find and believe that these factors control the world, sometimes invisibly, from the top down. Souls, spirits, ghosts, gods, demons, angels, aliens, intelligent designers, government and corporate conspiracists, and all manner of invisible agents with power and deliberate intent are believed to haunt our world and control our lives. For example, subjects watching reflective dots move about in a darkened room, especially if the dots take on the shape of two legs and two arms, infer that they represent a person or an intentional agent.[44] Children believe that the sun can think and follows them around. When asked to draw a picture of the sun, they often add a smiley face to give agency to it.[45] Subjects in an experiment conducted by Peter Brugger and Christine Mohr at the University of Bristol in England who were given dopamine—a chemical transmitter in the brain involving rewards and reinforcements for learning and finding patterns—are more likely to find significance in coincidences and pick out meaning and patterns where there are none.[46] In another study, Brugger and Mohr compared 20 self-professed believers in ghosts, gods, spirits, and conspiracies to 20 self-professed skeptics of such claims.[47] They showed all subjects a series of slides consisting of people's faces, some of which were normal, while others had their parts scrambled, such as swapping out eyes or ears or noses from different faces. In another experiment, real and scrambled words were flashed on a screen. In general, the scientists found that the believers were much more likely than the skeptics to mistakenly assess a scrambled face as real, and to read a scrambled word as normal.

Combined with our propensity to find revelatory patterns in both meaningful and meaningless noise, patternicity and agenticity form the basis of conspiratorial cognition (why people believe conspiracies), along with the conspiracy effect (why smart people believe blatantly wrong things for apparently rational reasons). Conspiracy theories predictably include hidden agents at work behind the scenes, puppet masters pulling political and economic strings as we dance to the tune of the Deep State, the Rothschilds, the Rockefellers, or the Illuminati. For example, psychologists Joshua Hart and Molly Graether, in their research on conspiracy personality types (discussed in chapter 2), they found that people who were more likely to believe in conspiracy theories "were also more likely to say that nonhuman objects—triangle shapes moving around on a computer screen—were acting intentionally, as though they were capable of having thoughts and goals they were trying to accomplish. In other words, they inferred meaning and motive where others did not."[48] That's patternicity and agenticity at work.

Finally, how paranoid are conspiracy believers? That is the question asked by Roland Imhoff and Pia Lamberty in their "more fine-grained understanding of the connect and disconnect between paranoia and belief in conspiracy theories." These researchers examined one meta-analysis and two correlational studies to provide an estimate for an association between the two, reaching the following conclusions:

> Although both assume sinister intentions of others, beliefs in conspiracy theories are more specific in who these others are (powerful groups) than paranoia (everyone). In contrast, paranoia was more restricted in terms of who the target of the negative intentions is (the self) than conspiracy theorizing (society as a whole). In light of this and distinct associations of conspiracy beliefs with political control and trust but not (inter-)personal control and trust (like paranoia), we propose to treat the two as distinct (albeit correlated) constructs with conspiracy beliefs reflecting a political attitude compared to paranoia as a self-relevant belief.[49]

Paranoia and constructive conspiracism are not exactly the same, or else we could just employ one term. But their influence overlaps in the mind of conspiracists, which is undeniable—and sometimes deadly.

• - - • - - •

The consequences of combining constructive conspiracism with Type II errors—that is, false negatives, or failing to recognize a conspiracy—can be as deadly as it is for prey animals who fail to recognize the rustle in the grass as a dangerous predator. Examples from history are abundant:

1. *The Yom Kippur War.* On October 6, 1973, a coalition of Arab states, led by Egypt and Syria, launched a surprise attack on Israel on the holiest day in Judaism, Yom Kippur (the Day of Atonement), crossing the Suez Canal and advancing virtually unopposed into the Sinai Peninsula. It took days for Israel to scramble a defensive response and repulse the attack, but that failure to recognize a conspiracy on the part of a potential enemy resulted in Israel now being hypervigilant about any potential threats to its existence.[50] That is constructive conspiracism.

2. *Operation Barbarossa.* This is the code name for the surprise Nazi invasion of the Soviet Union on Sunday, June 22, 1941. The normally paranoid Soviet dictator Joseph Stalin, who saw conspiracies afoot everywhere he looked, was not constructively paranoid enough to recognize that Adolf Hitler, his partner in the Molotov-Ribbentrop Pact guaranteeing peace between Nazi Germany and the USSR, would betray him, despite the fact that the Germans were amassing hundreds of thousands of troops and equipment near the Soviet border, and the British high command had signaled this fact to Stalin.[51] Stalin was not constructively conspiratorial enough.

3. *Operation Z, or the Hawaii Operation:* The Japanese surprise attack on Pearl Harbor on December 7, 1941, caught most of the US military off guard. Although it was evident enough from the actions of the Japanese military that war with the United States was immi-

nent, inasmuch as the former was already at war with China and diplomatic relations with the United States had broken down, most American leaders believed that the conflict would take place in the Far East, not thousands of miles closer to America, in Hawaii. With hindsight bias in full operation, many conspiracy theorists can't believe that President Franklin D. Roosevelt could not have realized the attack coming, so they have suggested he was either in on it or let it happen. The deeper problem was simply that he wasn't constructively paranoid enough.[52]

Although these examples come from military history, this should not distract from the deeper principle that the world is often a dangerous place, not just for nations, but also for individuals, so constructive conspiracism is often necessary. Applying our definition of a conspiracy (two or more people, or a group, plotting or acting in secret to gain an advantage or harm others immorally or illegally), even a cursory review reveals that conspiracies have dramatically influenced the course of history and may still be found at work in modern societies. A few examples from this arena will suffice to make the point, some of which I'll cover in more detail in the second half of the book:

- Julius Caesar was stabbed to death by a conspiracy of Roman senators on the Ides of March in 44 BC.
- The Gunpowder Plot of 1605 saw a group of provincial English Catholics attempting to assassinate King James I by blowing up the House of Lords during the State Opening of Parliament. The plot was discovered and thwarted only a few days beforehand, with the conspiracists caught, tried, convicted, hanged, drawn, and quartered.

- In 1776, an elite group of soldiers were assigned as George Washington's bodyguards, some of whom were plotting to assassinate the future first president of the United States at the behest of the governor of New York and the mayor of New York City, who were both Loyalists. Their plan was foiled, due to the ineptitude of the plotters in keeping it secret.
- Abraham Lincoln was assassinated by a conspiracy of white Southerners angered by the outcome of the Civil War, which itself was instigated by a Southern cabal to illegally secede from the United States, arguably the biggest conspiracy in US history.
- World War I exploded after a Serbian separatist secret society called the Black Hand conspired to assassinate Archduke Franz Ferdinand of Austria, leading to an arms race that erupted in the guns of August and the start of a conflict that resulted in the deaths of millions.
- In the 1950s, conspiratorially minded Senator Joseph McCarthy, in his now-infamous congressional hearings, launched a witch hunt to ferret out what he was certain was a Communist conspiracy to destroy America.
- In the 1960s, Operation Northwoods was a document produced under the Kennedy administration, proposing a number of false-flag operations—which themselves are a type of conspiracy—that might be carried out in order to justify military intervention in Cuba. Among the proposals were such ideas as staging a fake attack on the US military base at Guantanamo Bay, employing a fake Russian MIG aircraft to buzz a real US civilian airliner, faking an attack on a US ship to make it look like Cubans did it, and developing "a Communist Cuban terror campaign in Miami." None of these crazy ideas were

implemented, but the fact that members of Kennedy's administration considered them—even in the context of a meeting with people just spitballing ideas—reveals the lengths to which even high-ranking people in government are willing to conspire against others to get their way.

- In the 1970s, Watergate stands out as a conspiracy of dunces, and the Pentagon Papers revealed the extent to which the Kennedy, Johnson, and Nixon administrations conspired to escalate the Vietnam War without congressional knowledge, much less approval. We now know that Kennedy conspired to have Fidel Castro assassinated, Johnson conspired to cover up that fact when he took office, and Nixon secretly recorded conversations in the Oval Office that revealed his distinctive view of presidential power—a view that he later summarized in an interview with David Frost: "Well, when the president does it, that means that it is not illegal."[53]

- In the 1980s, the Iran-Contra arms-for-hostages scandal was a conspiracy that embodied what conspiracists since World War I had been concerned about—the usurpation of power by conspirators who were legally elected to their positions, instead of hijacking government agencies through a coup, which was common in centuries past.

- In the 1990s, government overreach against Randy Weaver and his family in Ruby Ridge, Idaho, and against David Koresh and the Branch Davidians in Waco, Texas, led to the rise of the conspiratorially minded militia movement that culminated in Timothy McVeigh's bombing of a federal building in Oklahoma City.

- In the 2000s, the George W. Bush administration concocted a conspiracy theory that Iraq was developing weapons of mass destruction (WMDs) and used it as a justification for invading that country, which proved false when inspectors failed to find any WMDs. Wikileaks revealed the extent to which the National Security Agency and other governmental agencies conspired to spy on Americans and foreign leaders on the heels of 9/11.

As George Orwell warned us in a memorable commentary shortly after the Second World War, "To see what is in front of one's nose needs a constant struggle. . . . The point is we are all capable of believing things which we know to be untrue, and then, when we are finally proved wrong, impudently twisting the facts so as to show that we were right. Intellectually, it is possible to carry on this process for an indefinite time: the only check on it is that sooner or later a false belief bumps up against solid reality, usually on a battlefield."[54] Once again, reality bites.

CHAPTER 5

A Case Study in Conspiracism

The Sovereign Citizens Conspiracy Theory

On July 3, 2021, Americans awoke to a bizarre story about a group of heavily armed men arrested without incident by Massachusetts police after an overnight roadside standoff.[1] Law enforcement had come upon them on the side of the road at 1:30 AM on Interstate 95 north of Boston, the drivers attending to their vehicles on what they said was their journey to a "training" camp in Maine. Whatever it was they were going to train for apparently involved firearms, as state troopers confiscated three AR-15 rifles, two pistols, a bolt-action rifle, a shotgun, a short-barreled rifle, lots of ammunition, high-capacity magazines, and body armor, all unlawfully possessed. Unlawful, that is, if you're a citizen of the United States, which the members of this particular group—Black separatists called Rise of the Moors—claimed they were not. Of what country, you may ask, were they citizens? None. According to their website,[2] the group seeks "equal justice under our own law, and not under the United States government, as we are not citizens of the

United States." As such, "we owe no tax obligations to the government of the United States."

Watching the story unfold, I immediately thought of the Sovereign Citizens conspiracy theory, which I first encountered as a college undergraduate. My roommate and I attended a tax seminar where we were told that paying taxes was unnecessary, because the Sixteenth Amendment, which empowered Congress to levy an income tax, was never legally ratified. After a long and detailed history of the IRS, we were advised not to file a tax return and given instructions on what to do and say when the Feds came a-knockin'. This was a type of conspiracy theory, inasmuch as it involved a government agency illegally profiting from citizens without their knowledge. The slick presentation seemed internally coherent and logically plausible while I was sitting there in the room. It was not until later, after some reflection, that I figured it couldn't possibly be true, because if it were, then no one would pay income tax. Unfortunately, my roommate went for it and got away tax free for years, until the IRS caught up with him and he got his comeuppance.

I was thinking about this incident in August 2013, when I appeared in a Portland, Oregon, court as an expert witness on the psychology of why people fall for such schemes. The case, *United States of America v. Miles J. Julison*, involved a house flipper who lost big in the 2007 financial meltdown.[3] That year he reported $583,151 in "other income" to the IRS on his tax return, claiming that the entire amount was withheld as income taxes. Submitting eight IRS 1099-OID forms, Julison requested a refund of $411,773. According to the IRS, an OID, or Original Issue Discount, "is a form of interest. It is the excess of a debt instrument's stated redemption price at maturity over its issue price." A 1099-OID applies to debt instruments, such as bonds and notes, that were discounted at purchase, and the tax is the difference between the instrument's actual value and the discounted purchase price. A 1099-OID fraud consists of filing Form 1099-OID with false withholding information, in order to reduce taxable income. Amazingly, the IRS sent Julison a check in the amount of $411,773, which he spent on a home loan, credit card bills, a Mercedes-Benz, and a boat. Emboldened by his success, the next year Julison reported $2.3 million in interest income and demanded a refund of $1.5 million. This time, however, instead of a refund check, he got an IRS investigation that landed him in court and, after a guilty verdict, sent him to jail.

This particular tax scam is popular among tax resisters with a conspiratorial bent, especially those who call themselves Sovereign Citizens. These individuals hold that the US government is actually a corporation owned by the International Monetary Fund and English banks, and that there is a secret account holding $1 million for every child born in the United States, thereby rendering them slaves to a global financial system.[4] Sovereign Citizens think this money should be "refunded" to them, and the 1099-OID is one tool among many that they use. Sovereign Citizens believe that they are exempt from federal jurisdiction, because they are "natural citizens" who are granted their rights from God. The rest of us schlubs are what they call "Fourteenth Amendment citizens," slaves who were freed by this constitutional amendment but who have fewer rights. As such, Sovereign Citizens do not believe they are subject to federal jurisdiction, do not recognize government currency (gold is popular among such far-right groups), and insist that taxation is illegitimate. Many do not believe in federal laws, and some even post "Sovereign Land" signs on their property, explaining that trespassers, including law enforcement agents, would be committing an "act of war." The FBI labels them a domestic terrorist threat, and the Southern Poverty Law Center estimates that there are about 100,000 "hardcore sovereign believers."[5]

As a self-proclaimed Sovereign Citizen, Miles J. Julison did not recognize the court's right to try him, declined to represent himself, and refused to work with his court-appointed lawyer—the attorney who brought me in on the case—who repeatedly urged him to plead guilty, with a reduced sentence, in the face of overwhelming evidence against him, if for no other reason than that he had a wife and two children who needed him. Instead, as it shows in the court records, and as I heard Julison repeatedly say in the courtroom, he voiced variants on the following:

> For and on the record, I am here under express duress *in propria persona*. I am Miles Joseph, creation of Christ Jesus. I reserve all of my unalienable rights without prejudice, UCC 1-308, Declaration of Independence, *nunc pro tunc*, *praeterea preterea* and without the state. My jurisdiction is in harmony with the common law, UCC 1-103. I refuse for cause all testimony of this court, as it is not under penalty of perjury, 28 U.S.C. 7146, Clause 1. My silence does not preclude a contract whatsoever.[6]

UCC is the Universal Commercial Code, enacted into law in 1952 to govern business transactions and standardize US business law to be uniform in every state. Julison repeated this language and these codes as if they were talismans—magical objects that would work if repeated in just the right sequence to set him free. During a lunch break outside the courtroom, Julison happened to walk past me, so I took the opportunity to ask him if he really believed all these Sovereign Citizen claims or if he was just in it for the money. As my testimony was done and I was heading home, I hoped for honesty. He was as unequivocal in his conviction as he was adamant in his mannerisms as he replied, "The United States is a corporation in the state of Delaware. I have their registration papers printed right off their web site. Before anything can be argued there has to be a jurisdiction established." So, I inquired, referencing my own testimony in court, which stated that I did not think he was just a con man pretending to be a Sovereign Citizen, but instead was a true conspiracist, "Is my description of you as a true believer true?" Julison responded, biblically, "I believe in the blood of the Lamb."

• - - • - - •

Sovereign Citizens is but a recent instantiation of larger and older conspiracy theories, in this case the Posse Comitatus (Latin for "force of the country"), an American right-wing populist movement named after the common law practice of a group of people mobilized by law enforcement to suppress lawlessness or defend a territory or country (as seen in Western films like The Magnificent Seven, in which a "posse" of gunslinging citizens are recruited to hunt down a Mexican outlaw).[7] The Posse Comitatus Act, passed in 1878 by Congress and signed into law by President Rutherford B. Hayes, limited the power of the federal government to employ federal troops to enforce domestic laws, but among conspiracists it is more closely associated with the spontaneous formation of a citizens' posse in the Wild West to track an errant scofflaw.[8] By the 1960s, this form of self-help justice morphed into a ragtag group of citizens, calling themselves Posse Comitatus, who took to the woods to practice survivalism (today's "preppers"). This, in turn, inspired the rise of the militia movement in the 1990s, following government overreach at Ruby Ridge and Waco. You can see where all this is heading.

The Posse Comitatus conspiracy theory holds that the county—not the country—is the highest level of legitimate government, and that county sheriffs are the highest-ranking law enforcement agents. This leads its members to not only repudiate all debts and refuse to pay federal and state taxes, but also to reject government-issued driver's licenses, issue bogus legal and financial documents, and concoct elaborate conspiracy theories involving the gold standard, the Federal Reserve, and international bankers. Posse Comitatus, in turn, is associated with the white-supremacist Christian Identity movement, whose stated mission was well captured by the Posse's primary founder, William Potter Gale, in a radio sermon in which he declared, "This nation and this government were founded by white men and white women who were Christians. They fought their way across the wilderness and built a great nation. In the name of the God of our Fathers, this nation will remain a white man's land and a white man's government."[9]

As a result of these and related conspiracy theories, members of the Sovereign Citizens, Posse Comitatus, and Christian Identity movements do not recognize federal and state law enforcement as legitimate. In yet another example of how beliefs drive actions, as well as the dangers of believing false conspiracy theories, on May 20, 2010, in West Memphis, Arkansas, violence resulted when Sovereign Citizen Jerry Kane was pulled over by two state police officers for a routine traffic stop. As he engaged in fisticuffs with the police, Kane's 16-year-old son lept out of the vehicle with his father's AK-47 rifle and shot both cops dead. Father and son were subsequently chased down and cornered in a Walmart parking lot, where they were killed by police.[10] Talk about having the courage of your convictions (however delusional they may be)! Further down the conspiratorial rabbit hole, some of these conspiracists consider federal buildings to be bases of a Jewish "enemy government," sometimes rendered as ZOG, or Zionist Occupation Government. So it should come as no surprise that Christian Identity movement member Terry Nichols aided and abetted Timothy McVeigh in blowing up the Alfred P. Murrah Federal Building in Oklahoma City in 1995. Far beyond being fringy, conspiracism can be deadly.

How does someone come to believe in such a conspiracy theory? I attempted to answer this question in another court case in Hawaii that was similar to the Sovereign Citizens conspiracy theory one in Oregon. This trial involved a scheme claiming that paying income tax is voluntary. Among the dozens of documents and videotaped lectures I reviewed in the case, one was from a tax consultant who told his audience that "filing of a US Individual Income Tax Return Form 1040 is completely voluntary. A person working in the private sector is not required to file or pay income taxes because there is no provision in the Internal Revenue Code which specifically and unequivocally requires an individual to pay income taxes."[11]

One citizen of Hawaii who believed this conspiracy theory did not pay income taxes for many years and accumulated a tax debt of $4,527,614. The case was ultimately settled out of court with the IRS, whom I presume got the money due, plus interest and penalties. (As I was about to board a plane to Hawaii I was told to stand down, as a settlement had been reached, which often happens in such cases.) For the record, paying income taxes is *not* voluntary. For this case, I was tasked by the defense to put together a primer on belief, consisting of ten components that explain precisely how and why someone can come to believe a conspiracy theory. As an overview of the psychology of conspiracism, the following are those ten components.[12]

1. *The brain is a belief engine.* Humans evolved to be skilled pattern-seeking creatures, but as we saw in the previous chapter, we are left with the legacy of two types of thinking errors: a Type I error (believing a falsehood), and a Type II error (rejecting a truth). In some cases, neither of these will automatically get us killed, so we can live with them.[13] The belief engine is an evolved mechanism to help us survive, because, in addition to committing Type I and Type II errors, we also engage in what we might call a Type I hit

(not believing a falsehood) and a Type II hit (believing a truth). Thus a belief engine is a domain-general processor with specific modes of making hits and misses. We have to believe *something* about our environment, and these beliefs are learned through experience, but the process of forming beliefs is genetically hard wired. It is in our nature to believe, so since we make both Type I and II errors, along with Type I and II hits, under the right conditions a great many false beliefs will pass through our skeptical filters. The rest of the components of belief below outline those conditions.

2. *Beliefs are reinforced by authorities.* We are a hierarchical social species who look up to authorities for guidance, starting with our parents, which is wise when you are young and inexperienced. We feel a sense of duty or obligation to people in positions of authority. This is why advertisers of pharmaceutical products employ doctors to front their campaigns, and why most of us will do most things that our manager requests. Job titles, uniforms, and even accessories like cars or gadgets can lend an air of authority and can persuade us to accept what these people say.[14]

Obedience to authority was the basis for the famous shock experiments conducted by psychologist Stanley Milgram at Yale University, in an attempt to understand how ordinary good Germans became extraordinarily evil Nazis.[15] Milgram obviously could not have his experimental subjects gas or shoot people, so he chose electric shock as a legal, nonlethal substitute. Looking for subjects to participate in what was billed as a "study of memory," Milgram advertised on the Yale campus and also in the surrounding New Haven, Connecticut, community. He said he wanted "factory workers, city employees, laborers, barbers, businessmen, clerks, construction workers, sales people, [and] telephone workers," not just undergraduates, who are the usual guinea pigs of this type of science lab.

Milgram then assigned his subjects to the role of "teacher" in what was purported to be research on the effects of punishment on learning. The protocol called for the subject to read a list of paired words to the "learner" (who was, in reality, a shill working for Milgram), then present the first word of each pair again, upon which the learner was to recall the second word. Each time the learner's response was incorrect, the teacher was to deliver an electric shock from a box with toggle switches in 15-volt increments (from 15 volts all the way up to 450 volts) and featured such labels as "Slight Shock," "Moderate Shock," "Strong Shock," "Very Strong Shock," "Intense Shock," "Extreme Intensity Shock," and "DANGER: Severe Shock, xxxx." Despite the predictions of 40 psychiatrists that Milgram surveyed before the experiment, who figured that only 1 percent of the subjects would go all the way to the upper end of the range, 65 percent of those who completed the experiment flipped that final toggle switch to deliver a shocking 450 volts.

Who was most likely to go the distance in maximal shock delivery? Surprisingly—and counterintuitively—gender, age, occupation, and personality characteristics mattered little in the outcome. Similar levels of punishment were delivered by the young and the old, by men and women, and by blue-collar and white-collar workers alike. What mattered most was physical proximity and group pressure. The closer the learner was to the teacher, the less of a shock the latter delivered. When Milgram added more confederates, to encourage the teacher to administer ever more powerful shocks, most teachers complied. But when the confederate themselves rebelled against the authority figure's instructions, the teacher was equally disinclined to obey. Nevertheless, 100 percent of Milgram's subjects delivered at least a "strong shock" of 135 volts.[16]

Application: If a college psychologist can get ordinary people to deliver dangerous shocks to innocent people by merely emphasizing the authority of the person giving the orders, how much easier must it be for a cult leader or conspiracy theorist to convince people of the validity of their claim if they deliver it in an authoritative manner?

3. *Beliefs are reinforced by peers (social proof)*. This principle relies on people's sense of "safety in numbers." For example, we're more likely to work late if others on our team are doing the same, put a tip in a jar if it already contains money, or eat in a restaurant if it's busy. Here, we're assuming that if lots of other people are doing something, then it must be okay. We're particularly susceptible to this principle when we're feeling uncertain, and we're even more likely to be influenced if the people we see seem to be similar to us. That's why commercials often use moms, not celebrities, to advertise household products, and TV shows employ canned laughter. Social proof is a shortcut to the knowledge and wisdom garnered by others. We make fewer mistakes by acting in accord with social evidence than by acting contrary to it. Like "Poll the Audience" on *Who Wants to be a Millionaire?*, for simple tasks, such as guessing the number of jelly beans in a jar, a decent-sized audience will average a guess within a couple of percentage points of the correct answer.[17]

Application: Conspiracy theories are often conveyed in groups of people, either in person in a hotel conference room or online in chat rooms. There's a sense of camaraderie among the members that provides social proof that the claims have some validity to them.

4. *Beliefs are reinforced by liking and by the similarity of other beliefs*. We're more likely to be influenced by people we like. Likability comes in many forms—people might be similar or familiar to us, they might give us compliments, or we may just simply trust them. Companies that use sales agents from within the community employ this principle with huge success. People are more likely to buy from people

like themselves, from friends, and from people they know and respect.[18]

Application: Conspiracy theories often play up the similarities among members, particularly in contrast to some other group—usually a government agency or corporation or evil clan—that wants to harm our "good" group.

5. Beliefs are reinforced by payoffs, success, and happiness. The group you join helps you quit your addiction, break your bad habits, fix your marriage, find you a job, make money, and so forth. By definition, a reinforcement is anything that causes someone to repeat a behavior. As B. F. Skinner showed in his classic experiments, all of us are motivated to seek rewards and avoid punishments. So anything that reinforces a behavior related to a belief only strengthens that belief.[19]

Application: Conspiracy theories, particularly those of a financial sort that I've discussed above, promise believers that they will be rewarded for accepting the conspiracy theory as real, either directly (through financial reward) or indirectly (through the reinforcement of inside knowledge and secret powers to come).

6. Beliefs are reinforced by confirmation bias. As noted in the previous chapter, confirmation bias is the tendency to seek and find corroborating evidence in support of already existing beliefs and ignore or reinterpret disconfirming evidence. We remember the hits and forget the misses.[20] Another study will suffice to reinforce this point. In 1981, psychologist Mark Snyder tasked subjects with assessing the personality of someone whom they were about to meet, but only after they reviewed a profile of that person.[21] One group of subjects were given a profile of an introvert (shy, timid, quiet), while another group of subjects were given a profile of an extrovert (sociable, talkative, outgoing). When asked to make a personality assessment, those subjects who were told that the person would be an extrovert tended to

ask questions that would lead to that conclusion; the introvert group did the same in the opposite direction.

Application: Conspiracy theories are the very embodiment of confirmation bias, directing believers to look for and find evidence that validates the conspiracy theory and ignore or rationalize away evidence that rebuts the theory. We saw how this worked in great detail with 9/11 Truthers and JFK assassination conspiracists.

7. Beliefs are reinforced by optimism and over-optimism biases. Optimism bias is the tendency to see oneself as better than average and as more likely to succeed than the odds warrant. According to psychologist Daniel Kahneman in *Thinking, Fast and Slow,* "people tend to be overly optimistic about their relative standing on any activity in which they do moderately well."[22] But optimism can slide dangerously into over-optimism. For example, Kahneman cited research showing that chief financial officers (CFOs) "were grossly overconfident about their ability to forecast the market" when tested by Duke University professors, who collected 11,600 CFO forecasts and matched them to market outcomes. They found a correlation of less than zero!

This overconfidence can be costly. Kahneman's study of CFOs "showed that those who were most confident and optimistic about the S&P index were also overconfident and optimistic about the prospects of their own firm, which went on to take more risk than others."[23] As he explained, "One of the benefits of an optimistic temperament is that it encourages persistence in the face of obstacles." But a "pervasive optimistic bias" can be detrimental, since "most of us view the world as more benign than it really is, our own attributes as more favorable than they truly are, and the goals we adopt as more achievable than they are likely to be."

Application: Conspiracy theories fuel optimism bias and usually tip it over into over-optimism, to the point where reality is distorted. For example, who in their right mind would believe paying taxes is purely voluntary? Over-optimistic conspiracists, that's who.

8. *Beliefs are reinforced by self-justification bias.* Self-justification bias is the tendency to rationalize decisions after the fact, to convince ourselves that what we did was the best thing we could have done. Once we make a decision about something in our lives, we carefully screen subsequent data and filter out all contradictory information related to that decision, leaving only evidence in support of the choice we made. This bias applies to everything from career and job choices to mundane purchases. One of the practical benefits of self-justification is that no matter what decision we make—to take this or that job, to marry this or that person, to purchase this or that product—we will almost always be satisfied with the decision, even in the face of contrary objective evidence.

For example, political scientist Philip Tetlock, in *Expert Political Judgment*, reviewed evidence about the ability of professional experts in politics and economics.[24] He found that even though all of them claimed to have data in support of their predictions and assessments, when analyzed after the fact, such expert opinions and predictions turn out to be no better than those of nonexperts—or even chance. Yet, as self-justification bias would predict, experts are significantly less likely to admit they are wrong than nonexperts.[25] Or, as I like to say, smart people believe weird things because they are better at rationalizing the beliefs they hold for non-smart reasons.

Application: Conspiracy theories traffic in self-justification, and proponents of conspiracy theories almost always consider themselves experts.

9. *Beliefs are reinforced by sunk-cost bias.* Sunk-cost bias is the tendency to believe in something because of the cost sunk into that belief. We hang on to losing stocks, unprofitable investments, failing businesses, and unsuccessful relationships. With attribution bias throttled up, we concoct rational reasons to justify those beliefs and behaviors in which we have made sizable investments.[26] This bias leads to a basic fallacy: why should a past investment influence future decisions? If we were rational, we should just compute the odds of succeeding from this point forward and then decide if any additional investment warrants the potential payoff. But we are not rational beings—not in business, certainly not in love, and most especially not in war.

Application: Conspiracy theories depend heavily on maintaining their membership rolls by getting people to commit to that theory. The more an individual sinks into that belief, the harder it is to let it go, whether it is a financial commitment or a psychological investment.

10. *Beliefs are reinforced by an endowment effect.* The psychology underlying sunk-cost bias is what economist Richard Thaler calls "endowment effect," or the tendency to value what we own more than what we do not possess. In his research on this topic, Thaler found that owners of an item value it roughly twice as much as potential buyers of the same item.[27] In one experiment, subjects were given a coffee mug valued at $6 and were asked what they would take for it if someone offered to buy the mug. The average price below which they would not sell was $5.25. Another group of subjects were asked how much they would be willing to pay to buy the same mug, and they gave an average price of $2.75. Ownership endows value by its own virtue, and nature has endowed us to hold dear what is ours.

Application: Conspiracy theories are further reinforced by endowing believers with secret knowledge, which they believe gives them power they would otherwise not have. With power comes confidence, and then overconfidence.

• – – • – – •

In this chapter we have looked at how belief in a conspiracy theory—including and especially ones as delusional as doctrines that the United States doesn't actually exist as a sovereign nation, and that paying taxes is optional—can be personally harmful. This brings part I of the book—our exploration of the psychology of why people believe conspiracy theories—to a close. We will return to this topic in the book's coda, which presents the results of my Skeptic Research Center study on conspiracy theory beliefs.

In part II we will consider how to determine which conspiracy theories really are true, since it is evident that one reason for conspiracism is that enough conspiracy theories are true, so it pays to believe most of them are—just in case. In subsequent chapters, we will then apply these skeptical principles of truth determination in detail to a number of conspiracy theories, most of which readers will already be familiar with. In this next part, I am shifting from a neutral scientist trying to understand the psychology of conspiracism to a skeptical activist making an assessment and, where appropriate, debunking conspiracy claims I judge to be unreasonable, invalid, or unsupported by the evidence, even while recognizing that some conspiracy theories are real. Those latter we will also consider in detail.

PART II

How to Determine Which Conspiracy Theories Are Real

We should care because conspiracy theories about past events usually carry with them a political agenda for today. Erroneous or downright mythical views of the past can have important, even crucial influence on the present. The coming to power of the Nazis, German rearmament, ultimately World War II might not have happened without widespread German belief in the stab-in-the-back conspiracy. Widespread acceptance by the American people of the "merchants of death" conspiracy thesis about our entry into World War I was a prelude to the ill-fated, nearly disastrous neutrality legislation of the 1930s. The unhappy consequences of McCarthyism would not have come about had the American people rejected his conspiracy thesis about the triumph of Communism in China.

STEPHEN E. AMBROSE, "Writers on the Grassy Knoll," *New York Times Book Review*, 1992

CHAPTER 6

The Conspiracy Detection Kit

How to Tell If a Conspiracy Theory
Is True or False

In 1997 I appeared on the late G. Gordon Liddy's radio talk show while on a media tour for my first book, *Why People Believe Weird Things*. Liddy asked me if I thought conspiracy theories are weird beliefs and if we should be skeptical of them. It was a set-up question that he himself answered after I hesitated in responding to the man who was behind the Watergate conspiracy. Most conspiracy theories are false, he told me, for two reasons: (1) competency and (2) leakage. Most conspiracists, Liddy continued, are bumbling, fumbling nincompoops who can't keep their mouths shut. Three people can keep a secret, he added, echoing Benjamin Franklin, if two of them are dead.

Since, as we have seen, some conspiracy theories are true, we cannot just dismiss them all out of hand. So how can we tell the difference between a true and a false conspiracy theory? What metric, algorithm, or rule of thumb could we apply to determine whether such a theory is most likely

Figure 6.1. A 2×2 choice matrix for a signal detection problem. *Source:* Matrix graphic by Pat Linse.

true, probably false, or undecidable? Think of it as a signal detection problem in a 2×2 matrix, illustrated in figure 6.1. *Signal detection theory* aims to assess if a signal, or information, represents a true or false signal. Our decision about whether the signal is true or false allows us to diagram a 2×2 choice matrix. The upper left cell represents conspiracy theories that are true, which you correctly identify as such. This is called a hit. The upper right cell represents conspiracy theories that are true, but which you incorrectly identify as false. This is called a miss, or a false negative, or a Type II error. The lower left cell represents conspiracy theories that are false, which you correctly identify as such. This is called a correct rejection, another type of hit. The lower right cell represents conspiracy theories that are false, but which you incorrectly identify as true—that is, you think the theory represents a true conspiracy, when it doesn't. This is called a false positive, or a Type I error.

As we consider the many factors that go into determining whether a conspiracy theory is true, think about which of the four cells you would put your assessment in, based on these criteria. Keep in mind that because conspiracy theories are so varied, there is no single set of criteria that can accurately assess the verisimilitude of every such theory. So think of this 2×2 matrix as a heuristic, a rule of thumb, a way to come at the problem of assessing the truth about a claim. It is not foolproof, but neither is it a random guess, starting with the fact that conspiracy theories fall along a spectrum of plausibility. An example of such a spectrum may be seen in a list compiled by researcher Mick West, who places conspiracy theories on a scale from 1 (mainstream) to 10 (extreme).[1] The closer to 1 a conspiracy theory falls, the more likely it is to be true, and the closer to 10, the less likely. What follows is West's list of ten conspiracy theories, ranked according to this assessment scale, with my own summaries and commentary.

1. *Big Pharma*: the theory that pharmaceutical companies conspire to maximize profits by selling drugs that people do not actually need. We know for a fact that this sometimes happens, and the recent crisis with the opioid epidemic that is killing more Americans every year than die in automobile accidents is a grim example. As investigative journalist Gerald Posner demonstrated in his 2020 book, *Pharma: Greed, Lies, and the Poisoning of America*, it now appears that some of the pharmaceutical companies—most notably Perdue Pharma and the Sackler family—conspired to downplay or deceive physicians and the public about just how addictive these drugs can be.[2] That doesn't mean that everything Big Pharma does is conspiratorially evil, however. We have to take it one case at a time.

2. *Global warming hoax*: the theory that climate change is not caused by man-made carbon emissions, and that there's some other motive for claiming this is the case. Global warming is real, and it is human caused. That much we know with great confidence, because of the multiple lines

of evidence from many different and independent sciences that study various aspects of the environment.[3] There's no realistic way thousands of scientists from around the world could meet, conspire, and create a hoax for such a phenomenon. For many decades, some environmental groups appear to have conspired to exaggerate the dire effects of human action with regard to overpopulation, the rain forests, peak oil, precious minerals, and many other doomsday predictions that have not materialized, including a bet that environmentalist Paul Ehrlich lost to economist Julian Simon over the future of Earth's resources.[4] Given these thus-far failed predictions, it is understandable why more conspiratorially minded people might think that global warming is a conspiracy, especially after the issue became politicized when Vice President Al Gore's film, *An Inconvenient Truth*, bundled the science with liberal politics.

3. *JFK assassination*: the theory that people other than Lee Harvey Oswald were involved in the assassination of John F. Kennedy. In a later chapter, I will make the case that this political assassination, unlike many in history that were orchestrated by a conspiracy, was the result of a lone gunman. But given the many strange anomalies and the magnitude of the event, it is understandable why so many people—many prominent scholars and investigators among them—are still convinced that there was a second shooter, and maybe more.

4. *9/11 inside job*: the theory that the events of 9/11 were arranged by elements within the US government. I will also cover this one in detail in a subsequent chapter, but suffice it to note here that we begin to slide into the improbability of so many different actors having to coordinate their covert operations in such a way as to pull off so many precise acts at the right time. This is extremely unlikely.

5. *Chemtrails*: the theory that the water vapor contrails formed behind commercial airplanes are actually toxic

chemicals released either by big corporations or by big government agencies as part of a secret program. Now we're moving into paranoia, where entire government agencies, corporations, and commercial airline operators would have to be in cahoots. It isn't even clear how these conglomerations would benefit—the *cui bono* test of any conspiracy theory—leaving one bewildered about how anyone could believe it.

6. *False-flag shootings*: the theory that mass public shootings, like those at Sandy Hook in 2012 and Las Vegas in 2017, either never happened or were arranged by people in power. Paranoia again—the belief that people whom we otherwise trust to run the apparatus of government suddenly turn evil and decide to commit mass murder of innocent citizens, in order to rescind the Second Amendment. This is never going to happen. No politician seeking reelection would propose otherwise, and gun sales actually go *up* after mass public shootings.

7. *Moon landing hoax*: the theory that the moon landings were faked in a movie studio takes us into the theater of the absurd, once you think about what would be required to pull this off. It would be cheaper and easier to simply go to the moon and film it there.

8. *UFO cover-up*: the theory that the US government has contact with aliens or crashed alien spaceships and is keeping it secret. Actually, the opposite is true: the discovery of extraterrestrial intelligence would be the greatest find in history. So any government lucky enough to have made that discovery would shout it from the rooftops, and any scientists or science agencies would do so as well, as it would enhance their status and funding.

9. *Flat Earth*: the theory that Earth is really flat, but governments, business, and scientists all pretend it is a globe. This theory generally bit the dust centuries ago, but it limped along on the thin margins of society until it got a

twenty-first century boost via social media. It garnered so much media attention that we felt compelled to devote a 2019 *Skeptic* magazine cover story to who says Earth is flat and why they say it.[5]

10. *Reptile overlords*: the theory that the ruling classes are a race of shape-shifting, transdimensional reptiles. Although bizarre almost beyond belief, this one also carries an anti-Semitic element that appeals to some on the Far Right. At this end of the credibility scale, I am reminded of psychiatrist Milton Rokeach's *The Three Christs of Ypsilanti*, the story of three of his patients, each of whom believed himself to be Jesus Christ.[6] Inspired by another case where two women who both were convinced they were the Virgin Mary met each other, Rokeach brought his three "Christs" together, each of whom instantly recognized the other two as delusional. Hoping the encounter might attenuate his patients' fantasized state, Rokeach acknowledged that the only thing cured was "my godlike delusion that I could manipulate them out of their beliefs."

Admittedly, there is a certain amount of subjectivity in evaluating conspiracy theories along this spectrum, but in general, what we are looking for is a *line of demarcation*—or where to draw the line—between possibly true and probably false for any one conspiracy theory. Mick West noted that this line of demarcation may shift within a single conspiracy theory, depending on which elements of it might be true or false. For example, 9/11 Truthers who think George W. Bush let it happen on purpose (LIHOP) reject the 9/11 Truthers who think Bush made it happen on purpose (MIHOP). Those who think explosive charges were used to bring down the World Trade Center buildings and accept that planes also hit the buildings reject the claims of the "No Planers"—those who contend that there were no planes involved in 9/11 at all. (They aver that videos we've all seen of the planes hitting the buildings were either CGI fakes or holograms.[7]) Where the demarcation line lands for various conspiracy theories very much depends on which theory is being examined. As West pointed out:

> Conspiracists have a demarcation line on their own personal version of the conspiracy spectrum. We all have our lines, and our perception of the claims on the more extreme side of the lines is that it's just false information. We might disagree about the reasons for that false information existing, but we all think the stuff on the extreme side of the line is wrong. Helping people out of the rabbit hole can equate to simply moving that line gradually down the extremeness spectrum. But to move their line you've got to understand exactly where that line of demarcation lies.[8]

• – – • – – •

This line of demarcation issue is an old one from the philosophy of science, usually rendered as the "demarcation problem" and first introduced in 1934 by renowned philosopher of science Karl Popper in *The Logic of Scientific Discovery*.[9] The demarcation problem asks, Where do we draw the boundaries between science and pseudoscience, or between science and non-science? The problem is that it is not always—or even usually—clear where to draw such a line. Whether a particular claim should be put into the set labeled "science" or "pseudoscience" will depend not only on the claim per se, but also on other factors, such as the proponent of the claim, the claim's history and methodology, the coherence of the claim with other theories, its internal consistency, attempts to test it, and the like. Popper's solution to the problem of demarcation was the criterion of falsifiability. Theories are "never empirically verifiable," he said, but if they are falsifiable, then they belong in the domain of empirical science. "In other words," he wrote, "I shall not require of a scientific system that it shall be capable of being singled out, once and for all, in a positive sense; but I shall require that its logical form shall be such that it can be singled out, by means of empirical tests, in a negative sense: it must be possible for an empirical scientific system to be refuted by experience."[10]

Although most scientists intuitively sense whether a claim is scientific or pseudoscientific, we need to translate such intuitions into a more formalized set of questions to ask when encountering a claim. Here is a list I made that I call the "baloney detection kit," inspired by Carl Sagan's name for his own list, which he put together in his 1996 book *The Demon-Haunted World*.[11] For this chapter, in place of "pseudoscientists," I've used "conspiracists":

1. *How reliable is the source of the claim?* All scientists make mistakes, but are the mistakes random, as one might expect from a normally reliable source, or are they directed toward supporting the claimant's preferred belief? Scientists' mistakes tend to be random; conspiracists' mistakes tend to be directional, usually in support of their preferred theory.

2. *Does the claimant often make similar claims?* Conspiricists have a habit of going well beyond the facts, so when individuals make numerous extraordinary claims, they may be more than just iconoclasts. What we are looking for here is a pattern of fringe thinking that consistently ignores or distorts data.

3. *Have the claims been verified by another source?* Typically, conspiracists will make statements that are either unverified or are verified by a source within their own belief circle. We must ask who is fact-checking the claims, and even who is checking the fact-checkers.

4. *How does the claim fit with what we know about how the world works?* An extraordinary claim must be placed

into a larger context, to see how it fits. For example, when people aver that the Egyptian pyramids and the Great Sphinx were built over 10,000 years ago by a super-advanced civilization of humans (or by extraterrestrials, in the "ancient aliens" scenario), they are basing this entirely on unexplained anomalies in the current paradigm and presenting no additional evidence for that earlier civilization. Where are the works of art, weapons, clothing, tools, and trash of this lost civilization?

5. *Has anyone gone out of the way to disprove the claim, or has only confirming evidence been sought?* Confirmation bias—or the tendency to seek confirming evidence and reject or ignore disconfirming data—is powerful and pervasive. This is why the methods of science that emphasize checking and rechecking, verification and replication, and, especially, attempts to falsify a claim, are so critical. Conspiracists are notorious for cherry-picking examples and only presenting evidence that supports their conspiracy theory. We must also ask, "What would falsify the conspiracy theory?"

6. *Does the preponderance of evidence converge on the claimant's conclusion, or on a different one?* For example, JFK assassination conspiracy theorists ignore all the evidence that leads to the conclusion that Lee Harvey Oswald acted alone in killing Kennedy, and none of the evidence points to any other person or agency. Instead, they focus on anomalies that don't seem quite right, and fragments of possibilities that converge on nothing or no one.

7. *Is the claimant employing the accepted rules of reason and tools of research, or have these been abandoned in favor of others that lead to the desired conclusion?* UFOlogists suffer from this fallacy in their continued focus on

a handful of unexplained atmospheric anomalies and visual misperceptions by eyewitnesses, while conveniently ignoring that the vast majority of UFO sightings are fully explicable. This is called *anomaly hunting*, or looking for anything unusual, especially if it is unexplainable, and then glomming on to that anomaly as "evidence" for one's conspiracy theory. Anomalies do not a theory make.

8. *Has the claimant provided a different explanation for the observed phenomena, or is it strictly a process of denying the existing one?* This is a classic debate strategy—criticize your opponent but never affirm what you believe, in order to avoid criticism of your own position. For conspiracists, this is the "I'm just asking questions" ploy, and it is an unacceptable stratagem in science.

9. *If the claimant has proffered a new explanation, does it account for as many phenomena as the old one does?* For a new theory to displace an old one, it must explain not only what the old theory did, but also the anomalies not covered by the old theory. Conspiracy theories always fail on this front. For example, 9/11 Truthers offer no new explanation to counter the government's theory that al-Qaeda did it, short of the nebulous and untestable "the Bush administration." We must always ask of the conspiracist, "Who, exactly, did it—name names and provide specifics."

10. *Do the claimants' personal beliefs and biases drive the conclusions, or vice versa?* All scientists hold social, political, and ideological beliefs that could potentially slant their interpretations of the data, but at some point (usually during the peer review process), such biases and beliefs are rooted out, or the paper or book is rejected for publication. A good question for conspiracy theorists is, "What would it take to

change your mind?" This usually stops them in their tracks, because most have never thought about that question.

• - - • - - •

The primary difference between science and pseudoscience—and here I will add between a true and a false conspiracy theory—is the presumption made about a claim before going into the research protocol to test it. Science begins with a null hypothesis, which assumes that the claim under investigation is not true until proven otherwise.[12] Suppose you declare that you have developed a cure for COVID-19, in the form of a drug that can eliminate 100 percent of the SARS-CoV-2 virus in a body. Before the FDA will approve your drug for sale to the public, you must provide substantial evidence that your claim is true in the scientific sense—that is, to reject the null hypothesis that you do not have such a drug. When people tell me UFOs are real and the government is conspiring to hide them, I say, "Show me the spaceship or alien body and I'll believe; otherwise I remain skeptical." In this example, the null hypothesis is that UFOs and aliens do not exist.

In addition, assuming a null hypothesis means that the burden of proof is on the person asserting a positive claim. The requirement is not for skeptics to disprove it. I once appeared on *Larry King Live* to discuss UFOs (a perennial favorite of the late talk-show host), along with a table full of UFOlogists. "How do you explain X, Dr. Shermer?" is the standard question I get, with X being whatever the latest grainy video or blurry photograph is, under the assumption that if I can't explain X, it means UFOs represent actual alien contact. No so. Most media sources miss this central tenet of science. It isn't up to the skeptics to disprove UFOs. The burden of proof is on UFOlogists to make their case, although, as I argued earlier in the book, such beliefs often tap a deeper emotional, religious, or political motive that makes them impervious to demands for evidence.

Then there is what's called a *residue problem*: no hypothesis or theory in any field can give a reason for 100 percent of the phenomena under investigation. This means that no matter how comprehensive a theory is, there will always be some anomalies for which it cannot account. The most famous case in the history of science is that Newton's gravitational theory could not adequately define the precession of the planet Mercury's orbit, which was subsequently explained by Einstein's theory of relativity. Darwin's theory of evolution by means of natural selection could not account for anomalies like the peacock's large and colorful tail (it would be a bull's-eye for the bird's predators, such as mongooses, jungle cats, and even stray dogs), a problem which kept Darwin up late nights. The solution was his theory of sexual selection, demonstrating how females choose mates, based on certain traits males develop to stand out from other males and attract females.

So why don't scientists accept the residue of unexplained anomalies as evidence of justified true belief? The answer is found in the principle of *proportional evidence*, where we allocate our beliefs according to the evidence in support of them. The common expression for this principle is that extraordinary claims require extraordinary evidence, or ECREE. The principle has been around at least since the eighteenth century, when Scottish philosopher David Hume, in his 1748 *An Enquiry Concerning Human Understanding*, wrote, "A wise man proportions his belief to the evidence."[13] Carl Sagan popularized ECREE in his 1980 television series *Cosmos*, in the episode on the possibility of extraterrestrial intelligence existing somewhere in the galaxy, or of aliens having visited Earth.[14]

ECREE means that an ordinary claim only needs ordinary evidence, but an extraordinary claim requires extraordinary evidence. The assessment of a claim as being ordinary versus extraordinary is necessarily subjective, but it can be quantified along the lines of what the baloney detection kit (described above) proposes. If you embrace a conspiracy theory asserting that some politicians are corrupt and take bribes, that's an ordinary claim for which ordinary evidence—such as a paper trail to the source, revealed in a court case—will probably suffice to convince me of its veracity. But if you tell me about a conspiracy theory that states politicians are conspiring to hide crashed UFOs and alien bodies in Area 51, we're going to need extraordinary evidence—such as a paper trail of government documents without redacted (i.e., blacked out) paragraphs and indications therein that extraterrestrial contact has been made and that the government has conspired to hide them— because we know that governments keep secrets for a host of reasons related to military intelligence and national security. (Blacked out paragraphs in documents obtained through the Freedom of Information Act are not uncommon.) Terrestrial secrets do not equate to extraterrestrial cover-ups. Before we accept this extraordinary claim as true, we're going to need clear and unmistakable photographs and videos that are accessible to all media sources, mainstream and otherwise, and verified by august scientific bodies, like the National Science Foundation, and respected scientific journals, like *Science* and *Nature*.

The ECREE principle also means that belief is not a discrete state of belief or disbelief, like an on-off switch. It's more like a dimmer dial, a continuum on which you can place confidence in a belief according to the evidence: more evidence leads to more confidence, and less evidence, less confidence. Applying the ECREE principle to conspiracy theories goes a long way toward determining where to draw the line of demarcation between true and false.

The ECREE principle itself is a specific form of *Bayesian reasoning*, or Bayes' Rule, invented in the eighteenth century by Reverend Thomas Bayes.[15] Roughly speaking, Bayesian reasoning has to do with the strength of evidence for a claim, and the reasoning rule has to do with how much we should revise our estimation of the probability of a claim being true, based on the evidence. When the evidence changes, we should change our probability estimates accordingly. These estimations of probabilities, which arrive from prior knowledge of conditions related to the claim, are called *priors*, or our initial degree of belief. The probability of something being true determines the *credence*—the credibility, or strength, of the belief. Think of credence, or the probability of something being true, as a percentage. For example, you should believe with 50 percent credence that a fair coin toss will land on heads, based on your priors that flipped coins land 50/50 on heads or tails. Or, if a bag contains four red marbles and one blue marble, and you withdraw one marble at random, then you should believe with 80 percent credence that the random marble will be red.

To put it a different way in this context, an extraordinary claim—for example, that the conspiracy theory that UFOs represent extraterrestrial intelligences (ETIs) hidden by the government—has a low Bayesian prior, because of the poor quality of the evidence for it. Thus the credence for the hypothesis that UFOs = ETIs remains low, unless better evidence emerges. Until then, we should have lower credence for the claim of being visited by ETIs. But we should keep an open mind, so if new evidence emerges to change our priors, we should be willing to also change our credence in the truth value of the conspiracy theory, assuming such new evidence is extraordinary. So by all means keep looking, but be skeptical unless the evidence *does* becomes extraordinary.

• — — • — — •

Paralleling the baloney detection kit above, what follows is a 10-point list for a conspiracy detection kit. The more a conspiracy theory manifests the following characteristics, the less likely it is to be a real conspiracy:

1. *Patternicity.* Proof of a conspiracy supposedly emerges from a pattern of "connecting the dots" between events that need not be causally linked. When no evidence supports these connections except the allegation of a conspiracy, or when the evidence fits equally well with other patterns—or with randomness—the conspiracy theory is likely to be false.

2. *Agenticity.* The agents behind the pattern of a conspiracy would need nearly superhuman power to pull it off. Most of the time, under most circumstances, people, agencies, and corporations are not nearly as powerful as we think they are. If a conspiracy theory involves superpowerful agents, it most likely is false.

3. *Complexity.* If a conspiracy theory is complex, its successful completion demands a large number of elements coming together at just the right moment and in the proper sequence. The more elements involved, and the more delicate the timing of the sequence in which they must come together, the less likely a conspiracy theory is to be true.

4. *People.* The more people involved in a conspiracy theory, the less likely it is to be true. Conspiracies involving large numbers of people who would all need to keep silent about their secrets typically fail. People can be incompetent and emotional. They screw up, chicken out, change their minds, have moral scruples. Conspiracy theories treat people as

automata or Manchurian candidates, operating like programmed robots carrying out the commands they are given. That is unrealistic.

5. *Grandiosity.* If a conspiracy theory encompasses some grandiose ambition for control over a nation, economy, or political system, and especially if it aims for world domination, it is almost certainly false. The bigger the conspiracy, the more likely it is to fail, for the above reasons concerning complexity and people.

6. *Scale.* When a conspiracy theory ratchets up from small events that might be true to much larger events that have much lower probabilities of being true, it is quite likely false. Most real conspiracies involve very specific events and targets—such as insider trading on Wall Street, price fixing in an industry, tax evasion by a corporation or individual, government aid to a political ally in one country, and, yes, the assassination of a political leader—but they always have a narrow goal of grabbing power or ending tyranny.

7. *Significance.* If a conspiracy theory assigns portentous and sinister meanings and interpretations to what most likely are innocuous or insignificant events, it probably is false. Again, most conspiracies are narrowly focused and significant only to those who will benefit from or be hurt by them. Most real conspiracies do not change the world, although there are exceptions, as we shall see in the chapter on the conspiracy that launched the First World War.

8. *Accuracy.* If a conspiracy theory commingles facts and speculations without distinguishing between the two and without assigning degrees of probability or factuality for the components of its claim, it is likely to be false. Conspiracists are notorious for sprinkling in a handful of verifiable facts amid a

vast array of conjectures and suppositions, which blur reality and confuse listeners into thinking there is more to the theory than there actually is.

9. *Paranoia.* Many conspiracy theorists are extremely and indiscriminately suspicious of any and all government agencies or private corporations, which suggests a lack of nuance in understanding how the world works. Yes, sometimes "they" really are out to get you, but usually not. When you combine the above elements in a conspiracy theory, what looks like a portentous conspiracy almost always is either randomness or something that has a far more prosaic explanation.

10. *Falsifiability.* Conspiracy theorists typically refuse to consider alternative explanations, rejecting all evidence contrary to their theory and blatantly seeking only confirming evidence to support what has a priori been determined as the truth. To return to Karl Popper and the line of demarcation that is drawn regarding the falsifiability of a claim, if a conspiracy theory cannot be falsified, it is probably false.

To these factors we should add one more: the type of country or society in which the conspiracy is alleged to unfold. Open, transparent, and free liberal democracies make it more difficult to pull off a conspiracy, because of the apparatus in place to prevent illegal or immoral cabals from forming to cheat the system (think of all the checks and balances designed by the founders of the United States—it was various forms of political conspiracies they were concerned about). In contrast, closed, autocratic societies protect and even enable conspiratorial shenanigans, and in some cases the government itself is the most dangerous conspiracy citizens face. Researchers have found that conspiracy theories about the government are especially rampant in autocratic societies, albeit unexpressed, out of fear of reprisals.[16]

• - - • - - •

Finally, part of the problem we all face in trying to determine whether a conspiracy theory is true is that we are not very good at understanding probabilities, as Las Vegas casino owners figured out long ago.[17] Here's an example. Examine these two series of heads (H) and tails (T) in coin flips and guess which series best represents randomness:

HTHTHTHTHTHTHTHTHTHTHTH

or

HHHTTHTTHTHHHHTTHHTTTTTTH

Most people would say the first series of alternating heads and tails looks like the most random arrangement. In fact, both computer simulations and actual coin-flipping experiments generate something much closer to the second series. The clusters of H's and T's are what randomness looks like. When subjects are asked to *imagine* flipping a coin and then are instructed to write down the sequence of outcomes, their guesses are highly nonrandom. That is, their string of heads and tails more closely resembles the predictable first string, not the less predictable and more (but not perfectly) random second string.[18]

There's a famous story about what happened when Apple first introduced the iPod, with its "random" music shuffle feature. People complained that it wasn't random, because some songs came up more often than others, which, to most people, doesn't intuitively seem random.[19] But that's what randomness is: clusters of things. If you toss a handful of coins in the air and watch where they land on the ground, they will not be perfectly distributed, with even spaces between them. They will be clustered into what looks to our mind like patterns, similar to the random scattering of stars in the sky. But stars don't look random to our eyes. Instead, they appear to be constellations of familiar figures, such as eagles, rams, fish, lions, bears, chariots, and dippers (big and little).[20] This problem has plagued cancer researchers, who look for clusters of people with cancers, to see if there's some clearly related cause, such as contaminated air or water near a factory. The problem also bedevils conspiracists, who see something sinister in the apparent clusters in their minds, rather than simply the randomness of life. This is why the conspiracism principle I introduced in chapter 2 bears repeating: never attribute to malice what can be explained by randomness or incompetence.

The fact that politicians sometimes lie, or that corporations occasionally cheat, does not mean that every event is the result of a tortuous, preplanned conspiracy. Much of the time, stuff just happens, and our brains connect the dots into meaningful patterns, even when those patterns are illusory. But the idea of powerful patterns is enough to make them real in people's minds, as novelist John Crowley had one of his characters explain in his fantasy novel Ægypt: "Can't you see, he'd said, the truth is so much more interesting: secret societies have not had power in history, but the notion that secret societies have had power in history has had power in history."[21] It's a point well made by David Aaronovitch in his concluding remarks in Voodoo Histories: The Role of the Conspiracy Theory in Shaping Modern History: "I have written this book because I believe that conspiracies aren't powerful. It is instead the idea of conspiracies that has power."[22]

In the coming chapters, we will begin our journey down the rabbit hole into conspiracies, real and imagined, and apply elements of my conspiracy detection kit to consider which ones are probably real and which are powerful fantasies created by our imagination.

CHAPTER 7

Truthers and Birthers

The 9/11 and Obama Conspiracy Theories

Following a public lecture in 2005 that I delivered at the Los Angeles Public Library, I was buttonholed by a documentary filmmaker with ambitions to expose the true conspiracy behind 9/11.[1] I told him I agreed that 9/11 was a conspiracy, in which 19 members of al-Qaeda, directed and funded by Osama bin Laden, conspired to fly hijacked planes into buildings. But that is not what he had in mind. "That's what they *want* you to believe," he said. "Who are *they*?" I queried. "The government," he whispered, as if *they* might be listening at that very moment. At this point in the conversation I declined to be interviewed, knowing precisely the 9/11 Truther talking points that were coming next:[2]

- The Pentagon was hit by a missile.
- Air Force jets were ordered to "stand down" and not intercept Flights 11 and 175, which struck the twin towers. The twin towers were razed by demolition explosives, timed to go off soon after the impact of the planes.

- A mysterious white jet shot down Flight 93 over Pennsylvania.
- New York Jews were ordered to stay home that day (Zionists and other pro-Israeli factions, of course, were involved).
- And, behind it all, 9/11 was orchestrated by George W. Bush, Dick Cheney, Donald Rumsfeld, and the CIA, in order to implement their plan for global domination and a New World Order, to be launched by a Pearl Harbor–like attack on the World Trade Center and the Pentagon, thereby providing the justification for war and galvanizing Congress and the public to back an invasion of Iraq.

In this chapter, we will review the two most prominent political conspiracy theories of the twenty-first century (until QAnon and the rigged election conspiracy theories displaced them)—the 9/11 Truthers and the Obama Birthers. We will consider their claims in some detail, to see not only why they're wrong, but also how conspiracists think in the teeth of contradictory evidence.

• - - • - - •

The 9/11 Truther movement began in 2002, when noted French left-wing activist Thierry Meyssan's 9/11 conspiracy book, L'Effroyable imposture ("The Big Lie"), became a bestseller in France.[3] American conspiracists soon joined the fray, producing such books as Inside Job by Jim Marrs, The New Pearl Harbor and 9/11 Unmasked by David Ray Griffin, and 9/11: The Great Illusion by George Humphrey.[4] Meyssan then wrote a 2019 sequel, Before Our Very Eyes, Fake Wars, and Big Lies: From 9/11 to Donald Trump.[5] A number of organizations arose, devoted to uncovering the "truth" about what really happened on 9/11, such as Architects & Engineers for 9/11 Truth, 9/11 Truth, Scholars for 9/11

Truth, Scholars for 9/11 Truth & Justice, and 9/11 Citizens Watch.[6]

Note the linguistic shift from the pejorative "conspiracy theory" to the loftier search for "truth." In his analysis of the 9/11 Truther movement, law professor Mark Fenster analyzed this shift, which he called "reverse labeling": "the official account, they argue, itself constitutes a conspiracy theory that is at once overly simple and excessively complex."[7] Like the *Warren Commission Report's* conclusion that JFK was killed by a lone assassin, the 9/11 Commission Report "posits one mastermind, Osama bin Laden, and a rickety story composed of multiple madmen and an absent civilian and military air defense." Fenster noted that Truther David Ray Griffin counted no less than 38 coincidental failures that would have had to happen for the attacks to have been pulled off by al-Qaeda, as we're told they did. Fenster also stated that Truthers consider *themselves* to be the true patriots, operating in the tradition of the Founding Fathers, who were constructively paranoid about the conspiratorial machinations of the British government. This puts those of us who accept the 9/11 Commission's conclusion that Osama bin Laden orchestrated the conspiracy in the position of patsies, going along with the story manufactured by the authorities.

With so many people digging into the rubble of 9/11 for the past 20 years, they must have amassed enough evidence to convict the true terrorists. Let's see what they've uncovered, beginning with where many 9/11 Truthers start: the melting point of steel. According to the organization 9–11 Research, steel melts at a temperature of 2,777 degrees Fahrenheit, but jet fuel burns at only 1,517 degrees Fahrenheit. No melted steel, no collapsed towers.[8] Thus, Truthers surmise, explosive devices must have been used to bring down the World Trade Center (WTC) buildings. Wrong.

In an article in the *Journal of the Minerals, Metals, and Materials Society*, M.I.T. engineering professor Thomas Eagar and a colleague explained why.[9] Steel loses 50 percent of its strength at 1,200 degrees Fahrenheit, and 90,000 liters (L) of jet fuel ignited other combustible materials, such as rugs, curtains, furniture, and paper, which continued burning after the jet fuel was exhausted, raising temperatures above 1,400 degrees Fahrenheit and spreading the fire throughout the building. Temperature differentials of hundreds of degrees across single steel horizontal trusses caused them to sag, straining and then breaking the angle clips that held them to the vertical columns. Once one truss failed, others followed suit. When one floor collapsed (along with the 10 stories above it) onto the next floor below, that floor then gave way, creating a pancaking effect that triggered the 500,000-ton building to collapse. Their conclusion was as follows:

> No designer of the WTC anticipated, nor should have anticipated, a 90,000 L Molotov cocktail on one of the building floors. Skyscrapers are designed to support themselves for three hours in a fire even if the sprinkler system fails to operate. This time should be long enough to evacuate the occupants. The WTC towers lasted for one to two hours— less than the design life, but only because the fire fuel load was so large. No normal office fires would fill 4,000 square meters of floor space in the seconds in which the WTC fire developed.

For a special issue of *Skeptic* on 9/11,[10] we consulted demolition expert Brent Blanchard, who is director of field operations for Protec Documentation Services, a company that documents the work of building demolition contractors. Since the rise in popularity of 9/11 conspiracy theories, he has been inundated with requests to explain why the WTC buildings appeared to have "collapsed as if by a controlled demolition." Actually, if you search "building de-molition" on YouTube, you will find hundreds of video clips of buildings collapsing by means of controlled demo-lition. I could not find one that collapsed from the top down, as did the World Trade Center buildings, including building 7. Instead, you see what demolition experts tell us about how controlled demolition is done: the charges are set to ex-plode from the bottom up, the opposite of what was seen on 9/11.

Blanchard and his team of experts at Protec have worked with all major American demolition companies, and many foreign ones, to study the controlled demolition of over 1,000 of the largest and tallest buildings around the world. Their duties include engineering studies, structural analyses, vibration/air overpressure monitoring, and photographic services. On September 11, 2001, Protec had portable field seismic-monitoring systems operating at other sites in Man-hattan and Brooklyn. In addition, demolition specialists were hired to clean up Ground Zero and remove the re-maining damaged structures, and these experts called on Blanchard's company to document both the deconstruction and the debris removal. The following are nine of the best arguments made by 9/11 conspiracy theorists, and their re-buttals by Protec:[11]

> Claim #1. The collapse of the towers looked exactly like controlled demolitions.
> Answer: No, they did not. The key to any demolition investigation is in finding out the "where"—the actual point at which the building failed. All photo-graphic evidence shows World Trade Center build-ings 1 and 2 failed at the point of impact. Actual implosion demolitions always start with the bottom floors. Photo evidence shows the lower floors of WTC 1 and 2 were intact until destroyed from above.

Claim #2. The World Trade Center buildings fell right down into their own footprint.

Answer: Not exactly. They followed the path of least resistance, and there was a lot of resistance. Buildings of 20 stories or more do not topple over like trees or reinforced towers or smokestacks, primarily because they are mostly empty space designed for offices, with 95 percent of the structure's interior consisting of nothing but air. Imploding demolitions fall into a footprint because lower stories are removed first. WTC debris was forced out away from the building as the falling mass encountered intact floors. Moreover, the collapse began on the side where the planes impacted, so the building was tilted slightly toward that weakened collapse point, which you can clearly see in the numerous videos of the collapsing buildings.

Claim #3. Explosive charges are seen shooting out of windows from several floors just prior to the collapse.

Answer: Air and debris can be seen being violently ejected from the building, but not because of explosive charges. Rather, this is a natural and predictable effect of rapid structure collapse of the upper floors onto the lower floors, thereby pushing out smoke from the burning fires. Moreover, the impact and explosion of the two airplanes crashing into the buildings knocked off most of the fireproof drywall material surrounding the steel beams, considerably increasing their vulnerability to flames.

Claim #4. Witnesses heard explosions.

Answer: All seismic evidence from many independent sources on 9/11 showed none of the sudden vibration spikes that result from explosive detonations. What people might have heard are common office items

that explode in massive fires, such as cleaning sup-
plies, CRT TVs and computer monitors, large motors
with an oil reservoir for lubrication (e.g., elevator lift
motors), tires in vehicles in the parking structure,
and propane tanks.

Claim #5. A heat-generating explosive (thermite?)
melted steel at Ground Zero.
Answer: No demolition workers reported encountering molten steel, cut beams, or any evidence whatsoever of explosions or explosive charges.

Claim #6. Ground Zero debris—particularly the large
steel columns from towers 1 and 2—were quickly
shipped overseas to prevent scrutiny.
Answer: Not according to those who handled the steel.
The chain of procession is clearly documented, first at
Ground Zero by Protec, and later at the Fresh Kills site
by Yannuzzi Demolition. The time frame (months)
before the steel was shipped to China was normal.

Claim #7. World Trade Center building 7 (WTC 7) was
intentionally "pulled down" with explosives. The
building owner himself was quoted as saying he
decided to "pull it."
Answer: Building owners do not have authority
over emergency personnel at a disaster scene. Demolition experts have never heard "pull it" used to refer
to an explosive demolition. Demolition explosive
experts anticipated the collapse of WTC 7, and they
also witnessed it from a few hundred feet away. No
one heard detonations.

Claim #8. Steel-framed buildings do not collapse due to
fire.
Answer: Many steel-framed buildings have done so.
For example, on May 13, 2008, a large part of the tall,

concrete-reinforced steel Faculty of Architecture tower at Delft University of Technology in the Netherlands caught fire and burned. Shortly thereafter, it collapsed nearly straight down, falling almost precisely into its own footprint.

Claim #9. Anyone who denies that explosives were used is ignoring the evidence.

Answer: Most of our comments apply to the differences between what people actually saw on 9/11 and what they should have seen, had explosives been present. The hundreds of men and women who worked to remove debris from Ground Zero were some of the country's most experienced and respected demolition veterans. They, of all people, possessed the experience and expertise to recognize evidence of controlled demolition—if it existed. None of these people have come forward with suspicions that explosives were used.

The collapse of World Trade Center building 7 has grown in importance to conspiracy theorists, especially since standard nonconspiracy explanations for the demise of WTC buildings 1 and 2 became accepted. WTC 7 refers to two buildings at the World Trade Center site, very near WTC buildings 1 and 2, all developed by Larry Silverstein (who comes into conspiratorial play later). At 47 stories high and built of red granite masonry, WTC 7 differed significantly from WTCs 1 and 2. When those two buildings collapsed, their falling debris caused significant damage to WTC 7, which included extensive fires that burned all day. Since building 7 was not struck by a plane, and it did not collapse until 5:20 PM on 9/11—hours after the twin towers collapsed—conspiracists say the cause of its collapse must be different from that of WTCs 1 and 2. According to the WTC7.net website, "Fires were observed in

Building 7 prior to its collapse, but they were isolated in small parts of the building, and were puny by comparison to other building fires."[12] Any damage from falling debris from WTC 1 and WTC 2 would have needed to be symmetrical, in order to trigger the pancaking collapse of WTC 7.

In point of fact, the fires burning in building 7 were extensive, not isolated. The 9/11 conspiracy theorists tend to only show the north side of WTC 7, which does not look nearly as damaged as the other side. The building burned all day, and emergency response workers realized that collapse was imminent. At 3 PM that day, they began an evacuation of all emergency personnel. According to New York City Fire Department chief Daniel Nigro, he and his firefighters noticed structural deformations of building seven hours before its collapse. He later said, "I feared a collapse of WTC 7 (as did many on my staff)."[13] When the building did collapse, the south side went first, which is where the most extensive damage occurred from the falling debris of WTC buildings 1 and 2.

For my money, the oddest of all the 9/11 conspiracy theory claims involves the Pentagon. The idea, first floated in Thierry Meyssan's book, L'Effroyable imposture, was that the Pentagon was struck by a missile, because the damage was too narrow and too limited to be the result of an impact from a Boeing 757. In the conspiracy film Loose Change 9/11, dramatic reenactments are presented, arguing that the hole in the Pentagon was too small to have been made by American Airlines Flight 77.[14] "How does a plane 125 ft. wide and 155 ft. long fit into a hole which is only 16 ft. across?" asked the reopen911.org website.

First, how would any of us know how big a hole a plane should make when colliding with a massive building like the Pentagon? These conspiracists are talking through their hats in what philosophers calls an "argument from ignorance" (a proposition that has not been proven false must be true), or an "argument from personal incredulity" (a proposition must be false if it contradicts one's personal beliefs).[15] In point of fact, one of the wings of the American Airlines jet was sheared off on impact with the Pentagon building, while the other wing hit the ground and was torn off before the impact. The fuselage of the plane plowed into the concrete structure and almost instantly disintegrated.

Second, according to structural engineer Allyn E. Kilsheimer, who arrived on the scene shortly after the impact, "I saw the marks of the plane wing on the face of the building. I picked up parts of the plane with the airline markings on them. I held in my hand the tail section of the plane, and I found the black box."[16] Photos of plane wreckage inside and outside the building back up Kilsheimer's eyewitness account. He then added, "I held parts of uniforms from crew members in my hands, including body parts. Okay?" Figure 7.1 shows a piece of the American Airlines commercial airliner on the lawn next to the Pentagon.

Most of the 9/11 conspiracy claims can also be refuted this easily. For example, regarding the Pentagon "missile strike," I queried the documentary antagonist I mentioned at the start of this chapter about what happened to Flight 77, which disappeared at the same time the Pentagon was struck. "The plane was destroyed and the passengers were murdered by Bush operatives," he solemnly revealed. "Do you mean to tell me," I rejoined incredulously, "that not one of the thousands of conspirators needed to pull all this off is a whistle-blower who would go on TV or write a tell-all book?" Think about the countless examples of disgruntled government bureaucrats and ex-politicians who can't wait to go public with their insider information that we taxpayers will, presumably, want to know about. During Donald Trump's administration, as well as since he left office, a

Figure 7.1. A piece of the downed American Airlines plane on the lawn next to the Pentagon.

stream of books have poured off the presses about what it was "really like" in the White House or the Pentagon, laundering the reputations of the authors in the process and leading to lucrative careers outside of government. Not one of these 9/11 insiders, witnesses to what would arguably be the greatest conspiracy and cover-up in the history of the United States, wants to go on CNN or 60 *Minutes* to reveal their secret? Not one of them wants to cash in on what would surely be one of the bestselling books of the year? Not one of them, after a couple of drinks and a twinge or two of guilt, has leaked to a friend (or a friend of a friend) their deep secret? No pillow talk with intimates? Nothing?

In response to this aspect of the 9/11 conspiracy theory, filmmaker Brian Dalton and I produced a short video spoof called "You Can't Handle the Truther," in which we played out all the scenarios on offer from conspiracists.[17] These included (1) doctoring a cruise missile to look like an American Airlines jet; (2) operatives going into the twin towers to plant explosive devices under cover of elevator repairs; (3) disposing of all the passengers on that jet in a secret base in Canada, thus permanently ensuring that they couldn't talk; (4) creating fake phone calls to their families; (5) and, with our tongues pressed firmly in our cheeks, suggesting that every single conspiracist involved signed a nondisclosure agreement (NDA), adding that since "no one in history has ever violated an NDA," the conspiracy's secrets were safe. Besides, we concluded, who would ever imagine that one of the most complicated conspiracies in history could have been pulled off by the George W. Bush administration. As Bush himself said in a different context, mangling a popular idiom, "Fool me once, shame on . . . shame on you. Fool me . . . you can't get fooled again."[18]

Then there is the conspiracy theory that the North American Aerospace Defense Command supposedly told fighter jets to "stand down" and let the commercial jets reach their targets, thereby implicating the US military in the conspiracy. What actually happened was reported in a special issue of *Popular Mechanics* on 9/11: "On 9/11 there were only 14 fighter jets on alert in the contiguous 48 states. No computer network or alarm automatically alerted the North American Air Defense Command (NORAD) of missing planes. And NORAD's sophisticated radar . . . ringed the continent, looking outward for threats, not inward."[19]

Remember the definition of hindsight bias: "the belief that an event is more predictable after it becomes known than it was before it became known."[20] Before 9/11, hijackers of planes typically demanded ransom or insisted that some political action be taken. Then they would land the plane at some predetermined destination. Hijacking a plane and flying it into a building was something new, which almost no one anticipated. Also, on 9/11, the hijackers disabled the onboard radar transponders, making the planes much harder to track. Without those signals, NORAD would have had to search 4,500 identical radar blips on its screens, not knowing precisely which ones were hijacked planes.

Another conspiracy claim is that there was a suspiciously high volume of "put" trading of airline stocks in the days just before 9/11.[21] A put trade is a bet that the price of a stock will decrease, which is why this is sometimes called "selling a stock short." Conspiracists think a lot of trading insiders knew the attacks were coming on 9/11, so they bet airline stocks would decline afterward. But the level of put trading in the days before 9/11 was not so different from other peaks earlier in the year. In addition, American Airlines had recently released a report predicting possible losses in the coming quarter. When that happens, put traders increase their trading activity. The 9/11 Commission investigated this claim and reached the following conclusion:

> Some unusual trading did in fact occur, but each such trade proved to have an innocuous explanation. . . . A single U.S.-based institutional investor with no conceivable ties to al-Qaeda purchased 95 percent of the UAL [United Airlines] puts on September 6 as part of a trading strategy that also including buying 115,000 shares of American [Airlines] on September 10. Similarly, much of the seemingly suspicious trading in American on September 10 was traced to a specific U.S.-based options trading newsletter, faxed to its subscribers on Sunday, September 9, which recommended these trades. The SEC and FBI, aided by other agencies and the securities industry, devoted enormous resources to investigating this issue, including securing the cooperation of many foreign governments. These investigators have found

that the apparently suspicious consistently proved innocuous.[22]

This is yet another example of hindsight bias at work. After the fact, conspiracists go in search of anything unusual, reading far more into randomness and complexity than they would if 9/11 had not happened.

Then there's the matter of cell-phone calls made from the planes, which conspiracists claim could not have happened in 2001, given the technology of the day. First, some passengers used the in-flight cell phones then available on seat backs. Second, cell-phone calls in 2001 could be made from high-altitude flights, although coverage was spotty as the plane moved past various ground-based tower cells. According to Paul Guckian, vice president of engineering for cell-phone maker Qualcomm, "at the altitude for commercial airliners, around 30,000 or 35,000 feet, phones would still get a signal."[23]

Dozens more 9/11 conspiracy claims go on and on in what skeptics call *anomaly hunting*—chasing around for anything unusual, while ignoring more obvious explanations—all grounded in the argument of personal incredulity: "If I can't think of an explanation for anomaly X beside being a conspiracy, then that proves there is a conspiracy." No, it doesn't. It just means you can't think of an explanation.

A final argument that proves 9/11 was not an inside job—indeed, that it *could not have been* an inside job—comes straight out of cognitive psychology. It is called the *conjunction fallacy*, identified by psychologists Amos Tversky and Daniel Kahneman.[24] They asked subjects to imagine they were looking to hire someone for their company and were considering the following candidate for employment: "Linda is 31 years old, single, outspoken, and very bright. She majored in philosophy. As a student, she was deeply concerned with issues of discrimination and social justice, and also participated in anti-nuclear demonstrations." The subjects were then asked, "Which is more likely? 1. Linda is a bank teller. 2. Linda is a bank teller and is active in the feminist movement." When this scenario was presented to their study's subjects, 85 percent chose the second option.

Mathematically speaking, this is the wrong choice, because the probability (p) of two independent events occurring together (i.e., in conjunction) will always be less than or equal to the probability of either one occurring alone. In this thought experiment, it is far more likely that Linda is a bank teller than that she is both a bank teller and active in the feminist movement. For example, what if you chose a very low probability for Linda being a bank teller, say p (Linda is a bank teller) = 0.05, and a high probability that she would be a feminist, say p (Linda is a feminist) = 0.95. Then, assuming variable independence, p (Linda is a bank teller and Linda is a feminist) = 0.05×0.95, or 0.0475, which is lower than p (Linda is a bank teller), which has a probability of 0.05.

Let's apply the conjunction fallacy to the conspiracy theory that 9/11 was an inside job by the George W. Bush administration. The 9/11 Truthers claim that explosive devices were used to bring down the World Trade Center buildings. We all saw that planes hit the buildings, causing massive fires that burned for over an hour before the buildings fell. The probability that this happened and that explosive devices were planted in the buildings at the precise location where the planes hit is less than the probability of either one of these independent events. Since we know with 100 percent certainty that planes hit the buildings, we cannot logically accept the conspiracy theory that explosive devices were also used.

Another theme I've tracked in this movement is that 9/11 Truthers complain they aren't taken seriously. Not so. As I have just demonstrated, a large number of people and organizations have looked hard enough at these claims to research and rebut them all. The problem for Truthers is that their claims are rejected because both evidence and logic are lacking. An observation by famed attorney Vincent Bugliosi, whom we will meet in the next chapter for his work in refuting all the JFK conspiracy theories, applies to most conspiracists, including and especially 9/11 Truthers:

> The conspiracy community regularly seizes on one slip of the tongue, misunderstanding, or slight discrepancy to defeat 20 pieces of solid evidence; accepts one witness of theirs, even if he or she is a provable nut, as being far more credible than 10 normal witnesses on the other side; treats rumors, even questions, as the equivalent of proof; leaps from the most minuscule of discoveries to the grandest of conclusions; and insists, as the late lawyer Louis Nizer once observed, that the failure to explain everything perfectly negates all that is explained.[25]

Investigative journalist Jonathan Kay discovered this effect firsthand when he went among the Truthers for his book. After carefully studying the details of their conspiracy theory, Kay engaged prominent Truthers with facts that refuted their claims, which, he discovered, was entirely useless, "because in every exchange, the conspiracy theorist inevitably would ignore the most obvious evidence and instead focus the discussion on the handful of obscure, allegedly incriminating oddities that he had memorized. No matter how many of these oddities I managed to bat away . . . my debating opponent always has more at hand."[26]

• – – • – – •

All that said, I ask again, was 9/11 a conspiracy? Yes, it was. Say what? Recall that I defined a conspiracy as two or more people, or a group, plotting or acting in secret to gain an advantage or harm others immorally or illegally. By definition, 19 members of al-Qaeda plotting to fly planes into buildings without warning us about this constitutes a conspiracy. The ultimate failure of the 9/11 conspiracy theorists is their inability to explain away the overwhelming evidence of the *real conspiracy* by Osama bin Laden, al-Qaeda, ISIS, and other terrorist organizations past and present that routinely conspired (and still conspire) to attack the United States and its foreign assets. The following are but a few incriminating events:

- The 1983 attack on the Marine barracks in Lebanon by a radical Hezbollah faction.
- The 1993 truck bomb attack on the World Trade Center.
- The 1995 attempt to blow up 12 planes heading from the Philippines to the United States.
- The 1995 bombings of US Embassy buildings in Kenya and Tanzania, which killed 12 Americans and 200 Kenyans and Tanzanians.
- The 1996 attack on Khobar Towers in Saudi Arabia, which killed 19 US military personnel.
- The 1999 failed attempt to attack Los Angeles International Airport by Ahmed Ressam.
- The 2000 suicidal boat attack on the USS *Cole*, which killed 17 sailors and injured 39 others.
- The well-documented evidence that Osama Bin Laden was a major financier for and the leader of al-Qaeda.
- The 1996 fatwa by Bin Laden that officially declared a jihad against the United States.
- The 1998 fatwa by Bin Laden, calling on his followers "to kill the Americans and their allies—civilian and military is an individual duty for any Muslim who can do it in any country in which it is possible to do it."

Given this background, since Osama bin Laden and al-Qaeda officially claimed responsibility for the attacks of 9/11, we should take them at their word that they did it.

In conclusion, what bothers me most about the 9/11 Truther movement is that it is a distraction from the real conspiracy of al-Qaeda, ISIS, Boko Haram, the Taliban, and other such extremist organizations plotting to kill Westerners in Europe and America through countless low-level, nearly indefensible targets, such as streets, subways, theaters, stadiums, Christmas markets, churches, and any other place where large crowds of people gather. Those are real conspiracies, organized and implemented by genuine conspirators. Let's not lose sight of them while anomaly hunting among the rubble of 9/11.

• - - • - - •

President Barack Obama was a busy man during his eight years in office. Among other things, he allegedly (1) concocted a fake birth certificate to hide his true ID; (2) created "death panels" for who would live and who would die under his healthcare plan; (3) conspired to destroy religious liberty by mandating contraceptives for employees of religious institutions; (4) blew up the Deepwater Horizon offshore drilling rig to garner support for his environmental agenda; (5) masterminded Syrian gas attacks as a pretext to war; (6) orchestrated the shooting of a TSA agent to strengthen that agency's powers; (7) ordered the Sandy Hook Elementary School massacre to push through gun-control legislation; (8) built concentration camps for Americans who resist change; (9) attended a Christian church to hide his secret Islamic faith; and (10) contrived to have the stock market increase in value by 142 percent, to conceal the fact that he's a socialist.[27]

Do people really believe these things about Obama? Yes, some do. Not a majority of all Americans, but, if you break it down by political preference, a majority of Republicans (72 percent) said they believed one or more of these conspiracy theories and generally endorsed the Birther conspiracy theory.[28] As a result, conspiratorial rumors plagued Obama's administration throughout his presidency.[29]

The Birther conspiracy theory began in 2008, when Barack Obama won the primary election for the Democratic Party's presidential nomination and people—most notably Donald Trump—floated the idea that he wasn't born on US soil, a constitutional requirement for the presidency. After his election to the highest office in the land, the conspiracy theory continued. So a "Certification of Birth" of Barack Hussein Obama, stating that he was born on August 4, 1961, at 7:24 PM in Honolulu, Hawaii, was authenticated and released by Hawaii's governor, Neil Abercrombie, along with that state's attorney general and the chief of its Health Department.

The conspiracy theory continued, so the *Honolulu Advertiser* posted a copy of its August 13, 1961, edition announcing births that week, including that of the president-to-be. The conspiracy theory lingered, so on October 31, 2008, Dr. Chiyome Fukino, director of the Hawaii Department of Health, issued this statement:

> There have been numerous requests for Sen. Barack Hussein Obama's official birth certificate. State law prohibits the release of a certified birth certificate to persons who do not have a tangible interest in the vital record. Therefore I . . . along with the registrar of Vital Statistics who has statutory authority to oversee and maintain these type of vital records, have personally seen and verified that the Hawaii State Department of Health has Sen. Obama's original birth certificate on record in accordance with state policies and procedures.[30]

The conspiracy theory persisted, so the new governor of Hawaii, Linda Lingle, a Republican who, at that time, was campaigning for John McCain against Obama in his first quest for the presidency, publicly stated that the birth certificate was legit. And McCain himself famously upbraided a woman who was on stage at one of his campaign rallies in 2008 when she expressed her opinion that Obama was "an Arab." "No, ma'am," McCain retorted, taking the microphone back. "He's a decent family man, a citizen that I just happen to have disagreements with on fundamental issues, and that's what this campaign is all about."[31]

The conspiracy theory kept on, with conspiracists countering that this was the "short-form" document and not the more legitimate "long-form" certificate that would include more details about the birth. So a spokeswoman for the Hawaii Department of Health, Janice Okubo, issued a statement about the "long" and "short" forms: "They're just words. That [what was posted on the Internet] is considered a birth certificate from the state of Hawaii. There's only one form of birth certificate. When you request a birth certificate, the one you get looks exactly like the one posted on his site. That's the birth certificate."[32]

Numerous lawsuits challenging the birth certificate were filed, and lower courts threw them all out. The conspiracy theory persisted, and in time the legal submissions migrated all the way to the US Supreme Court, which heard and dismissed three additional suits filed in the case. The conspiracy theory continued, so at long last the president—with more important matters on his White House agenda—released his long-form birth certificate.

Nevertheless, Birthers insisted that the document was a forgery. As they went anomaly hunting through the document, conspiracists wondered where the embossed seal and the registrar's signature were on the certificate, why the shade of color allegedly was different from other Hawaii birth certificates, why there was no crease in the certificate from being folded and mailed, and why it looked

Photoshopped. In what PolitiFact calls the most widely read article in their history, its fact-checkers addressed each of these Birther claims and more, concluding, "If this document is forged, a U.S. senator and his presidential campaign have perpetrated a vast, long-term fraud. They have done it with conspiring officials at the Hawaii Department of Health, the Cook County (Ill.) Bureau of Vital Statistics, the Illinois Secretary of State's office, the Attorney Registration & Disciplinary Commission of the Supreme Court of Illinois and many other government agencies."[33]

Again employing the tools of my conspiracy detection kit, in an open society like ours, it simply isn't possible for this many people to pull off such a meticulous conspiracy without outsiders learning about it, or without one of their members slipping up or gaining moral scruples.

There are many more such challenges to Obama's birth location,[34] but at some point normal skepticism morphs into abnormal denialism, in which one's ideological stance is so entrenched that no amount of evidence can ever dissuade one from the certitude of belief. Why? In many ways the Obama Birther movement is the political doppelganger of the 9/11 Truther movement—albeit on the opposite end of the political spectrum. And the Birthers are as immune to contradictory facts as the Truthers. So one explanation is to be found in normal political tribalism, in which each side goes in search of and finds support for their own political party or representative, while pulling out any conceivable argument against the other, as evidenced by the fact that Birthers tend to be Republicans, while Truthers tend to be Democrats (with a smattering of conspiracy-minded libertarians among both conspiracy theory camps).

Because of these factors, plus confirmation bias (in which we look for and find confirming evidence in support of what we believe), it is almost impossible to objectively view contradictory evidence. Thus the Birthers, like the Truthers before them, will never be dissuaded from their beliefs. *Plus ça change, plus c'est la même chose.*

In the case of the Birthers, Obama's foreign-sounding name, his international family history, and his cosmopolitan background and education make it easy to glom onto a claim such as this, misinterpreting the probability of a certificate of live birth and a newspaper announcement both being false if the central claim was true. Now that the actual birth certificate has been released, the odds of all three being faked are beyond astronomical. Nevertheless, rumors about Obama's birthplace persist, with a significant percentage of Americans stating that they believe Obama was not born in the United States, was raised a Muslim, or both. Even after his presidency ended in 2016, a December 2017 YouGov poll found that 31 percent of Americans said they believed it was possible that Obama was born outside the United States with, predictably, 51 percent of Republicans assenting to this claim.

Finally, there is a darker element at work in the Birther movement—racism. In their analysis of "The Genesis of the Birther Rumor," Ashley Jardina and Michael Traugott noted that, especially among white Americans, "birther beliefs are uniquely associated with racial animus."[35] In their study, they merged this finding "with other work which shows that rumors are more strongly endorsed by the individuals most motivated and capable of integrating them among their pre-existing attitudes and beliefs. We find, therefore, that it is white Republicans who are both racially conservative and highly knowledgeable who possess the most skepticism about Obama's birthplace."[36]

Unfortunately, racist conspiracy theories continued to haunt the political landscape long after Obama left office in 2016, culminating in Charlottesville, Virginia, and the "Unite the Right" rally that tragically ended in the death of a white protestor who was there to counter these ugly forces in American culture, which do not appear to be going away any time soon. It reinforces my earlier point—conspiracy theories do not exist on the margins of society, but are deeply ensconced in mainstream culture. Thus, eternal vigilance is not only the watchword of freedom, but also the mantra of a sane and rational society.

CHAPTER 8

JFK Blown Away

The Mother of All Conspiracy Theories

Before 9/11 Truthers, Obama Birthers, and QAnon Trumpers, the mother of all conspiracy theories involved the assassination of President John F. Kennedy on November 22, 1963. In response to this tragedy, the new president, Lyndon B. Johnson, assembled a blue-ribbon commission of investigators, headed by US Supreme Court Justice Earl Warren, which produced a comprehensive 889-page report concluding that Lee Harvey Oswald was the lone assassin.[1] Since then, exhaustive investigations of the assassination have been conducted, including the thorough 1979 report of the House Select Committee on Assassinations; the definitive 2002 book on Oswald by Gerald Posner, *Case Closed*; Vincent Bugliosi's 2007 encyclopedic 1,600-page *Reclaiming History*, which addressed nearly every claim made by JFK conspiracy theorists; and Michel Jacques Gagné's recent *Thinking Critically About the Kennedy Assassination*.[2] All of these corroborated the original finding of the *Warren Commission Report* that Oswald acted alone.

Since Oswald himself was assassinated two days after he killed Kennedy, there was no trial, and the case was closed until 1969, when New Orleans district attorney Jim Garrison put local businessman Clay Shaw on trial as a co-conspirator. Shaw was alleged to have links to Oswald, who had lived for a short time in New Orleans. As Garrison was also a JFK assassination conspiracy theorist, he hoped a trial would uncover elements within the US government that had conspired to kill the president. By his reckoning, the most likely candidate was the CIA, in cahoots with the military-industrial complex, because, he reasoned in contrived hindsight, Kennedy wanted to get out of Vietnam. (As JFK assassination researcher Michel Gagné told me, "Vietnam did not figure prominently in Garrison's theories during the sixties. At first he claimed it was a sadist[ic] homosexual plot involving David Ferrie and Clay Shaw; then he began blaming the FBI; then he moved on to say that the CIA killed JFK because he intended to make peace with Cuba, not knowing that JFK had given his consent to the CIA plots to murder Castro.")[3] "In a very real and terrifying sense," Garrison proclaimed, "our government is the CIA and the Pentagon, with Congress reduced to a debating society."[4] Unfortunately for Garrison, the jury acquitted Shaw in under an hour.[5]

Conspiracy theories swirling around the president's assassination arose from day one, but interest was reignited after Watergate eroded public trust in the government in the early 1970s. Then Abraham Zapruder's 8mm movie camera film was made public in 1975, so everyone could see the president's head appear to snap *back and to the left*, as if the bullet came from the grassy knoll to the president's right, instead of the Texas School Book Depository Building where Oswald was located, placing Oswald behind JFK when the shot was fired. So, in 1976, the government reopened the case. The House Select Committee on Assassinations hired 250 investigators and spent $5.5 million dollars and 30 months to get to the bottom of who really killed JFK. After issuing a colossal 12-volume report, the committee concluded that Oswald was guilty and that no agency within the US government was involved.[6]

The only tidbit conspiracy theorists got out of the report was that an audio tape from the Dictabelt recording device, placed within the motorcade in Dealey Plaza, suggested that a fourth bullet was fired. Subsequent analysis, however, determined that whatever sound was recorded on the Dictabelt device happened a full 90 seconds after the assassination, long after the president's motorcade had accelerated out of Dealey Plaza and rushed to Parkland Memorial Hospital. Moreover, it was not even the sound of a gunshot. "My team has proven beyond a shadow of a doubt, for the first time," concluded Larry Sabato, head of the Center for Politics at the University of Virginia, upon the unveiling of a comprehensive study of police radio transmissions that day, "that the main conclusion of the House Select Committee on Assassinations—that a Dallas police Dictabelt recording shows four shots, not three, were fired in Dealey Plaza—is simply wrong."[7]

A decade later, in 1986, the London Weekend television show hosted a mock trial in which Vincent Bugliosi—the acclaimed prosecutor who convicted Charles Manson and his cult followers for murder—posthumously tried Lee Harvey Oswald. Oswald was defended in absentia by equally illustrious defense attorney Gerry Spence, known for defending Randy Weaver, the gun-loving, anti-government isolationist whose family was killed by FBI agents in a botched raid at his home in Ruby Ridge, Idaho, in 1992. After a 20-hour trial, the jury deliberated for six hours in what Time magazine called the closest "to a real trial as the accused killer of John F. Kennedy will probably ever get."[8] The jury convicted Oswald as the lone assassin. A 2013 PBS

Nova series special, "Cold Case JFK," shows definitively that only Oswald's Mannlicher-Carcano rifle could have caused the wounds suffered by Kennedy and Governor John Connally.[9] A 2019 documentary film, *Truth Is the Only Client: The Official Investigation of the Murder of John F. Kennedy* (the main title comes from Earl Warren's direction to the commission members) is long (nearly two and a half hours), but it is based on the comprehensive *Warren Commission Report* and subsequent studies. The film comes to the same conclusion: Lee Harvey Oswald acted alone.[10] Case closed.

In the mind of the public, however, the case is still not closed. Polls taken since the mid-1960s have consistently found that at least half of all Americans believe there was more than one shooter in Dealey Plaza. A 1997 Fox News poll found that a little over half of Americans considered it either "very likely" or "somewhat likely" that US officials were directly involved in the president's death.[11] A 1998 CBS News poll reported that 76 percent said they thought JFK was killed by a cabal of assassins.[12] A 2003 ABC News poll found that only 32 percent of American adults accepted that Lee Harvey Oswald acted alone.[13] A 2013 Gallup poll found that 61 percent of Americans specifically believed that there was a conspiracy.[14] A 2016 Chapman University survey found that half of all Americans believed that the government was covering up what they knew about the JFK assassination.[15] And a 2021 poll that my Skeptic Research Center, in conjunction with Anondah Saide and Kevin Mc-Caffree, conducted of over 3,000 Americans found that 36 percent said they slightly, moderately, or strongly agreed that "individuals within the United States government have hidden the truth about who was really responsible for the assassination of John F. Kennedy," with another 28 percent uncertain.[16]

So ubiquitous are JFK assassination conspiracy theories that there's even a joke featuring a conspiracist who dies and goes to heaven, where God offers to reward him for a life well lived by answering any question he'd like to ask.

CONSPIRACIST. "Who actually killed John F. Kennedy?"
GOD. "Lee Harvey Oswald, acting alone, using his own Carcano M91 rifle."
CONSPIRACIST. "This goes even higher than I thought."

Speaking to a conference of top-notch lawyers shortly after Oliver Stone's film JFK was released in 1992, attorney and JFK assassination expert Vincent Bugliosi asked how many of them did not believe the findings of the Warren Commission that a lone assassin killed JFK. Nearly everyone in the room raised their hands. When asked how many had seen Oliver Stone's film, roughly the same number of hands shot up. Bugliosi then asked how many had read the Warren Commission Report: "It was embarrassing. Only a few people raised their hands. In less than a minute I had proved my point. The overwhelming majority in the audience had formed an opinion rejecting the findings of the Warren Commission without bothering to read the Commission's report."[17] These were professional lawyers, passing judgment on a murder case while knowing next to nothing about it.

There has been so much published on the JFK assassination that I could fill this entire book with nothing but different conspiracy theories about the event. And once you go down that rabbit hole, a problem becomes apparent. Most of the theories contradict each other, and none have identified a second shooter, much less a conspiring organization, so the lone-assassin theory keeps rising to the top as the inference for the best explanation. For example, those who think organized crime was behind the assassination are in conflict with those who opine that the FBI orchestrated it. If you posit that the CIA did it, then it can't have been done by the CIA's Russian opposite, the KGB. Oliver Stone's film

JFK implicates just about everyone, including the Dallas Police Department, the Secret Service, Vice President Lyndon Johnson, the FBI, the CIA, anti-Castro Cuban exiles, organized crime, and especially the military-industrial complex.[18] If everything is a conspiracy and everyone a conspiracist, then nothing is explained.

My own opinion on the matter has changed over time. When I hadn't read much on the subject, I just assumed that the *Warren Commission Report*'s conclusion that Oswald acted alone was correct. But after I saw Oliver Stone's film, based on Jim Garrison's trial of Clay Shaw, I came to suspect that there might be more to the story—possibly even a real conspiracy to assassinate the president. That is the power of film, and who can forget Kevin Costner, as Jim Garrison, running the Zapruder film over and over for the jury, showing Kennedy's head snap "*back* and to the left . . . *back* and to the left."[19]

But after I read Gerald Posner's and Vincent Bugliosi's books, I updated my priors and reestablished my credence in the lone-assassin theory, which was later reconfirmed for me after I edited a special edition of *Skeptic* magazine in 2013, on the fiftieth anniversary of the assassination, in which we debunked the most common conspiracy theories.[20] So let's start this analysis with Lee Harvey Oswald, whom even most conspiracy theorists agree was involved in the shooting of the president. There are entire books, documentaries, and dramatic films about Oswald—by far the best is the PBS *Frontline* series, "Who Was Lee Harvey Oswald?"[21]—but below are the core facts that implicate him.[22]

• - - • - - •

Lee Harvey Oswald was born in New Orleans in 1939 and joined the US Marines in the 1950s, where he received riflery training. Contrary to what Oliver Stone had one of his characters say in his film—that Oswald "shot Maggie's drawers," meaning he couldn't even hit the target—Oswald scored the second highest rating possible in riflery, making him a sharpshooter. And if you go to Dealey Plaza and visit the sixth floor of the former Texas School Book Depository Building, which is now a museum, you can look out a window adjacent to the sniper's nest window and see just how close it was to where bullets hit the president, marked by two white X's on the highway below, denoting the neck shot and the head shot.

Politically, Oswald was an avowed Communist who defected to Russia in 1959, worked in a radio factory in Minsk for two years, and married a Russian woman named Marina. After he grew disenchanted with the USSR, in 1962 he moved to Dallas, Texas, shortly after telling friends he wanted to relocate to Cuba to join Castro's Communist revolution. This background helps establish a motive for killing Kennedy, as the president was avowedly anti-Communist and, after the failed Bay of Pigs invasion of Cuba, also clearly anti-Cuban and anti-Castro.

Temperamentally, Oswald was emotionally unhinged and suffered from delusions of grandeur, telling people he had ambitions to someday do something to make himself famous. He very likely was a sociopath, and quite possibly expressed the personality traits of psychopathy, narcissism, and Machiavellianism—the "Dark Triad"—dark because the combination often leads to malevolent actions.[23]

While in Dallas, Oswald encountered anti-Communist crusader Edwin A. Walker, a retired general who was something of a conspiracy theorist himself, once accusing US Supreme Court Justice Earl Warren of plotting to destroy the United States by banning prayer in schools and promoting civil rights for minorities. In April 1963, just eight months before he assassinated Kennedy, Oswald attempted to kill General Walker by shooting at him from around 100 feet outside his home. Walker was struck with bullet fragments in his forearm and survived. After the Kennedy assassination, it was determined that Oswald used the same firearm for both: an Italian-made 6.5mm Mannlicher-Carcano bolt-action rifle, which he purchased by mail order in March 1963, along with a .38 Smith & Wesson revolver, leaving a paper trail investigators later uncovered. That same Mannlicher-Carcano rifle was found among some boxes near the sniper's nest on the sixth floor of the Texas School Book Depository Building, and three spent Mannlicher-Carcano cartridges were scattered on the floor in the sniper's nest.

After Oswald tried to kill General Walker, he told his wife Marina what he had done. According to her, he also planned to assassinate Richard Nixon when the former vice president (and future president) visited Dallas, but she locked him in the bathroom to stop him. (After the JFK assassination, the Warren Commission determined that it was Oswald who attempted to murder General Walker.)

That summer, Oswald created the New Orleans chapter of the pro-Castro organization called Fair Play for Cuba (he was its only member), and he was arrested for getting into fights with anti-Castro Cubans—further evidence of his violent tendencies.

In September 1963, after his wife talked him out of hijacking a plane to Cuba, Oswald traveled to Mexico City in order to procure a visa to travel to Cuba, but the Cuban embassy said they would only give him a visitor's visa if he would be returning to the Soviet Union with his family, which he refused to do. So he went to the Soviet embassy, where he encountered three undercover KGB agents, who later reported that Oswald seemed unhinged, so they put him off.

Oswald then returned to Dallas, where, on October 16, he started work at the Texas School Book Depository Building. Conspiracy theorists have made much of the fact that the building was on Kennedy's parade route, but that route wasn't determined until the week before the president's visit to Dallas, well after Oswald got the job there (again reinforcing a central theme of this book—so many actual conspiracies turn on chance, coincidence, and contingency).

Coworkers saw Oswald on the sixth floor of the Texas School Book Depository Building shortly before JFK's motorcade arrived and saw him exit shortly after the assassination. The sniper's nest on the sixth floor of the Texas School Book Depository Building was constructed out of boxes, which had Oswald's fingerprints on them. Three bullet casings were found in the sniper's nest, indicating that he took three shots. This matches what 81 percent of the eyewitnesses in Dealey Plaza reported hearing—three shots.

Subsequent tests with a Mannlicher-Carcano rifle, particularly that mentioned in the 1979 House Select Committee Report, found that three shots can easily be taken in the eight seconds that Oswald had to get off the shots (some researchers put it at 10 seconds). With the first bullet already chambered, it would have taken only 3.3 seconds to squeeze off three shots.

The three shell casings found in the sniper's nest carry distinct ballistic markings on them, indicating that they were fired from Oswald's rifle. The one recovered bullet at Parkland Memorial Hospital, where Kennedy and Texas's Governor Connally—who was also hit by the first bullet to strike JFK—were taken, showed matching ballistic markings, indicating it had been fired from that rifle.

After killing Kennedy, Oswald went home and picked up his .38 Smith & Wesson revolver and left again. Shortly thereafter, he was stopped by Dallas patrolman J. D. Tippet. Oswald killed him with four bullets, an act witnessed by 10 observers, and the bullet casings at the scene matched Oswald's .38 Smith & Wesson.

Oswald then fled the scene and ducked into a nearby theater, without paying. The police were summoned to the theater, where they confronted Oswald. Oswald pulled out his revolver and attempted to shoot the first officer, but the gun was wrestled away from him and he was arrested, saying, "Well, it is all over now."

Actually, it was all over for Oswald two days later, when, at 11:21 AM CST on Sunday, November 24, Dallas nightclub operator Jack Ruby walked into Dallas Police Headquarters when Oswald was being transferred to the city jail and shot him dead at point-blank range. In yet another eerie coincidence, Oswald was rushed to Parkland Memorial Hospital and pronounced dead, two days to the hour after President Kennedy died in that same hospital.

• - - • - - •

There is no doubt whatsoever that Lee Harvey Oswald shot John Fitzgerald Kennedy, and anyone who would join a Fair Play for Oswald Committee needs a reality check. What conspiracists contend is that *someone else*, or *several others*, also shot Kennedy, or conspired to order the hit, or bankrolled the job, or orchestrated the shooters in Dealey Plaza, or something. (For those who think Oswald was a patsy set up by the CIA, the KGB, or the Mob, one need only recall the above facts about the man and ask yourself, "Who in their right mind would select someone this unstable and deranged to carry out an assassination of this magnitude?") Since there is no solid evidence fingering anyone other than Oswald, conspiracists have to go anomaly hunting to find something that does not quite seem to fit the lone-assassin theory. What should we do with such anomalies? Nothing. No theory explains everything, and here our conspiracism principle applies: never attribute to malice what can be explained by randomness or incompetence.

A perfect example of this is the man who shot Oswald, Jack Ruby, who has also been a prime suspect for conspiracists, particularly because of his affiliation with the Mob.

Ruby told investigators exactly why he shot Oswald: in order to save "Mrs. Kennedy the discomfiture of coming back to trial." He said his decision was a spur of the moment thing after recovering from two days of grief-stricken sadness, saying of Kennedy, whom Ruby loved as his president, that he did not understand "how a great man like that could be lost." Those who knew Ruby described him as temperamental and periodically violent. Vincent Bugliosi summarized what many people said about Oswald's assassin: "FBI agents may have interviewed close to one hundred people who knew Ruby well, and in their published reports in the Warren Commission volumes the reader would be hard-pressed to find one interviewee who did not mention Ruby's temper, or at least how 'very emotional' he was."[24]

So much of conspiracy theorizing depends on eyewitness accounts, but we know from decades of research in cognitive psychology that memories are not an accurate, high-fidelity recording of events. As psychologist Elizabeth Loftus has shown in experimental settings and real-world cases, peoples' memories can be easily manipulated by simple suggestion. For example, the choice of adjectives eyewitnesses to an automobile accident used to describe it—such as "smashed" instead of "collided"—influenced the witnesses' estimates of the speed at which they remembered the cars traveling.[25] Loftus's most famous experiment involved planting a false memory in an adult of getting lost in a mall as a child. A third of her subjects "remembered" being lost in the mall, most filling in rich details of what the mall looked like, what people were wearing, what happened and when, and even the emotions of being lost and then found.[26] This for an event that never even happened!

Emotionally charged events distort memory even more—and being present during the assassination of a president whose head is blown open by a bullet surely counts as an affecting event. This is probably why spectators in Dealey

Plaza gave such differing accounts of what happened. Some heard shots from behind Kennedy's limousine, while others thought they heard shots from in front of it or to the right, on the grassy knoll. Three witnesses said the shots came from *inside the president's car*. Another witness said that she "saw some men in plain clothes shooting back," which never happened. An early press bulletin reported that one of Kennedy's Secret Service agents had been killed—also untrue. According to *Dallas Morning News* reporter Hugh Aynesworth, who was at Dealey Plaza and saw the assassination, "I remember interviewing people that said they saw certain things; some did, some didn't. Even then there were people making up things. I remember interviewing a young couple where the guy was telling me that he had seen this and he had seen that, and his wife said, 'You didn't see that! We were back in the parking lot when it happened!' Even then!"[27]

Nevertheless, 81 percent of eyewitnesses reported hearing three shots, whereas only 5 percent said they heard four shots.[28] Most JFK conspiracy theories depend on four shots. Figure 8.1 is instructive, because it visually demonstrates a convergence of eyewitness testimony to the three-shot theory, whereas those who thought they heard four or more shots compose a mere five percent, which has garnered the lion's share of attention—another example of conspiracists chasing anomalies.

The directionality of the shots is another matter entirely, as experts on firearm investigations say it is very difficult to determine directionality from sound alone. Add to that factor the observation that Dealey Plaza is a small environment, encased with buildings and walls that cause echoes, and you have a recipe for misperception. Yet only a handful of people said that they'd heard shots from more than one direction.

Then there are the Parkland Memorial Hospital observations, made by the attending physicians and nurses, who

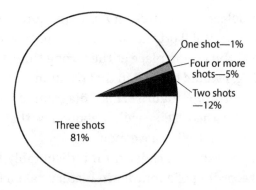

Figure 8.1. The number of gunshots witnesses heard at Dealey Plaza is instructive, because it shows that all JFK conspiracy theories depend on the tiny 5 percent of individuals who thought they heard four or more shots. *Source:* Graph by Pat Linse.

could not seem to agree on the directionality of the bullets from the nature of the wounds. Some said that the president's throat looked like it had an entrance wound, thereby placing the shooter in front of, not behind, Kennedy. Someone else reported that it was the back of his head that was blown off, not the side above the ears, as the *Warren Commission Report* says. And so on. But a more formal autopsy of Kennedy's body after it was returned to Washington, DC, determined that both shots entered his back and head from behind, the first exiting his throat and hitting Governor Connally, and bullet and skull fragments indicating the second went from back to front.

The weirdest anomaly of all was Louie Steven Witt, aka the Umbrella Man, who went to Dealey Plaza holding his umbrella as a sign of political protest against Kennedy, based on the fact that JFK's father, Joseph Kennedy, was a supporter of British Prime Minister Neville Chamberlain, who often carried an umbrella and went down in history as the man who appeased Hitler when the Führer still could have been stopped. Conspiracists have obsessed over the Umbrella Man's role in the assassination, but as Witt told the House Select Committee on Assassinations, "I think if the *Guinness Book of World Records* had a category for people who were at the wrong place at the wrong time, doing the wrong thing, I would be No. 1 in that position, without even a close runner-up."[29] Figure 8.2 is a diagram of what some JFK conspiracy theorists speculate about how that umbrella might have been used as a weapon.

Then there's the Zapruder film, indisputably the most analyzed recording of a murder in history, taken by Dallas clothing manufacturer Abraham Zapruder, who was perched atop a four-and-a-half-foot tall concrete pillar with his 8mm movie camera to capture his president rolling past. "This is the key shot," says Kevin Costner, as Jim Garrison, in Oliver Stone's film *JFK*. "Watch it again. The president going back to his left. Shot from the front and right. Totally inconsistent with the shot from the Depository."

Was it? Our intuitions about how bullets and bodies interact would make it seem so, and that's what happens in the movies, which is where most of us get our knowledge about firearms. But numerous studies since have shown

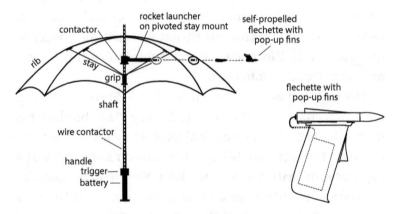

Figure 8.2. The alleged assassination weapon of Louie Steven Witt, aka the Umbrella Man, said to be a second shooter, using his umbrella as a gun. No such weapon was ever found. *Source:* Rendering by Pat Linse.

that what is seen in the Zapruder film is exactly what happens to a person when shot from behind—namely, the body's involuntary reaction to the sudden pain and shock of being hit by a bullet, causing Kennedy's head to lurch back after first being propelled forward (plus, Kennedy was wearing a back brace that prevented his body from lurching forward). In the clinical language of a study on the "transfer of momentum and kinetic energy" of the bullet impact, "the observed motions of President Kennedy in the [Zapruder] film are physically consistent with a high-speed projectile impact from the rear of the motorcade, these resulting from an instantaneous forward impulse force, followed by delayed rearward recoil and neuromuscular forces."[30]

Let's consider the three shots that Oswald fired. According to Dale Myers, a computer animator who produced an exact simulation of the Zapruder film, at frame 160, the first shot is fired, and Governor Connally starts to turn to his right—later Connally said he thought the shot came from behind. At frame 224, you can see Connally's jacket pop out as Oswald's second shot entered Kennedy's back, emerged from his throat, and then struck Connally.[31] In frame 247, you can see Kennedy's hands go up toward his throat in response to that second shot, along with Connally's reaction, wincing in pain after being hit; in frame 275, you can see Connally turn around to see what has happened to Kennedy (figure 8.3). Both men were hit by the same bullet, which conspiracists call the "magic bullet theory" but forensic analysts call the "single-bullet theory."

Here is another example of misinformation fueling a conspiracy theory. The assumption conspiracists make is that Kennedy and Connally were perfectly lined up in the limousine, with their seats at the same height, so a bullet fired from the sixth floor of the Texas School Book Depository Building would have had to enter Kennedy's back, exit his

Figure 8.3. Frame 247 (top) of the Zapruder film corresponds to Oswald's second shot, which passed through Kennedy's neck and into Connally (*seated in front of JFK*), who grimaces in agony. In frame 275 (*bottom*), Connally turns to see what has happened behind him.
Zapruder Film © 1967 (renewed 1995), used with permission from The Sixth Floor Museum at Dealey Plaza.

throat, make a right turn, then a left turn, and then enter Connally, which is clearly impossible (and is why it's called a "magic bullet"). But as Myers showed in his reenactment, based on the plans for Kennedy's limo, Connally was sitting on a small jump seat placed a few inches to Kennedy's left and three inches lower than the President, which means that a shot from the sniper's nest was at an angle that perfectly matched the wounds in Kennedy and Connally, without any "magical" twists and turns of the bullet. As Myers concluded, the "single-bullet theory" should be renamed the "single-bullet fact."[32] Figure 8.4, by *Skeptic* magazine's art director, Pat Linse, illustrates what really happened with the second bullet as it struck and passed through both Kennedy and Connally.

Another argument conspiracists make is that the bullet recovered at Parkland Memorial Hospital was "pristine," evidence they say shows it was planted there by operatives, who were apparently so dumb they didn't bother to bang up the bullet a little. But the bullet was not pristine, and it had rifling marks, proving that it was shot out of a rifle. Figure 8.5 shows that it was flattened, as if it had gone through a body, which it had—two bodies, in fact.[33]

Finally, the third and fatal shot that hit Kennedy's head in frame 313—when viewed in slow motion in the digitally enhanced, high-definition, slo-mo versions readily available online—clearly shows that the shot came from behind. If you pause the film at frame 313 (see figure 8.6), you can see skull, brain, and blood matter ejected in an upward and forward direction, as if the shot came from the sixth story of the Texas School Book Depository Building, which it did.[34]

Earlier in the book I introduced my concept of patternicity, or the tendency to find meaningful patterns in both meaningful and meaningless noise.[35] There is, perhaps, no better illustration of this phenomena than JFK conspiracists who think they are seeing patterns of intentional agents lurking in the shadows of Dealey Plaza, particularly above the grassy knoll. Figure 8.7 shows a Polaroid photograph taken by Mary Ann Moorman, who was standing on the opposite side of the road from Abraham Zapruder. Assassination conspiracists claim to have discovered in Moorman's blurry, grainy photograph evidence of multi-

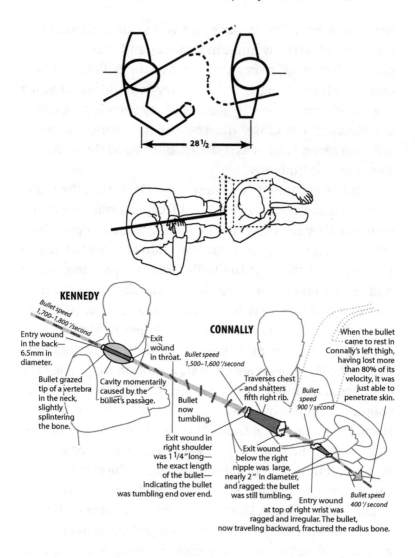

ple shooters. Look for yourself. The only thing I see is patternicity. The image also stands in for what so many conspiracy theories depend on: degraded data that can be interpreted in many different ways. Once the mind has determined what that set of information is, that person cannot see it as something else, including randomness.

• – – • – – •

I could go on and on in this vein for pages more, debunking conspiracy theory after conspiracy theory. Thousands of books have been published on the assassination, with around 95 percent of them skeptical of what seems obvious. The evidence overwhelmingly points to the conclusion that JFK was blown away by Lee Harvey Oswald, acting alone. Nevertheless, despite the evidence and logic that lead to this unmistakable conclusion, a great many people disagree. As political scientist and JFK conspiracy researcher John McAdams argued in *JFK Assassination Logic: How to Think About Claims of Conspiracy*, the most we can aim toward is that in teaching people how to think about conspiracies, "hopefully they will reject many bogus conspiracy arguments and evidence, even while holding out for a particular piece of evidence or some tantalizing 'unanswered question' that might be the tip-off to covert shenanigans."[36]

At this point, the burden of proof is on conspiracy theorists to provide positive evidence for a second shooter, rather than merely anomaly hunting, in the "just asking

Figure 8.4. Top: The inaccurate single bullet theory has Governor Connally facing straight forward and seated directly in line with President Kennedy. The shot line is also inaccurate, as it shows an extreme angle for the shot, which would have missed Connally, were it not for the "magic" twists and turns it would have had to take. Middle: Instead, Dale Myers's analysis shows that Governor Connally was seated on a small jump seat placed a few inches to Kennedy's left. At the time of the "single bullet" shot, Connally had shifted his upper body sharply to the right when he heard the first shot. Bottom: The path of the second bullet, with notations about speeds and rotational action after it passed through Kennedy's upper back and neck and then struck Connally in his right shoulder, before going through his wrist and into his leg. Source: Top and middle images redrawn by Pat Linse from Robert Groden and Harrison Edward Livingstone's book, *High Treason* (New York: Basic Books, 1998); bottom diagram (redrawn by Pat Linse) and captions labeling events of the bullet's passage through both bodies from Gerald Posner's book, *Case Closed* (New York: Random House, 1993), pages 478–479.

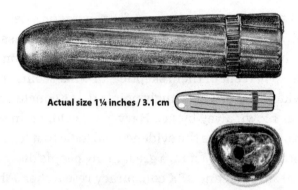

Actual size 1¼ inches / 3.1 cm

Figure 8.5. The so-called "pristine" bullet, allegedly found at Parkland Memorial Hospital, was anything but that. It shows the wear marks of a bullet that had traveled through a body. *Source:* Art by Pat Linse.

Figure 8.6. In this still of frame 313 of the Zapruder film, you can see the fatal shot as Kennedy's blood, brains, and pieces of his skull fly upward and to the front, as they would if he was shot from behind—not back and to the left, as Oliver Stone's film JFK claims. *Source:* Zapruder Film © 1967 (renewed 1995), used with permission from The Sixth Floor Museum at Dealey Plaza.

questions" vein. So why the skepticism, even paranoia, about the lone-assassin fact? There are at least four reasons, related directly to this particular conspiracy theory, with which I will end this chapter, and another three reasons, related to real conspiracies, with which I will begin the next chapter. All of these serve as a heuristic for understanding why conspiracy theories have become so mainstream in the past half century.

1. *Cognitive dissonance.* As we have seen earlier, cognitive dissonance plays a role in conspiracy theorizing, particularly when there is a mismatch between the size or importance of an event and its purported cause—again, a proportionality problem. In this case, the contention that a lone psychopath like Lee Harvey Oswald assassinated one of the most powerful people in the world doesn't gel. Hence the need to balance the cognitive scales by adding conspiratorial agents, such as the FBI, the CIA, the KGB, the Cubans, the Mafia, and the military-industrial complex.

2. *Fame and popularity.* Having tried many murder cases, most notably the Manson murders, Vincent Bugliosi noted that as these matters go, the Kennedy murder was not that complicated. "I've personally prosecuted several murder cases where the evidence against the accused was far more circumstantial and less robust than the case against Oswald," Bugliosi wrote, adding that "the case against Oswald himself is overwhelming and relatively routine. As Earl Warren himself observed: 'As district attorney of a large metropolitan county for years . . . I have no hesitation in saying that had it not been for the prominence of the victim, the case against Oswald could have been tried in two or three days with little likelihood of any but one result.'"[37]

3. *Camelot.* When famous people die, their fans and supporters often elevate them to mythic status. After JFK's death, Jackie Kennedy mentioned that he had enjoyed the

Figure 8.7. This grainy Polaroid photograph (*this page*) shows Kennedy, who has just been shot through the upper back and neck, in the rear seat of the vehicle. Jackie (seated to his *left*) is leaning toward him to find out what has happened. The photo was taken by Mary Ann Moorman, who was standing on the opposite side of the road from Abraham Zapruder, who can be seen at the *farthest right*, standing on top of a concrete pillar. The enlarged images (*next page*) of circled areas in the photo represent "evidence" of multiple shooters that assassination conspirators claim to have discovered within Moorman's blurry photograph. *Source:* Photo from Wikimedia; art by Pat Linse.

soundtrack from the Broadway musical *Camelot*, and it became a nostalgic descriptor of his administration, echoing Kennedy's favorite stanza from the play: "Don't let it be forgot that once there was a spot / For one brief shining moment that was known as Camelot."[38] Had Kennedy lived and served a second term, he probably would have been judged in less mythic tones. Elevated to near god-like status, however, his murder has also been raised to mythic proportions.

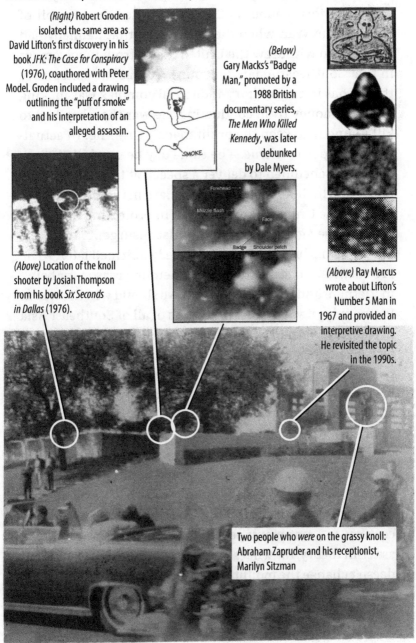

Below: A few of the potential assassination conspirators "discovered" in the Moorman photo.

(Right) Robert Groden isolated the same area as David Lifton's first discovery in his book *JFK: The Case for Conspiracy* (1976), coauthored with Peter Model. Groden included a drawing outlining the "puff of smoke" and his interpretation of an alleged assassin.

(Below) Gary Macks's "Badge Man," promoted by a 1988 British documentary series, *The Men Who Killed Kennedy*, was later debunked by Dale Myers.

(Above) Location of the knoll shooter by Josiah Thompson from his book *Six Seconds in Dallas* (1976).

(Above) Ray Marcus wrote about Lifton's Number 5 Man in 1967 and provided an interpretive drawing. He revisited the topic in the 1990s.

Two people who *were* on the grassy knoll: Abraham Zapruder and his receptionist, Marilyn Sitzman

4. Politics. Arguably the most popular of the many conspiracy theories about JFK emerged after the turmoil of the Vietnam War, when the idea spread that Kennedy had intended to withdraw the United States from involvement in that Southeast Asian quagmire. But, as the conspiracy theory has it, the military-industrial complex was making so much money from conducting the war that they had to kill Kennedy to keep the profit machine rolling. In actuality, the opposite is true. The same day he was killed, Kennedy was scheduled to deliver a speech at the Dallas Trade Mart, in which he was going to declare his commitment to keeping the United States involved in protecting the South Vietnamese against the Communist insurgents from the north. As his brother Robert Kennedy affirmed later, "The President . . . had a strong, overwhelming reason for being in Vietnam and [in believing] that we should win the war in Vietnam [as it would mean] the loss of all of Southeast Asia if you lost Vietnam . . . [which would] have profound effects as far as our position throughout the world, and our position in a rather vital part of the world." When asked if his brother had given any consideration to pulling out, RFK curtly replied, "No."[39]

In the next chapter, I will have more to say about real conspiracies and how they lead people to be constructively paranoid about their government, but the point here is that we should not be surprised if, in the second half of the twentieth century—and continuing well into the twenty-first century—a great many people have doubted the JFK lone-assassin theory, for what seemed to be rational reasons. That doesn't change the mountain of facts supporting the lone assassin theory, but it does explain the continued interest—almost obsession—in this particular conspiracy theory.

CHAPTER 9

Real Conspiracies

What If They Really Are Out to Get You?

In the previous chapter, I hope I convinced you that President John F. Kennedy was assassinated by a lone gunman named Lee Harvey Oswald, even while acknowledging the psychological desire for there to be a conspiratorial cause proportional in importance to the effect—namely, the leader of the free world should have been cut down by a force matching his in size or importance. That he wasn't feels wrong, but the facts say otherwise, and we should follow the facts, not our feelings.

In this chapter I want to explore another, deeper reason why so many people think that the conspiracy theories surrounding not just the JFK assassination, but many other assassinations and related political events, carry such psychological weight. The answer I offer in this chapter—an extension of what I've called constructive conspiracism earlier in the book—is because there really are conspiracies, and sometimes *they really are out to get you.* As American writer and poet Delmore Schwartz noted,

"Even paranoids have real enemies."[1] Let's begin with three broad historical trends.

• - - • - - •

Real Political Assassinations

Historically, regime change through political assassination was not all that uncommon. For example, in a study of 1,513 European monarchs who ruled between 600 and 1800 AD, criminologist Manuel Eisner found that 227 of them, or about 15 percent, were assassinated in coup d'états.[2] That's a large enough number to make most of us constructively conspiratorial about the machinations of backroom operatives plotting the overthrow of a leader or administration. This particular type of conspiracy is common enough to have a name: regicide.

The assassination of Archduke Franz Ferdinand of Austria in the summer of 1914, which triggered the First World War, is a glaring example, about which I'll have more to say in the next chapter on how conspiracies really work. In 1917 in Russia, after overthrowing the Tsarist regime, Lenin and his Bolshevik conspirators assassinated the Romanov family in the early-morning hours of July 17, 1918, consisting of Tsar Nicholas II and his wife Alexandra, along with their five children: Olga, Tatiana, Maria, Alexei, and, most famously, Anastasia. Conspiracy theories abound that Anastasia survived the attack and lived a long life afterward. For a time, a woman named Anna Anderson claimed she was Anastasia and enjoyed some limelight as a media curiosity when she "recalled" her life as a Romanov. While DNA testing in the 1990s confirmed that the buried bodies in a grave were those of most of the family, two of the children, including Anastasia, could not be identified.[3] Finally, in the summer of 2007, a group of amateur archeologists uncovered remains in a second grave near the larger grave that contained most of the Romanov family, and DNA testing on these bodies proved conclusively that no one in the Romanov family survived the assassination, including Anastasia.[4]

In the United States, no fewer than four presidents have been assassinated while in office—Abraham Lincoln, James Garfield, William McKinley and, John F. Kennedy. Before Kennedy was killed, arguably the most famous political assassination was that of Lincoln. He was shot in the back of the head in Ford's Theater in Washington, DC, on April 14, 1865, unquestionably the result of a cabal led by famous actor John Wilkes Booth, in cahoots with his co-conspirators Lewis Powell, David Herold, and George Atzerodt. Powell and Herold were assigned to kill Secretary of State William H. Seward, while Atzerodt was supposed to murder Vice President Andrew Johnson. In other words, this conspiracy intended to decimate the Lincoln administration, not just get rid of the president, in the hope of reigniting the South's war of independence, better known as the Civil War.

As we shall see, real conspiracies are difficult to pull off, and that was the case here. Only Booth succeeded in his assignment. Atzerodt lost his nerve, got drunk, and entirely abandoned his mission to kill Johnson. Powell lied his way into Seward's home, where the secretary of state was in bed, recovering from a carriage accident. After overpowering Seward's son, Powell managed to stab Seward with a knife, but the neck splint for the secretary of state's injuries prevented the knife from slicing open his jugular vein, and he survived. Powell ran out the door screaming, "I'm mad! I'm mad!" After a 12-day manhunt, Booth was trapped in a barn and—with seemingly cosmic justice—was shot in the back of the head, a wound from which he died two hours later. The other conspirators were captured by the end of the month, tried, found guilty, and executed, along with Mary Surratt, convicted as a co-conspirator for aiding and abetting the assassins, the first woman ever executed by the US government.[5]

President James Garfield was shot on July 2, 1881, at the Baltimore and Potomac Railroad Station in Washington, DC, where he was to deliver a speech before departing on a vacation. He died of his injuries 79 days later, on September 19, barely six months into his term, killed by a lone nut named Charles Guiteau. Guiteau believed he was personally responsible, in part, for Garfield's electoral defeat of Ulysses S. Grant and felt he was unrewarded for his role. Five years earlier, his own family had tried to have him permanently committed to an asylum, but he escaped. He then set himself the task of killing a US president, stating, "I leave my justification to God." After he shot Garfield, Guiteau declared, "I am a Stalwart of the Stalwarts! I did it and I want to be arrested! Arthur is President now," referring to Vice President Chester A. Arthur. As a result of this confession, conspiracy theories that Arthur was behind the assassination emerged, but they were never supported by evidence. During his trial, Guiteau invoked the newly introduced insanity plea and said he planned to run for president himself after he was acquitted. He was found guilty and hung on June 30, 1882, waving to the crowd and reciting a poem he wrote, titled "I am Going to the Lordy."[6]

President William McKinley was assassinated on September 6, 1901 at the Pan-American Exposition in Buffalo, New York. An anarchist named Leon Czolgosz, who was standing in the reception line where McKinley was shaking hands, shot the president. McKinley died eight days later from his wounds, and Czolgosz was sentenced to death by electric chair. Shortly thereafter, Congress passed legislation requiring Secret Service protection for all future presidents. Czolgosz was following in the tradition of European anarchists, who had assassinated (or attempted to assassinate) half a dozen members of royal houses in the late nineteenth century. After Czolgosz's execution, Buffalo police announced that they believed he had not acted alone, and they arrested several other anarchists on suspicion of conspiracy. These alleged cohorts were all eventually released when no evidence was presented to try them in a court of law, but subsequent suspicions of anarchists produced surveillance programs, leading to the formation of the Federal Bureau of Investigation, or FBI, in 1908.[7]

Unsuccessful presidential assassination attempts have included those on Andrew Jackson, Theodore Roosevelt, Franklin Roosevelt, Gerald Ford, and Ronald Reagan, all by lone unhinged sociopaths.[8] Their lack of success was largely due to luck and associated circumstances.

On January 30, 1835, President Andrew Jackson was fired upon outside the US Capitol building by a mentally ill house painter named Richard Lawrence, whose pistol misfired twice in the rainy weather. None other than Representative Davy Crockett wrestled the would-be assassin to the ground, whereupon President Jackson beat him with his cane. Conspiracy theories about the assassination attempt were proposed, fingering Jackson's arch rival, Senator John C. Calhoun, but no evidence of a plot was ever uncovered, and Lawrence spent the rest of his life in an insane asylum.

On October 14, 1912, former President Teddy Roosevelt was running again on a third-party ticket, the Progressive, or Bull Moose, Party. While campaigning in Milwaukee, Wisconsin, Roosevelt was shot by a saloonkeeper named John Schrank. Roosevelt survived because the bullet was slowed down by passing through his steel eyeglass case and a 50-page, twice-folded manuscript of the speech he was about to deliver, which he famously did in his blood-soaked shirt, for all to see. His opening line is classic: "Ladies and gentlemen, I don't know whether you fully understand that I have just been shot, but it takes more than that to kill a

Bull Moose."[9] Schrank was found legally insane and was institutionalized until his death.

On February 15, 1933, a disgruntled Italian immigrant named Giuseppe Zangara fired five shots at president-elect Franklin Roosevelt when the latter was giving a speech in an open car in Miami, Florida, but all the bullets missed their intended target. One hit and killed the mayor of Chicago, Anton Cermak, so conspiracy theories arose about who the "real" intended target was. Zangara plead guilty and confessed to the assassination attempt: "I have the gun in my hand. I kill kings and presidents first and next all capitalists." A month later, he was executed by electric chair.

On September 5, 1975, Charles Manson family cult member Lynette "Squeaky" Fromme took a shot at President Gerald Ford in Sacramento, California, to protest environmental pollution, but missed. She spent most of the rest of her life in prison, proclaiming her undying devotion to Manson: "The curtain is going to come down on all of us, and if we don't turn everything over to Charlie immediately, it will be too late."

On March 30, 1981, John Hinckley Jr. shot President Ronald Reagan in Washington, DC, in order, Hinckley said, to impress actress Jodie Foster after he became obsessed with her in the film *Taxi Driver*. Hinckley claimed he was insane at the time of the attempted assassination. Three government-appointed psychiatrists determined that he was sane, because of the extensive advance planning required to attempt a political assassination, but his defense-appointed psychiatrists diagnosed him with several severe mental disorders, including schizophrenia spectrum disorder and paradoxical rage. The jury agreed with the defense. Rather than being imprisoned for shooting the president, Hinckley was sent to St. Elizabeth's, a mental hospital in Washington, DC, where he was subjected to psychological observation and treatment.

All US presidents—just like heads of state throughout the world—routinely receive death threats and require extensive personal security. In some cases, the "they" out to get world leaders turn out to be deranged and delusional psychopaths, operating alone, but there are enough examples of political conspiracies resulting in regime change through violence that it is not paranoid to be wary of them. My next two broad historical trends are examples of the latter.

• - - • - - •

US Involvement in Political Assassination

After the Second World War, the CIA and other agencies of the US government became secretly engaged in the practice of international political assassination and regime change. Although this was against the United Nations Charter that the United States had recently signed, the practice went on for decades, until it was exposed in the 1970s.

For example, as mentioned previously, Kennedy's own administration discussed ways to assassinate Fidel Castro, with methods that were right out of a James Bond movie: an exploding cigar; a poisoned cigar; a scuba-diving wetsuit laced with tuberculosis bacillus; an exploding conch shell, planted on the sea bottom where Castro liked to dive; a ballpoint pen containing a hypodermic syringe preloaded with poison; and even a Mafia hit, to be conducted by infamous mobsters Sam Giancana and Santo Trafficante. As Castro famously said, "If surviving assassinations were an Olympic event, I would win the gold medal."[10]

Then there is the Kennedy-era document dubbed "Operation Northwoods," officially titled "Justification for US Military Intervention in Cuba."[11] It included numerous false-flag operations to be used as a pretext for killing Castro and overturning his Communist regime, such as staging a phony attack on the US military base at Guantanamo Bay, employing a fake Russian MIG aircraft to buzz a real US civilian airliner, hijacking planes, faking an attack on a US ship to make it look like the Cubans did it, and developing "a Communist Cuban terror campaign in the Miami area, in other Florida cities and even in Washington" that would harass US citizens, all to be blamed on Castro. The document, drafted by the Joint Chiefs of Staff, read, "The desired resultant from the execution of this plan would be to place the United States in the apparent position of suffering defensible grievances from a rash and irresponsible government of Cuba and to develop an international image of a Cuban threat to peace in the Western Hemisphere."

That President Kennedy rejected all of these proposals is beside the point here. As wrong as the Truthers are in their conspiracy theories about 9/11 being an "inside job" and a false-flag operation to justify a US-led regime change in Iraq, the "Operation Northwoods" document fueled the fires of constructive conspiracism. Ironically, "Operation Northwoods" only came to light in 1997, as part of a mountain of documents, totaling 1,521 pages, of once-secret records related to JFK's assassination.[12] This cautionary warning by the US Department of Defense is revealing for our understanding of how conspiracies really work: "Any of the contrived situations described above are inherently, extremely risky in our democratic system in which security can be maintained, after the fact, with very great difficulty. If the decision should be made to set up a contrived situation it should be one in which participation by US personnel is limited only to the most highly trusted covert personnel."[13] In other words, real conspiracies on this scale are extremely difficult to keep secret.

Another significant revelation in those documents was that Lyndon Johnson was eager for the Warren Commission to conclude that Oswald acted alone, not because he knew about an extant conspiracy (much less that he was in on one), but because he feared investigators would discover the Kennedy administration's plots to kill Castro, which could lead to tensions with the Soviet Union that could escalate into conflict and, possibly, even a catastrophic nuclear exchange. Nor was Castro the only target of the CIA. Over the decades, the agency was involved in many schemes to overthrow foreign leaders of countries not friendly toward the United States and American interests, including Patrice Lumumba of the Congo, Rafael Trujillo of the Dominican Republic, Ngo Dinh Diem of South Vietnam, Indonesia's President Sukarno, Chile's President Salvador Allende, and General Rene Schneider of Chile.[14]

Many of these conspiracies came to light in 1976 in the Senate Select Committee's report on foreign and military intelligence (also known as the Church Committee report), chaired by Senator Frank Church of Idaho.[15] In response, the following year President Gerald Ford signed Executive Order 11,905, which was later enshrined in President Ronald Reagan's Executive Order 12,333: "No person employed by or acting on behalf of the United States Government shall engage in, or conspire to engage in, assassination."[16] As Ford stated in a press conference, "Let me say at the outset that this Administration does not condone, under any circumstances, any assassination attempts."[17] Nevertheless, the United States has continued to be involved in regime change by overthrowing dictators, such as Libya's Muammar Gaddafi in 1986, Serbia's Slobodan Milosevic in 1999, and Iraqi president Saddam Hussein in 2003, albeit under quasi-legal means through the UN and with congressional approval. Loopholes in the Executive Order remain, however. During the Gulf War, President George H. W. Bush could have ordered the assassination of Saddam Hussein as an enemy combatant after the war began. Although Bush stated that "no one will weep when he's gone" and "there would be no sorry if he's not there,"[18] he affirmed that the Middle East should be governed by the "rule of law," not by the "law of the jungle."[19]

The Church Committee also discovered Operation SHAMROCK, which involved the National Security Agency (NSA) obtaining information and intelligence from the major telecommunications companies about both foreigners and US citizens, as well as a "mail covers" program by the CIA and FBI that involved opening and photographing hundreds of thousands of pieces of mail—without a search warrant or notification to the mail senders or receivers. While acknowledging that the country needs intelligence on potential enemies foreign and domestic, the Church Committee added this cautionary warning:

> If this government ever became a tyranny, if a dictator ever took charge in this country, the technological capacity that the intelligence community has given the government could enable it to impose total tyranny, and there would be no way to fight back because the most careful effort to combine together in resistance to the government, no matter how privately it was done, is within the reach of the government to know.[20]

Keep in mind that this was written in 1975, long before the internet and the Wikileaks revelations of what both the George W. Bush and Obama administrations were doing in the surveillance of American citizens.

• - - • - - •

Real Conspiracies That Eroded Public Trust in the Government

Now I want to develop further the idea that constructive conspiracism—paranoia about possibly dangerous people or situations—is rational, because of the many real conspiracies that have so dramatically influenced the course of history and may still be found at work in modern politics, economics, finance, business, and world affairs. These are often complex conspiracies, seemingly happening before our eyes in ways that are difficult to discern.

Let's start with one of the most famous US Supreme Court decisions in its long and storied history—that of the 1919 case of *Schenck v. United States*—in which Justice Oliver Wendell Holmes, writing the unanimous opinion of the court regarding where and when speech should be censored, issued these now-famous and oft-quoted lines:

> The most stringent protection of free speech would not protect a man in *falsely shouting fire* [italics added] in a theatre and causing a panic. . . . The question in every case is whether the words used are used in such circumstances and are of such a nature as to create *a clear and present danger* [italics added] that they will bring about the substantive evils that Congress has a right to prevent.[21]

What were the falsely shouted utterances that Justice Holmes feared constituted a clear and present danger? They were 15,000 fliers distributed to draft-age men during the First World War that encouraged them to "Assert Your Rights": "If you do not assert and support your rights, you are helping to deny or disparage rights which it is the solemn duty of all citizens and residents of the United States to retain." Rights to what? Freedom. Freedom from what? Slavery. Slavery? In 1919? Yes. According to the distributors of the fliers—Charles Schenck and Elizabeth Baer, who were members of the Executive Committee of the Socialist Party in Philadelphia—military conscription constituted involuntary servitude, which is strictly prohibited by the Thirteenth Amendment of the Constitution. As they wrote in their broadside "Long Live the Constitution of the United

States," "When you conscript a man and compel him to go abroad to fight against his will, you violate the most sacred right of personal liberty, and substitute for it what Daniel Webster called 'despotism in its worst form.'"[22]

For this "treasonous" act of voicing their opposition to the draft (and US involvement in the First World War), Schenck and Baer were convicted of violating Section 3 of the Espionage Act of 1917, passed shortly after US entry into the Great War, in order to prohibit interference with government recruitment into the armed services and prevent insubordination in the military or support for enemies of the United States during wartime.[23] This all sounds like an antiquated law applicable to a darker time in American history, employed as it was to silence such socialists as newspaper editor Victor Berger, labor leader and Socialist Party of America presidential candidate Eugene V. Debs, anarchists Emma Goldman and Alexander Berkman, communists Julius and Ethel Rosenberg, and Pentagon Papers revealer Daniel Ellsberg. The act is still used today as a cudgel against such whistleblowers as diplomatic cable-leaker Chelsea Manning and NSA contractor Edward Snowden, who remains on the lam in Moscow for his Wikileaks revelations about spying on both American citizens and foreign actors (including German chancellor Angela Merkel) by the US government.[24]

As an example of the severity of the lies told by the US government, consider a few passages from the Pentagon Papers—the government report on the history of the United States' political and military involvement in Vietnam from 1945 to 1967—and the gap between what the public was told versus what was really going on during our involvement in that Southeast Asian country.[25] On December 21, 1963, at a White House news conference, Defense Secretary Robert S. McNamara told the media, "We reviewed in great detail the plans of the South Vietnamese and the plans of our own military advisers for operations during 1964. We have every reason to believe they will be successful." Yet McNamara told President Lyndon B. Johnson something quite different in a memo that same day: "The situation is very disturbing. Current trends, unless reversed in the next 2–3 months, will lead to a neutralization at best and more likely to a Communist-controlled state."

In a televised address to the nation on August 4, 1964, about the Gulf of Tonkin incident that triggered an escalation of the war—itself an exaggeration of what really happened as a justification for further US involvement in Vietnam—President Johnson assured American citizens, "We still seek no wider war." That statement contradicted what was actually going on in the months before that date: "On 1 February 1964, the United States embarked on a new course of action. . . . On that date, under direction of the American military establishment, an elaborate program of covert military operations against the state of North Vietnam was set in motion."

Two years later, on January 13, 1966, in his State of the Union address, President Johnson told Congress and the American people, "The enemy is no longer closer to victory. Time is no longer on his side. There is no cause to doubt the American commitment. Our decision to stand firm has been matched by our desire for peace." Five days later, Assistant Defense Secretary John McNaughton told Defense Secretary Robert McNamara, in a memo, "The present U.S. objective in Vietnam is to avoid humiliation. The reasons why we went to Vietnam to the present depth are varied; but they are now largely academic."

With this level of mendacity, is it any wonder why people don't trust what their elected officials tell them? The credibility gap between public statements by politicians and their true beliefs about what is really going on has widened into a credibility canyon. There is, perhaps, no more poignant public display of this problem than Robert McNamara's mea culpa, in Errol Morris's gripping documentary film, *The Fog of War*, which was made all the more haunting by Philip Glass's soundtrack.[26] A few choice quotes make the point:

> We all make mistakes. We know we make mistakes. I don't know any military commander, who is honest, who would say he has not made a mistake. There's a wonderful phrase: "the fog of war." What "the fog of war" means is: war is so complex it's beyond the ability of the human mind to comprehend all the variables. Our judgment, our understanding, are not adequate. And we kill people unnecessarily.

How many people were killed needlessly? McNamara quantified it thusly:

> Any military commander who is honest with himself, or with those he's speaking to, will admit that he has made mistakes in the application of military power. He's killed people unnecessarily—his own troops or other troops— through mistakes, through errors of judgment. A hundred, or thousands, or tens of thousands, maybe even a hundred thousand. But, he hasn't destroyed nations. And the conventional wisdom is don't make the same mistake twice, learn from your mistakes. And we all do. Maybe we make the same mistake three times, but hopefully not four or five.

That Morris made a similar film, *The Unknown Known*,[27] a decade later—about Secretary of Defense Donald Rumsfeld and the lies told to the public about the invasion of Iraq, the torture and abuse of prisoners at Abu Ghraib, and more—suggests that the problem is endemic to the system of governance itself. Constructive conspiracism indeed.

In 2019, the British government arrested Wikileaks founder Julian Assange in London when the Ecuadorian embassy refused to allow continued asylum after years of protecting him.[28] Protecting him from what? Among other things, from the US government bringing him to trial for treason for leaking millions of secret documents. Some of them compromised intelligence agents abroad, while others revealed morally and legally questionable actions on the part of the US military, such as killing innocent Iraqi civilians.[29] The following are just a few of the documents WikiLeaks published that were unknown to the general public:[30]

- A copy of the 238-page *Standard Operating Procedures for Camp Delta*, the protocol employed by the US Army at the Guantanamo Bay detention camp in Cuba, revealing restrictions placed over detainees at the camp, including the designation of some prisoners as off-limits to the International Committee of the Red Cross when they came to inspect the camp.
- Classified US military footage from a series of helicopter attacks in Baghdad on July 12, 2007, that killed over a dozen people, including two Reuters news staff, which was posted on a website called "Collateral Murder." The video showed the helicopter crew laughing at the "dead bastards" and cajoling each other to "Light 'em up!" and "Keep shooting, keep shooting."
- Over 92,000 documents related to the war in Afghanistan between 2004 and 2009, which included instances of "friendly fire" and civilian casualties. They substantiated the deaths of over 109,000 people in Iraq, not counting the battle-related losses of coalition forces. Among those were 3,700 "friendly fire" killings of innocent civilians.
- The "War Logs" of 400,000 documents related to the Iraq War, which included information that the US government had ignored reports of the illegal use of

torture, most notably at Abu Ghraib prison, just outside Baghdad, that revealed the dark underbelly of US operations in Iraq. There was the female American soldier, sporting a pixie haircut, in fatigues and a t-shirt, dragging an Iraqi detainee down the hall on a leash. There was the pyramid of naked men, heads bowed in shame, with two American soldiers grinning in self-righteous triumph. There was the group of naked men milling about uncomfortably in a room, bags over their heads and hands feebly trying to cover their genitals. There was the faux fellatio scene between two Iraqi men. There was the terrified detainee about to be shredded by two unmuzzled Belgian Shepard dogs barely restrained by a couple of burly soldiers. And there was the now-iconic crucifixion-by-electricity scene, with a hooded man atop a box, arms outstretched and electrical wires wrapped about his neck, with electrical current flowing out of his hands and disappearing upward to who knows where.

I cannot adjudicate the Snowden and Assange cases here. Suffice it to say that but for their actions, the public would not have known to what extent our own government has conspired to take actions against foreign powers and peoples without our approval or knowledge (much less that of Congress), and even conspire to surveil its own citizens, again without our approval or knowledge. This is a type of conspiracy. Nearly everyone agrees that democracies must strike a balance between open transparency and keeping secrets in the interest of national security. Sharing our nuclear codes with the Russians clearly does not fall under the First Amendment's free speech and free press protections. But the NSA spying on US citizens without congressional approval is not exactly a stellar example of a transparent democracy, regardless of its justification. My larger point here is that ever since the First World War, nations have conspired to control information, often at the cost of transparency.

In the next chapter, we will look in more detail at the real conspiracy that triggered the Great War, in what could arguably be called the deadliest conspiracy in history.

CHAPTER 10

The Deadliest Conspiracy in History

The Trigger of World War I and How Conspiracies Really Work

So much of conspiracism is driven by power—who has it, who doesn't, and what that perceived difference does to corrupt people's thinking about conspiracies and conspiracy theories, ranging from QAnon on back through the twentieth century to what is arguably the result of the deadliest conspiracy in history. It began on June 28, 1914, which dawned clear and sunny in Sarajevo, the capital of Bosnia-Herzegovina, a small Balkan province. Annexed in 1908, it was under the imperial control of Austria-Hungary, governed by Franz Joseph, the aging Habsburg emperor. Franz Joseph's heir apparent—his 51-year-old nephew, Archduke Franz Ferdinand—was in town with his wife, Countess Sophie Chotek, to inspect the army's summer maneuvers, open a new state museum, and visit the local magistrates. He was also there to recognize St. Vitus's Day, the anniversary of the 1389 Battle of Kosovo, where Serbs were humiliated in their defeat, so not everyone in town was celebrating his visit.

The couple cruised down the historic Appel Quay in their Gräf & Stift Double Phaeton sports coupé, with the top down so the throngs of well-wishers could see royalty in the making. The couple were dressed in ostentatious finery of the day: he in a cavalry dress uniform consisting of a blue tunic, gold collar with three silver stars, and a helmet with green peacock feathers; she in a long white silk dress with red and white fabric roses, wearing a white hat and veil. They made this excursion despite warnings they received the day before, indicating that a terrorist attack was possible—even likely. Nevertheless, Sophie told one of her hosts, "Everywhere we have gone here, we have been treated with so much friendliness—and by every last Serb too—with so much cordiality and unsimulated warmth that we are very happy about it!"[1]

Among those with no intent of offering the royal couple a warm welcome were Serbian nationalists, who were not keen on being subjects of the Austro-Hungarian Empire. The 1908 annexation led to the radicalization of certain Serbian nationalist groups. Three years later, on March 3, 1911, a secret society called the "Black Hand" was formed in a Belgrade apartment. Serbia's independence was recognized at the Congress of Berlin in 1878, but Bosnian Serbs dreamed of uniting their country with Serbia, forming Greater Serbia. The forthcoming elevation of Franz Ferdinand to emperor was believed by Bosnian Serbs to pose a threat to their irredentist plans. In response, Black Hand operatives radicalized, armed, and positioned assassins among the crowd as the six automobiles in the archduke's motorcade glided down the boulevard. Their targets, in the second car, were impossible to miss. The assassins knew where to go, because the parade route was published in the local papers, to ensure a large welcoming crowd. Security forces were conspicuous by their absence.

The assassins included 28-year-old Muhamed Mehmedbašić, a carpenter from Herzegovina; 18-year-old Cvjetko Popović, a student in Sarajevo; 17-year-old Vaso Čubrilović, also a student in Sarajevo; and three 19-year-olds, who turned out to be the key players in the conspiracy. The latter were Trifko Grabež, the son of an Orthodox priest; Nedeljko Čabrinović, a high school dropout working with a printer in Belgrade; and Gavrilo Princip, another high school dropout, who sought refuge with Serbian guerrilla fighters and dreamed of one day freeing all southern Slavs. As Princip later explained at his trial, "I am a Yugoslav nationalist, aiming for the unification of all Yugoslavs, and I do not care what form of state, but it must be free from Austria."[2]

Since Princip was the key actor in the assassination, much of the follow-up investigation, looking into a possible conspiracy behind his actions, centered on this 19-year-old. Who was he and how far up did the conspiracy go? That is the subject of investigative journalist Tim Butcher's book, *The Trigger: Hunting the Assassin Who Brought the World to War*.[3] Gavrilo Princip was born in 1894 in a tiny hamlet in western Bosnia, the son of a dirt-poor feudal serf, who was effectively "owned" by two local lords. There was longstanding resentment against Austria-Hungary, which was seen as a foreign power occupying their land. As was not uncommon at the time, six of Gavrilo's siblings died in childbirth. In 1907 he escaped the grinding poverty of his home and moved to Sarajevo to attend school. Butcher tracked down Gavrilo's school reports, which showed him to initially be an A student, but his grades declined thereafter, when "he had fallen in with other young radicals who dared to think the unthinkable: doing away with Austria-Hungary." It was, therefore, seemingly foreordained that

Princip would be the trigger for what, in the end, was the demise of the Austro-Hungarian Empire.

Historian Christopher Clark, in *The Sleepwalkers: How Europe Went to War in 1914*, provided a detailed account of how the assassination conspiracy went down.[4] The assassins were given four Browning pistols and six small hand grenades with 12-second chemical fuses, which were stolen from the Serbian State Arsenal by Black Hand operatives (it was never determined precisely who they were), along with paper packets of cyanide powder, with which to commit suicide after their revolutionary mission. As the motorcade entered the kill zone, the first two assassins—Mehmedbašić, armed with a hand grenade, and Čubrilović, equipped with a pistol and hand grenade—lost their nerve and failed to act. The latter later explained, "I did not pull out the revolver because I saw that the Duchess was there. I felt sorry for her."

Next in line was Čabrinović, who grabbed his hand grenade and triggered the detonator by smacking it against a lamppost, giving him 12 seconds to aim and hurl it at the targeted second vehicle. The driver spotted the missile out of the corner of his eye and punched the accelerator, causing the grenade to skirt across the back of the car and land under the following vehicle before it detonated, wounding the passengers and a number of police and bystanders in the crowd. Franz Ferdinand was unharmed, while Sophie incurred a small cut on her cheek. As instructed, Čabrinović swallowed his cyanide powder and lept into the nearby Miljacka River, which was too shallow at that time of year for drowning. The cyanide only resulted in violent vomiting, and he was captured, beaten by the crowd, and hauled off to the police station.

The vehicles sped off to safety, while the other three assassins slunk away in defeat, the assassination conspiracy foiled by nerves, empathy, and bad luck. Even the best-prepared conspiracies rarely unfold according to plan, and this one was not over yet. Remarkably—and in hindsight, foolishly—Franz Ferdinand decided to complete his appointed rounds, explaining without an ounce of constructive conspiracism, "Come on. That fellow is clearly insane; let us proceed with our programme." The archduke and his associates continued on to the town hall reception for him, where Sarajevo's mayor bumbled his way through his original welcoming speech, apparently oblivious to how his words resonated on the heels of an attempted assassination of his guest: "All of the citizens of the capital city of Sarajevo find that their souls are filled with happiness, and they most enthusiastically greet Your Highness's most illustrious visit with the most cordial of welcomes."

Franz Ferdinand upbraided his host: "I came here as your guest and your people greet me with bombs!" The archduke then delivered his speech, acknowledging what he thought he saw in the faces of his audience: "an expression of their joy at the failure of the attempt at assassination." What happened next is illustrative of how successful conspiracies often turn on the quirkiest of contingencies. Franz Ferdinand then decided to visit the hospital where his wounded comrades were being treated. Sophie abandoned her plans to meet with a delegation of Muslim women at city hall and thought it best to join her husband, another fateful decision. The delegation once again headed down Appel Quay toward the hospital, but this time the couple's car turned right on Franz Joseph Street, heading toward the National Museum. Their driver apparently was unaware that the museum event had been cancelled. Realizing his wrong-turn error, the driver stopped, put the archduke's coupé into neutral, and allowed it to slide backward onto Appel Quay, as the vehicle lacked a reverse gear.

Meanwhile, dejected by the failed conspiracy, Gavrilo Princip meandered over to Moritz Schiller's delicatessen, on the corner of Appel Quay and Franz Joseph Street, for some private consolation. Looking up at the moment of the wrong turn, Princip was astonished to see his targets paused before him. Unable to disengage his grenade from his belt, he pulled out his 9mm semiautomatic Browning pistol and fired the first shot through the vehicle's door, hitting Sophie in the abdomen, severing her stomach artery and causing her to slump into her husband's lap. "As I saw that a lady was sitting next to him I reflected for a moment whether to shoot or not," Princip later explained to his interrogators, insisting that his intended target was only the archduke. Referring to the countess, Princip added, "At the same time I was filled with a peculiar feeling." Princip's moment of hesitation passed and he fired again, this time hitting Franz Ferdinand in the jugular vein of his neck. As the car sped off, the archduke proclaimed to his wife, "Sophie, Sophie, don't die. Stay alive for our children." As his plumed helmet slipped off his head, he said to his fellow passengers, "It's nothing, it's nothing." Those were his final words, as both he and his wife fell unconscious, bled out, and died soon after.

Princip, as he was trained, moved to shoot himself with his pistol and swallow his cyanide, but the crowd grabbed his limbs and started pummeling him into a pulp. He was rescued by the police and hauled off into custody. He was tried, jailed, and sentenced to 20 years of solitary confinement. He died four years later, "his body so badly ravaged by skeletal tuberculosis that his right arm had had to be amputated." That is unfortunate indeed, as a new conspiracy theory emerged shortly after Princip's capture—namely, that forces high up in the Serbian government conspired to assassinate the archduke. Here is what Princip's biographer, Tim Butcher, wrote about the conspiracy theory that launched the First World War:

Over the last century his voice has rarely been heard, drowned out by more powerful forces, not least Vienna which was desperate to use the assassination as a pretext to attack its small and potentially troublesome neighbour, Serbia. For this to work, Austria-Hungary worked to represent Princip and the assassination plot as the work of the Serbian government. And this alone is perhaps the greatest misrepresentation of the truth about Gavrilo Princip, with the historical record containing no convincing evidence to support the claim.[5]

A dramatic film of these events, titled simply *Sarajevo* and well worth watching for inculcating the political climate of the day, follows this conspiratorial thread through the eyes of the investigator—an Austrian judge named Leo Pfeffer—who was tasked with tracing the assassins to their source.[6] Historian Christopher Clark detailed what Pfeffer's investigation revealed.[7]

At first, Princip insisted that he acted alone, claiming he was surprised to hear the explosion from Čabrinović's grenade. Čabrinović contended that he was a lone assassin, having procured the explosive device from an anarchist in Belgrade. The next day, however, Čabrinović changed his story and admitted that he and Princip were accomplices who had planned the assassination together in Belgrade, explaining that they obtained their weapons from unnamed Belgrade partisans. With his explanation now cast into doubt, Princip admitted that he worked in cahoots with Čabrinović. They kept their revised story straight by communicating in prison through a code of knocks, which they learned about in a Russian novel.

A police dragnet uncovered one of the Black Hand operatives, Danilo Illić, who attempted a plea bargain to avoid the death penalty in exchange for revealing more conspiratorial details, starting with the fact that Princip and

Čabrinović were not the only assassins. Illić named the others and identified their whereabouts. The police nabbed a total of six of the seven conspirators.

The next step in the investigation was to determine if the plot could be traced all the way up to the Serbian government. The pistols were of Serbian manufacture, and the bombs were from a Serbian armory, so that was more than a little suggestive. Although many Serbs expressed delight that the disliked Archduke Franz Ferdinand was killed, as it delivered a blow to the hated Habsburg empire, additional information gathering uncovered no direct links to the Serbian state.

Although Judge Pfeffer concluded that this was not an officially state-sanctioned hit by the Serbian government, Leopold von Berchtold, the Austro-Hungarian foreign minister, was keen to find an excuse to squelch the rising ambitions of Serbia, since it was backed by its strong Slavic ally, Russia, with which the Habsburgs were not on good terms. Two days after the assassination, on June 30, Berchtold presented a "final and fundamental reckoning with Serbia" to the Austrian emperor, the 84-year-old Franz Josef, who agreed to consult with his ally, Kaiser Wilhelm of Germany. On July 5, the kaiser gave Berchtold what came to be known as the "blank check" promise that Germany would support Austria-Hungary if it attacked Serbia.

Given these underlying currents, it might not have mattered that on July 13, another investigator from the Austro-Hungarian Foreign Office, Friedrich von Wiesner, issued his unequivocal findings to Berchtold: "There is nothing to prove or even suppose that the Serbian government is accessory to the inducement for the crime, its preparation, or the furnishing of weapons. On the contrary, there are reasons to believe that this is altogether out of the question."[8] What all this means is that the Austro-Hungarian assumption of Serbian complicity in the assassination was very likely mistaken—or, worse, a contrived conspiracy theory for the purpose of justifying a war it was already bent on initiating—so the most atrocious war in the history of humanity up to that date was arguably pointless. Imagine how differently the twentieth century would have unfolded without the Great War, sparing the lives of tens of millions of people. Moreover, no World War I would almost certainly mean no Hitler, no Nazis, no World War II, and no Holocaust. Just imagine.

• - - • - - •

The consequences of the events in Sarajevo on June 28, 1914, cannot be exaggerated, and the details of what unfolded after the assassination are worth reviewing, not just for the consequences of conspiracism, but also for how contingent history can be, sometimes with tragic outcomes. At the time, treaties and alliances divided the great powers of Europe into two grand coalitions: the Triple Entente of Britain, France, and Russia, and the Triple Alliance of Italy, Germany, and Austria-Hungary. Once Austria-Hungary decided that the conspiracy to assassinate Franz Ferdinand was orchestrated by Serbia and was not solely the work of a rogue organization, the Black Hand, it retaliated a month later, on July 28, by bombarding the Serbian capital of Belgrade.

Russia was obligated by treaty to back Serbia, so it mobilized its troops on July 30. The next day, Austria-Hungary and Germany mobilized to counter the Russian buildup. On August 1, Germany declared war on Russia, in support of Austria-Hungary. The latter declared war on Russia five days later, on August 6. In support of Russia, France ordered full mobilization on August 2. Not wanting a two-front war, Germany invaded France through neutral Belgian, in hopes of defeating the French in four weeks, after which it could concentrate on the Russian front. Britain was obliged by treaty to defend Belgium, and, in support of France, it, too, declared war: first, on Germany on August 4, and second, on Austria-Hungary on August 12. It was a full-on Continental war.

As the war virus spread, Japan sided with the Triple Entente and seized German possessions in China and the Pacific. Over the ensuing months and years, much of the rest of the world—including the United States in 1917—joined the world's first global conflict, which ended four years later with a total body count of nine million combatants and seven million civilian deaths, plus tens of millions more deaths in related genocides and the horrific influenza pandemic of 1918 that struck weakened populations.

Sometimes real conspiracies can be catastrophic, and this one was the result of six seconds on a street corner in Sarajevo. This is how conspiracies really work—as messy events that unfold according to real-time contingencies and often turn on the minutia of chance and the quirkiness of human error.

In an earlier chapter, we discussed the two conspiracy theories about 9/11: that President George W. Bush made it happen on purpose (MIHOP), or that he let it happen on purpose (LIHOP). Neither one of these applies to what Austria-Hungary did in attacking Serbia after the assassination of Franz Ferdinand and Sophie Chotek. Instead, that nation acted as many countries have done when they want to accomplish something that would otherwise be immoral, illegal, or both—it turned to its advantage an event that happened for other reasons. Call it COWHOP—capitalized on what happened on purpose.

To that end, the real response to the 9/11 conspiracy was neither MIHOP nor LIHOP. It was COWHOP, which is actually so common in history that we might think of it as "politics by other means." After the first Gulf War in 1991 that successfully repelled the Iraqi invasion of Kuwait, the State

Department determined that Saddam Hussein's own people most likely would overthrow him in good time, and regime change like that is always better coming from within instead of without. When this didn't happen, and Hussein regained his power and continued harming his own people, including by using poison gas, there was a strong incentive to overthrow his abusive and dangerous dictatorship and try to install a democracy. Since nations can no longer legally just start wars and invade foreign countries—I will explain why shortly—the United States capitalized on the 9/11 tragedy: first, by correctly invading Afghanistan, which did harbor the real conspirators, and second, by invading Iraq, which had nothing to do with 9/11. George W. Bush capitalized on what happened on purpose, and the resultant instability in the Middle East after America's longest wars would make it appear that the entire enterprise was unjustified.

• - - • - - •

It will surprise most readers of this book, as it did me when I first heard about it, that war was outlawed in 1928. Say what? Yale University legal scholars Oona Hathaway and Scott Shapiro, in their 2017 book on how this happened and why, *The Internationalists: How a Radical Plan to Outlaw War Remade the World*,[9] begin with the contorted legal machinations of lawyers, legislators, and politicians in the seventeenth century, which made war, in the words of Prussian military theorist Carl von Clausewitz, "the continuation of politics by other means." Those means included a license to kill other people, take their stuff, and occupy their land. Legally. How did this happen?

In 1625, renowned Dutch jurist Hugo Grotius penned a 500-page legal justification for his country's capture of the Portuguese merchant ship *Santa Catarina* when those two countries were at war. The document was titled *The Law of*

War and Peace, and it argued, in short, that if individuals have rights that can be defended through courts, then nations have rights that can be defended through war. Why? Because there was no world court to adjudicate disputes between countries. As a consequence, for four centuries nations have felt at liberty to justify their bellicosity through "war manifestos"—legal statements outlining their "just causes" for "just wars." Hathaway and Shapiro compiled over 400 such documents into a database and then conducted a content analysis—that is, a catalog of reasons why countries said they had to fight. The most common rationalizations for war were self-defense (69 percent); enforcement of treaty obligations (47 percent); compensation for tortious injuries (42 percent); violations of the laws of war or the laws of nations (35 percent); stoppage of those who would disrupt the balance of power (33 percent); and protection of trade interests (19 percent).[10]

These war manifestos are, in short, an exercise in motivated reasoning, employing confirmation bias, hindsight bias, and other cognitive heuristics to justify a predetermined end. Instead of "I came, I saw, I conquered," these declarations read more like "I was just standing there minding my own business when he threatened me. I had to defend myself by attacking him." The problem with this arrangement is obvious. Call it *moralization bias*: the belief that our cause is moral and just, and anyone who disagrees is not simply wrong, but immoral.

In 1917, with the carnage of the First World War evident to all, Chicago corporate lawyer Salmon Levinson reasoned, "We should have, not as now, laws *of* war, but laws *against* war; just as there are no laws *of* murder or *of* poisoning, but laws *against* them."[11] With the support of American philosopher John Dewey, French foreign minister Aristide Briand, German foreign minister Gustav Stresemann, and US secretary of state Frank B. Kellogg, Levinson's dream of war outlawry came to fruition with the General Pact for the Renunciation of War, also known as the Peace Pact, or the Kellogg-Briand Pact, signed in Paris in 1928. War was outlawed.

Given the number of wars since 1928—not the least of which was the Second World War, exceeding its predecessor in carnage—what happened? Moralization bias was in full flowering, but there was also a lack of enforcement. That began to change after the ruinations of World War II, when the concept of "outcasting" took hold, the most common example being economic sanctions. "Instead of doing something to the rule breakers," Hathaway and Shapiro explained, noting that this usually involved attacking the offending nation, "outcasters refuse to do something *with* the rule breakers."[12] This principle of exclusion doesn't always work (think of Cuba and Russia today), but sometimes it does (think of Turkey and Iran today), and it is almost always better than war. The result, these researchers showed, is that "interstate war has declined precipitously and conquests have almost completely disappeared." Nonetheless, outcasting has yet to work with North Korea, and, as tempting as a military response may be to some, given that country's geographic locale, we might heed the words from Pete Seeger's Vietnam War protest song: "We were waist deep in the Big Muddy / But the big fool said to push on."[13] We know how that worked out.

Just because *outlawing* war has not *eliminated* war is no more reason to give up on outlawry than arguing that we should do away with laws against murder, just because homicide rates have not bottomed out at zero. These rates have, in fact, dropped precipitously over the centuries, as have international wars, so the system works, even if imperfectly. For example, the Correlates of War project—the best and most thorough dataset ever assembled on military conflict—shows that the more two countries trade with one another, the less inclined they are to fight. In a similar vein, the more democratic two nations are, the less likely they are to combat each other.[14] These are not perfect correlations—there are exceptions—but countries that are democratic and economically interdependent are less likely to allow political tensions to escalate to the point of conflict.

Hathaway and Shapiro used data from the Correlates of War project to make various calculations.[15] They found that between 1816 and 1928, on average there was approximately 1 conquest every 10 months, or 1.21 conquests per year. Another way to conceptualize this is that during this period, a nation had a 1.33 percent chance of being conquered, which translates into countries losing territory once in an ordinary human lifetime. The average amount of real estate lost was substantial: 295,486 square kilometers (114,087 square miles) per year, or about 11 Crimeas per year for over a century. That's a lot of land! (By comparison, California is 163,696 square miles, and Texas is 268,597 square miles.) The span from 1929 to 1948 wasn't much better: a 1.15 percent chance per year, or 1 conquest every 10 months, and an average loss of 240,739 square kilometers (92,949 square miles). But everything changed after the Second World War, when outcasting took effect—primarily through economic sanctions—and the average number of conquests fell to 0.26 per year, or 1 every 3.9 years, with an average loss of only 14,950 square kilometers (5,772 square miles) per year. As Hathaway and Shapiro concluded, "The likelihood that any individual state would suffer a conquest in an average year plummeted from 1.33 percent a year to [0].17 percent from 1949 on. After 1948, the chance an average state would suffer a conquest fell from once in a lifetime to *once or twice a millennium*."[16]

In the next chapter, we will explore a slew of conspiracies and conspiracy theories arising throughout the twentieth century and continuing into the twenty-first century. They began shortly after the First World War and accelerated in popularity as governments and corporations both grew in power. As we examine them, let us heed the words of historian John Emerich Edward Dalberg Acton, better known simply as Lord Acton, who penned this observation in a letter in 1887: "Power tends to corrupt, and absolute power corrupts absolutely. Great men are almost always bad men."[17] He wrote that at a time when democracies fought to get a toehold by climbing the precipitous cliff faces of absolute monarchies and other autocracies, whose influence and power peaked in the mid-twentieth century, but whose conspiratorial machinations continued, tempting even liberal democracies to follow suit.

CHAPTER 11

Real and Imagined Enemies

Conspiracies in Reality and in Our Imaginations

A central theme of this book is that conspiracy theories often enough are true, so it is not unreasonable for us to be constructively conspiratorial about people and organizations with power, especially when trust in them is low. It's a reality well documented by historian Kathryn Olmsted in *Real Enemies: Conspiracy Theories and American Democracy, World War I to 9/11.*[1] According to Olmstead, before the First World War, conspiracy theories were mostly directed toward religious, ethnic, and racial minorities—especially Jews—driven largely by fears that these outsiders were conspiring to use the government to their own end.

After World War I, "no longer were conspiracy theorists chiefly concerned that alien forces were plotting to capture the federal government; instead, they proposed that the federal government itself *was* the conspirator."[2] She then characterized the difference between pre–World War I conspiracy theories and those that came after: "The institutionalized secrecy of the modern U.S. government inspired a new type of conspiracy theories. These theories argued that government officials lied to citizens, dragged the peaceable American people into foolish wars, and then spied on and oppressed the opponents of war." Inasmuch as agencies of the US government *did do these things and continues the practice well into the twenty-first century*, it was not irrational for citizens to become skeptical of their own government. Examples are legion throughout the twentieth century and into the current one.

● ─ ─ ● ─ ─ ●

After John F. Kennedy's assassination, the country went through the tumultuous years of the Vietnam War. The *Pentagon Papers* and other documents revealed to what extent the federal government was lying to and spying on its citizens, including FBI wiretaps of Martin Luther King Jr. They recorded his extramarital trysts and tried to blackmail him into silence—even hinting he should take his own life—which didn't work. So his assassination in 1968—also by a lone assassin, James Earl Ray—looked suspicious, as did the murder of JFK's brother Bobby, right after winning the California primary in his bid for the presidency, gunned down by a dubious character named Sirhan Sirhan. As with JFK, no conspiracies were ever proven in these assassinations, but the point is that it was not unreasonable for a great many people to suspect that there were.

Then there was Watergate, and Richard Nixon's secret audiotapes that exposed the public to the uglier side of mainstream politics and politicians, in all their racist and bigoted conspiracy mongering, particularly the president's suspicions of Jews. Under Nixon's administration, Olmsted noted, "paranoia, conspiracy, and conspiracy theory became fundamental operating principles of the executive branch."[3] Nixon withheld vital information from the Joint Chiefs of Staff, so, in response, they had a National Security Council staffer steal documents from Secretary of State

Henry Kissinger's briefcase, in order to find out what was really going on in the administration. The government was spying on itself, further eroding trust in this sacred institution, designed to protect and defend the Constitution! "To the ordinary guy, all this is a bunch of gobbledygook," said Nixon's chief of staff, Bob Haldeman, of the *Pentagon Papers*. (It is worth noting here that the *Pentagon Papers* implicated the Kennedy and Johnson administrations, but not Nixon's, so his initial response was to be nonplussed.) "But out of the gobbledygook," Olmstead added, "comes a very clear thing: you can't trust the government; you can't believe what they say and you can't rely on their judgment; and the implicit infallibility of presidents, which has been an accepted thing in America, is badly hurt by this, because it shows that people do things the president wants to do even though it's wrong, and the president can be wrong." Consider again the underlying belief in the QAnon conspiracy theory that the Deep State government can't be trusted—in this context it doesn't seem so crazy. There's even a certain kind of rationality to it.

In 1976, the CIA's secret and illegal Program MKULTRA was exposed by Frank Church's congressional committee report, showing that since the 1950s, that agency had engaged in mind-control experiments, administering LSD and other mind-altering drugs to unsuspecting people, with an aim toward developing drugs and procedures that could be used in interrogations.[4] One of these unwitting victims was US Army biochemist Frank Olson, who jumped out of a New York City hotel window to his death. Or was he pushed? His son, Eric Olson, has long suspected that the CIA murdered his father. A gripping docudrama series, produced by acclaimed filmmaker Errol Morris—titled *Wormwood*, after the word Shakespeare's Hamlet used to describe his realization that his mother was complicit in the murder of his father—ends by playing out two possible scenarios:

suicide and murder.[5] A 1994 autopsy report on Olson's exhumed body suggested cranial injuries that might have happened before his fall—meaning he was knocked out first—but the government never admitted homicidal guilt and instead paid the family $750,000, because Olson's informed consent was not obtained for the LSD experiment. Either way, all we need to know is that the CIA was dosing unsuspecting citizens with mind-altering drugs, in order to understand why people believe conspiracy theories about powerful agencies. Parallel to the alleged "missile gap" between the United States and the USSR, some believed there was a "mind-control" or "brainwashing" gap between our intelligence agencies and those of other nations—most notably the USSR, but also Communist China and, especially, North Korea—in which these countries experimented on captured US soldiers during the Korean War.[6]

The Iran-Contra scandal under President Ronald Reagan in the 1980s further eroded public trust in what the US government was doing without the approval of Congress, much less without the knowledge of its own citizens. Senior administration officials secretly facilitated the sale of arms to Iran, which was illegal at the time, because of an arms embargo. The proceeds from the clandestine sale were used to fund the Contras in Nicaragua, who were perceived to be more favorable to American interests, in that they were a group of anti-Sandinista rebels fighting a socialist government whose policies were hostile to US foreign affairs. Congress prohibited support for such groups. As Olmsted noted, Iran-Contra "represented what conspiracy theorists since the First World War had feared the most: the ultimate executive usurpation of power. The Iran-contra conspirators had not subverted the government, they *were* the government."[7]

By the late 1980s, presidential and congressional approval ratings were in free fall, leading Senator Daniel Patrick Moynihan to observe that never in the history of the nation had there been "so massive a hemorrhaging of trust and in-tegrity."[8] This lack of trust and transparency engenders conspiratorial cognition, especially of both public and pri-vate authorities. By the time the television series X-Files aired in the 1990s, many of its otherwise patently absurd plots—involving cigarette-smoking men in back rooms running the world, aided by extraterrestrial overlords—didn't seem so ridiculous to many Americans, and the show became a massive hit.

• – – • – – •

As is now evident, the problem in discerning true from false conspiracy theories of these types is that governments do lie and cover up. A case in point is the set of perennially popu-lar conspiracy theories involving UFOs, which have once again surfaced as I complete this book in mid-2021. Videos of unidentified aerial phenomena (UAPs) began to recircu-late, featuring aircraft alleged to perform feats of physics and aerodynamics unknown to the US government agen-cies tasked with protecting our airspace. I have written about this extensively elsewhere,[9] but in this context it is noteworthy that yet again, conspiracy theories abound re-garding the government hiding information about these videos, especially since they were filmed by the US military, who admitted they are "real." That word is doing a lot of work here. When people hear "real," their brains autocor-rect to "aliens" or "Russian/Chinese assets" threatening our country, while the government simply meant that the vid-eos themselves are genuine, not fakes or hoaxes. In late June of 2021, the Office of the Director of National Intelligence fi-nally issued a long-awaited report about these UAPs, which predictably drew no firm conclusions about them—alien, foreign, or otherwise.[10] The report called for further re-search and, not surprisingly, requested more funding. The following are some highlights:

- Various forms of sensors that register UAPs generally operate correctly and capture enough real data to allow initial assessments, but some UAPs may be attributable to sensor anomalies.
- When individual UAP incidents are resolved, they will fall into one of five potential explanatory categories: airborne clutter, natural atmospheric phenomena, US government or US industry developmental programs, foreign adversary systems, and a catchall "other" bin.
- We were able to identify one reported UAP with high confidence. In that case, we identified the object as a large, deflating balloon. The others remain unexplained.
- UAP sightings also tended to cluster around US training and testing grounds, but we assess that this may result from a collection bias because of focused attention and greater numbers of latest-generation sensors operating in those areas.
- We currently lack data to indicate any UAPs are part of a foreign collection program or indicative of a major technological advancement by a potential adversary.

The report concluded, "Sociocultural stigmas and . . . reputational risk may keep many observers silent, complicating scientific pursuit of the topic." To understand why this stigma exists, let's put this latest wave of UFO sightings into historical context.

Our story begins on July 7, 1947, when William W. "Mac" Brazel, a rancher working just outside Roswell, New Mexico, discovered some unusual debris scattered on the ground. Brazel notified the local sheriff, saying he might have discovered the remains of "one of them flying saucers."[11] The reference was to a wave of UFO sightings that began the month before, on June 24, 1947, when Kenneth

Arnold was flying his private plane over the Cascade Mountains in Washington State and saw nine shiny objects moving quickly across the sky. Arnold initially described them as flying like "geese in formation"—which is what they probably were (I've seen such "UFOs" myself)—but then later added that the objects were "crescent shaped" and that they "moved like a saucer would if you skipped it across the water." An Associated Press (AP) story about the incident then misquoted Arnold as describing what he saw as "flying saucers." Arnold later complained, "They said that I'd said they were saucer-like. I said they flew in *saucer-like fashion.*" But, similar to most corrections of media errors, this one also flew under the public's fact-checking radar.

The "flying saucer" meme caught on when over 150 newspapers picked up the AP story. Soon afterward, hundreds of flying saucer reports appeared, with a peak of 850 sightings in the weeks following Arnold's report. The July 7 story told by "Mac" Brazel promptly reached the Roswell Army Air Field (RAAF), at which point Lieutenant Walter Haut sent out a press release, stating that a "flying disc" had been recovered at the ranch. Haut, in fact, had not seen the debris himself, so here begins the distortion of the most famous UFO case in history: the Roswell incident. This incident has nothing to do with extraterrestrial intelligence and everything to do with terrestrial surveillance. The following day, July 8, 1947, the *Roswell Daily Record* ran a now famous headline: "RAAF Captures Flying Saucer on Ranch in Roswell Region."

The next day, July 9, the *Roswell Daily Record* offered a more sobering description of what was found on the ranch: "When the debris was gathered up the tinfoil, paper, tape, and sticks made a bundle about three feet long and 7 or 8 inches thick, while the rubber made a bundle about 18 or 20 inches long and about 8 inches thick. In all, he [Brazel] estimated, the entire lot would have weighed maybe five

pounds." (Does anyone seriously imagine that technologically advanced aliens traversed the vast distances of inter-
stellar space in star ships made of tinfoil, paper, tape, and
sticks, all held together with rubber?)

The military described the debris as the remains of a
weather balloon, and that was that for the next 30 years, as
Roswell dropped off the UFO cultural radar. In 1967, *UFO
Wave of 1947*, a report published by pro-UFOlogist Ted
Bloecher, chronicled 853 UFO reports that year. Roswell
wasn't even on the list! Think about it—the most famous
UFO case in history wasn't even on the minds of UFOlogists
either at the time it happened or twenty years afterward.

Roswell, then, is really a story of modern myth-making,
starting in 1980, when the *National Enquirer* ran a sensation-
alist UFO story, followed by a popular television documentary, *UFOs Are Real*. The narrative was solidified with Charles
Berlitz and William L. Moore's book, *The Roswell Incident*,
outlining a government cover-up of the discovery of a
crashed alien spacecraft in the New Mexico desert. Shortly
thereafter, other bestsellers appeared, such as Kevin Randle
and Donald Schmitt's *UFO Crash at Roswell* and Don Berliner
and Stanton Friedman's *Crash at Corona*.[12] Since then, thousands of articles, books, television shows, and documentaries have kept the Roswell myth alive.

The following is what really happened. The debris discovered at the ranch in Roswell was not the remains of a
weather balloon, as reported by the military. It was wreckage from the crash of an experimental high-altitude spy
balloon, designed to detect acoustic signatures of Soviet
nuclear bomb tests in the upper atmosphere, part of a program called Project Mogul. In 1994, Charles B. Moore, a Project Mogul scientist, was even able to identify the specific spy
balloon, called NYU Flight 4, that crashed on "Mac" Brazel's
ranch:

When the wind information is coupled with the similarities in the debris described by the eyewitnesses—the balsa sticks, the "tinfoil," the tape with pastel, pinkish-purple flowers, the smoky gray balloon rubber with a burnt odor, the eyelets, the tough paper, the four-inch-diameter aluminum pieces and the black box—to the materials used in our balloon flight trains, it appears to me that it would be difficult to exclude NYU Flight 4 as a likely source of the debris that W. W. Brazel found on the Foster ranch in 1947.[13]

UFOlogists make much of the fact that the government lied about what happened at Roswell, mistaking military secrets for UFO evidence. Nonetheless, this was the Cold War, and the US government was understandably disinclined to publicly announce that it was carrying on surveillance of the Soviet Union's nuclear program.

Area 51 is shrouded in even more mystery, inasmuch as it has long been a top-secret military facility that prohibits UFOlogists, curious journalists, and skeptics like me from poking around inside to find out what is really going on at this site, 90 miles north of Las Vegas, Nevada, that was chosen for its isolation. It wasn't until 2013 that a Freedom of Information Act request resulted in the CIA revealing to the public for the first time what Area 51 was used for.[14] In 1955, the government constructed a long runway on the dry lake bed, in order to conduct test flights of the U-2 spy plane, a high-altitude aircraft equipped with high-resolution cameras to record military activities in the Soviet Union and its allies, such as Cuba. After Francis Gary Powers' U-2 was shot down over the Soviet Union, the CIA launched Project OXCART, another top-secret program to develop the next generation of spy planes—the Lockheed A-12—which eventually became the legendary SR-71 "Blackbird." Keep in mind that these planes are fast, traveling at over 2,000 miles per hour, and they fly at altitudes three times greater than commercial airliners, soaring as high as 90,000 feet. With over 2,850 OXCART A-12 flights at Area 51 and the surrounding territory, it is no wonder that there were so many sightings, which even experienced commercial pilots found baffling and mysterious. As one Area 51 veteran explained, "The shape of OXCART was unprecedented, with its wide, disk-like fuselage designed to carry vast quantities of fuel. Commercial pilots cruising over Nevada at dusk would look up and see the bottom of OXCART whiz by at 2,000-plus mph. The aircraft's titanium body, moving as fast as a bullet, would reflect the sun's rays in a way that could make anyone think, UFO."

Almost all UFO sightings have prosaic explanations such as this. It is in the residue of unexplained phenomena that conspiratorial cognition kicks into gear. For example, in *UFOs: Generals, Pilots and Government Officials Go On the Record*, UFOlogist Leslie Kean noted:

> Roughly 90 to 95 percent of UFO sightings *can* be explained [as] weather balloons, flares, sky lanterns, planes flying in formation, secret military aircraft, birds reflecting the sun, planes reflecting the sun, blimps, helicopters, the planets Venus or Mars, meteors or meteorites, space junk, satellites, swamp gas, spinning eddies, sundogs, ball lightning, ice crystals, reflected light off clouds, lights on the ground or lights reflected on a cockpit window, temperature inversions, hole-punch clouds, and the list goes on![15]

Thus the entire extraterrestrial hypothesis for explaining UFOs and UAPs is based on a residue of data left over after the above list has been exhausted. What remains? Not much. But never underestimate the conspiratorial mind in attributing to conspiracies what can better be explained by the normal operations of nature and governments.

• - - - • - - •

As amusing as such conspiracy theories can be, they are relatively harmless: grist for UFOlogists meeting in hotel conference rooms and for television screen writers. Other conspiracies are far more disturbing—even deadly. Consider two troubling examples from twentieth-century history whose effects are still felt today.

The first begins at the Nuremberg trials of Nazi war criminals shortly after the end of the Second World War, when their crimes against humanity were exposed. Starting in the mid-1930s, the Nazi regime sterilized tens of thousands of Germans decreed to be subject to such hereditary diseases as feeble-mindedness, schizophrenia, epilepsy, manic-depressive psychosis, and physical malformations.[16] Part of the Nazis' defense was to point to America as a precedent for their sterilization program. In the early twentieth century, so-called feeble-minded Americans—those at the bottom of the intellectual ladder in the newly developed field of intelligence testing—were believed to be draining the gene pool and pulling the country down. Eugenic policy at the time called for sterilization, and from 1907 to 1928, almost 9,000 Americans were sterilized. The most famous case was that of Carrie Buck, who lived, along with her mother, in Virginia's State Colony for Epileptics and Feeble-minded. (Yes, there was really a place in America with that title.) Carrie and her mother were both classified as feeble minded. Carrie soon gave birth to an illegitimate daughter. Since the science of the day dictated that three successive generations of a measurable trait constituted evidence of hereditary cause, it was determined that Carrie should be sterilized. The decision was challenged and went to the Virginia Supreme Court, where it was upheld in 1925. Challenged again, the case was argued before the US Supreme Court, where the justices voted in favor of sterilization. Justice Oliver Wendell Holmes passed judgment on Carrie Buck with these chilling words: "It is better for all the world, if instead of waiting to execute degenerate offspring for crime, or to let them starve for their imbecility, society can prevent those who are manifestly unfit from continuing their kind. The principle that sustains compulsory vaccination is broad enough to cover cutting the Fallopian tubes. *Three generations of imbeciles are enough* [italics added]."[17] Carrie Buck was sterilized, along with a thousand others at the Virginia State Colony, pushing the total in America to about 20,000 sterilizations by the mid-1930s, most without the recipients' knowledge or consent. That's a conspiracy.

My second example unfolded between 1932 and 1972, when the US Public Health Service purposefully, and without the consent or knowledge of the patients, withheld treatment for syphilis from 600 African American men. They were sharecroppers, recruited by Alabama Tuskegee University with the promise of medical care, meals, and—morbidly—free burial insurance if they participated in the study. This is the now-infamous "Tuskegee Study of Untreated Syphilis in the Negro Male," as the report was chillingly titled.[18] By the time the study ended in 1972—and that only happened because a whistleblower broke the story, which ended up on the front page of the *New York Times*—only 74 of the 600 men were still alive. Most of them died from syphilis or complications of the disease, along with at least 40 of their wives, who had contracted syphilis from their husbands, and at least 19 of their children, who were born with congenital syphilis.

One legacy of this horrific story is that this conspiracy against African American citizens of the United States—citizens whose rights were supposed to be protected by the Constitution—led to major changes in the laws and regulations of scientific research and the protection of subjects in experiments and clinical studies (such as informed consent and communication of the diagnosis). The other legacy is that—because of this tragic history—such nefarious governmental actions would loom large in the second half of the twentieth century, when African American communities embraced the conspiracy theory that the federal government was behind the crack cocaine epidemic that hit inner-city Blacks especially hard, as well as in the twenty-first century, when African Americans were vaccine hesitant during the COVID-19 pandemic (although not any more so than white Americans, albeit for different reasons).

• - - • - - •

Thus far in this chapter I've focused primarily on political and military conspiracies and conspiracy theories, but let's not let big business off the conspiratorial hook. I shall start this section with a question. What do tobacco, food additives, chemical flame retardants, and carbon emissions all have in common? The answer is that the industries associated with them and their ill effects have been remarkably consistent and disturbingly effective at planting doubt in the mind of the public, even in the teeth of scientific evidence. It's a type of conspiracy, inasmuch as these industries, and the corporations within them, knew about the harmful effects on unsuspecting customers and conspired to cover up that information, to the detriment of the public.[19]

It began with the tobacco industry, when scientific evidence began to mount that cigarettes cause lung cancer. A 1969 memo included this statement from an executive at the Brown & Williamson Tobacco Corporation: "Doubt is our product since it is the best means of competing with the 'body of fact' that exists in the minds of the general public."[20] For decades, the tobacco industry conspired to deceive the public on the health dangers of cigarettes. In 1999, the Justice Department sued tobacco companies for racketeering, seeking to force them to pay for their years of deception. In 2006, US District Judge Gladys Kessler ruled against them, issuing a scathing opinion:

Defendants have known many of these facts for at least 50 years or more. Despite that knowledge, they have consistently, repeatedly, and with enormous skill and sophistication, denied these facts to the public, to the Government, and to the public health community. Moreover, in order to sustain the economic viability of their companies, Defendants have denied that they marketed and advertised their products to children under the age of eighteen and to young people between the ages of eighteen and twenty-one in order to ensure an adequate supply of "replacement smokers," as older ones fall by the wayside through death, illness, or cessation of smoking. In short, Defendants have marketed and sold their lethal product with zeal, with deception, with a single-minded focus on their financial success, and without regard for the human tragedy or social costs that success exacted.[21]

The tobacco model was subsequently mimicked by other industries. As Peter Sparber, a veteran tobacco lobbyist said, "If you can 'do tobacco' you can do just about anything in public relations."[22] It was as if they were all working from the same playbook, employing tactics such as deny the problem, minimize the problem, call for more evidence, shift the blame, cherry pick the data, shoot the messenger, attack alternatives, hire industry-friendly scientists, and create front groups. Documentary filmmaker Robert Kenner encountered this last strategy while shooting Food, Inc., about harmful chemicals and preservatives in the foods we eat.[23] "I kept bumping into groups like 'Center for Consumer Freedom' that were doing everything in their power to keep us from knowing what's in our food." Kenner called them "Orwellian," because such front groups sound like neutral nonprofit think tanks in search of scientific truth but instead are funded by the for-profit industries associated with the problems they investigate.

Consider "Citizens for Fire Safety," a front group created and financed in part by chemical and tobacco companies to address the problem of home fires started by cigarettes. Kenner discovered this while filming his 2014 documentary, *Merchants of Doubt*, in which I appeared as an expert witness.[24] It is based on the 2010 book of the same title by historians of science Naomi Oreskes and Erik Conway. To misdirect regulators and the public away from the link between cigarettes and home fires, the tobacco industry hired Peter Sparber—the tobacco lobbyist mentioned above—to work with the National Association of State Fire Marshals to promote the use of chemical flame retardants in upholstery. A leaked memo read, "You have to fireproof the world around the cigarette." Suddenly, Americans' furniture was awash in toxic chemicals.

Climate change is the latest arena for these merchants of conspiracism, and the front group du jour is climatedepot .com, financed in part by Chevron and Exxon and headed by a colorful character named Marc Morano, who, in *Merchants of Doubt*, told filmmaker Kenner, "I'm not a scientist but I do play one on TV occasionally . . . hell, more than occasionally." Morano's motto in challenging climate science, about which he admitted he has no scientific training, was "Keep it short, keep it simple, keep it funny." Manufacturing doubt is not difficult, because in science, all conclusions are provisional, and skepticism is intrinsic to the process. But as Oreskes and Conway noted in their book, "Just because we don't know *everything*, that doesn't mean we know *nothing*." We *do* know a lot, and the heart of the problem concerns what we are aware of that some people *don't want us to know*. What can we do about this form of conspiracism?

Magicians have a saying, reiterated in *Merchants of Doubt* by prestidigitator extraordinaire Jamy Ian Swiss: "Once revealed, never concealed." In the film, Swiss demonstrated this axiom with a card trick in which a selected card that went back into the deck ended up beneath a drinking glass on the table. It is virtually impossible to see how this is done, but once the move is highlighted in a second viewing, it's virtually impossible *not* to see it thereafter. My hope with this form of corporate conspiracism—which has obvious political implications when it comes to big issues like climate change—is to expose the conspiracy for what it really is and hope the tricks of these magicians of doubt are no longer effective.

• - - • - - •

As we near the close of this section, I want to look forward to a growing problem I see with a new type of conspiracism, identified by political scientists Russell Muirhead and Nancy L. Rosenblum in A Lot of People Are Saying: The New Conspiracism and the Assault on Democracy.[25] Classic conspiracy theories are grounded in arguments and evidence, whereas more recent ones are simply asserted, usually without facts to support them. This new conspiracism is captured in the book's title, lifted from the 2016 presidential election and Donald Trump's recurrent phrase, "a lot of people are saying," which was typically followed by no evidence whatsoever for the pronouncement. Muirhead and Rosenblum offered an explanation in characterizing this new conspiracism:

> There is no punctilious demand for proofs, no exhausting amassing of evidence, no dots revealed to form a pattern, no close examination of the operators plotting in the shadows. The new conspiracism dispenses with the burden of explanation. Instead, we have innuendo and verbal gesture: "A lot of people are saying . . ." Or we have bare assertion: "Rigged!" . . . This is conspiracy theory without the theory.[26]

Then how does such conspiracism spread and catch hold? Through repetition. In the age of social media, what counts is not evidence, but retweets and re-posts. The new conspiracism is by no means only the product of Donald Trump, given that politicians—not to mention economists, scholars, opinion-page editorialists, cultural commentators, and ideologues of all stripes—have been making evidence-lacking assertions for generations, although admittedly without an audience of 60 million Twitter followers that the conspiracist-in-chief commanded (until he was kicked off social media). More importantly, Trump's conspiratorial assertions would go nowhere without a receptive audience, so the blame for the nefarious effects of the new conspiracism has to be spread much wider—to encompass all of social media, alternative media, and even some mainstream media outlets, which have stepped up their sensationalistic headlines in an effort to recapture the advertising dollars they've been losing to social and alternative media.

Most disturbing of all for the spread of conspiracy theories are internet trolls and bots, giving the false impression that there are far more adherents to a particular conspiracy theory than actually exist. This is called *pluralistic ignorance*, or the spiral of silence, in which everyone believes that everyone else believes something, even when very few people actually do.[27] When this happens, a particular idea that most individual members do not endorse can still take hold of a group.[28] A 2009 study by sociologist Michael Macy and his colleagues confirmed the effect: "People enforce unpopular norms to show that they have complied out of genuine conviction and not because of social pressure."[29] Laboratory experiments mentioned in their paper have demonstrated that people who conform to a norm under social pressure are more likely to publicly punish deviants from the norm, as a way of advertising their genuine loyalty instead of appearing to just be faking it.

Calling global warming a Chinese conspiracy is one such way to signal to your political tribe that you're a solid team player. Endorsing one's belief in QAnon and the big "rigged election" lie is another. This helps explain why otherwise rational people appear to believe irrational things. Cognitive scientist Hugo Mercier pointed out that most people who appear to believe irrational things do not have the courage of their convictions when it comes time to do something about it.[30] As I noted earlier, if you truly believed that there was a secret, satanic cult of pedophiles operating out of the basement of a Washington, DC, pizzeria, wouldn't you call the local police to investigate, or perhaps go there yourself to confirm it and then call in the authorities to break it up? That's what Edgar Welch did, when he assaulted the Comet Ping Pong pizzeria, but most people went online to leave a one-star review of the restaurant and complain about the pizza. That's not what would happen if they truly believed a crime was occurring.

Mercier also pointed out that conspiracists who claim a belief in all-powerful government agencies and corporate entities that have censorious powers to silence anyone who speaks out nonetheless openly meet at hotel conferences, swap ideas through emails, and publish their conspiracy theories openly in books, magazines, and documentary films. Dissidents in autocracies like North Korea, where conspiracies are real, would never be able to speak openly, out of fear of imprisonment or death. Psychologist Steven Pinker, invoking distinctions made by Mercier and psychologist Dan Sperber, distinguishes between a reality mindset and a mythology mindset,[31] which I characterize as the difference between empirical truth claims that are falsifiable and verifiable, and mythic truth claims that are neither falsifiable nor verifiable. To Bertrand Russell's observation that "it is undesirable to believe a proposition when there is no ground whatsoever for supposing it is true," Pinker pointed out that this is not the default position, but instead is an anomaly in human history, during which "there were no grounds for supposing that propositions about remote worlds were true. But beliefs about them could be empowering or inspirational, and that made them desirable enough." Conspiracy theories occupy neural networks in our brains that didn't evolve to seek truth and understand reality. Therefore, Pinker explained, "Russell's maxim is the luxury of a technologically advanced society with science, history, journalism, and their infrastructure of truth-seeking such as archival records, digital datasets, high-tech instruments, and communities of editing, fact-checking, and peer review. We children of the Enlightenment embrace the radical creed of universal realism: we hold that *all* our beliefs should fall within the reality mindset."

This is what makes the new conspiracism so troubling. Most conspiracy theorists at least try to muster facts and logic to convince you that a cabal is afoot. In my correspondence with conspiracists over the years, they routinely send me reams of documents, articles, books, and papers, as well as links to websites, documentary films, and demonstrations, all in hopes of convincing me, through reason and empiricism, that they're right to be constructively conspiratorial. The new conspiracists who have emerged since 2016 don't even bother to try. For them, it's truth by assertion: "A lot of people are saying . . ." And if there are political or social consequences in demanding evidence, people in positions of power who could break the spiral of silence by speaking out don't do so, because of fear.

If you thought this would all go away after the November 2020 election, or after the Capitol insurrection on January 6, 2021, or after President Biden's Inaugural Address on January 20, 2021—which I thought it would—that does not appear to be the case. As I write in the summer of 2021, a sizable minority (29 percent) of Republicans still believe that "the storm" is coming and Donald Trump will return to the White House any day now to take his rightful place on the throne of power.[32]

• - - • - - •

Fortunately, there is a way to break the bonds of pluralistic ignorance and the spiral of silence: knowledge and transparency. For example, Michael Macy and his colleagues found that when skeptics are scattered among true believers in a computer simulation of a society in which there is ample opportunity for interaction and communication, social connectedness acted as a safeguard against a takeover by unpopular norms.[33]

Knowledge and transparency are the keys to combating both conspiracies and conspiracy theories, including the new conspiracism. Free inquiry, free speech, and, especially, a free press are vital to the stability of a liberal democracy, one in which all citizens have access to all available knowledge, and politicians must operate under a transparent dome, with every one of us looking in, to ensure that conspiracies do not corrupt society, and that conspiracy theories do not corrupt society absolutely.

I am confident that through knowledge and transparency, the conspiracies and conspiracy theories of today, like those of the past, will be revealed for what they are, and that our civilization will continue its long path of progress, with the arc of the moral universe continuing to bend toward truth, justice, and freedom (even if we never eliminate all forms of bigotry and prejudice). In part III, I will consider how we can do that, both in talking to individual conspiracy believers and in rebuilding trust in the institutions on which each of us individually—and liberal democracies generally—so depend for determining what we should believe as truth.

Talking to Conspiracists and Rebuilding Trust in Truth

The Constitution of Knowledge is the most successful social design in human history, but also the most counterintuitive. In exchange for knowledge, freedom, and peace, it asks us to mistrust our senses and our tribes, question our sacred beliefs, and relinquish the comforts of certitude. It insists that we embrace our fallibility, subject ourselves to criticism, tolerate the reprehensible, and outsource reality to a global network of strangers. Defending it every day, forever, against adversaries who shape-shift but never retreat, can be . . . exhausting, upsetting, and deeply stressful. My biggest worry is Lincoln's biggest worry: "If destruction be our lot, we must ourselves be its author and finisher."

JONATHAN RAUCH, *The Constitution of Knowledge*, 2021

Talking to Constituents and Rebuilding Trust in Truth

CHAPTER 12

How to Talk to Conspiracy Theorists

Engaging with People with Whom We Disagree

Over my many years on the conspiracy beat, I have talked to and corresponded with a great many conspiracy theorists. After *Skeptic* magazine published an investigative article on the 9/11 "Truth Movement" and analyzed their claims—which we found wanting—I encountered a number of 9/11 Truthers who insisted that my skepticism was misplaced and that we should all be skeptical of the official government explanation for 9/11. At public events, 9/11 Truthers would show up during the question-and-answer period, challenging me to explain some alleged anomaly related to the attacks on September 11, 2001, such as the supposedly inexplicable collapse of World Trade Center building 7 or the purported missile strike on the Pentagon.

I also receive a fair amount of correspondence from conspiracists, where a common theme is that I am a conspiracist myself, conspiring to spread disinformation as a means of distracting the public from "the truth." And not just by 9/11 Truthers. UFOlogists have suspected as much when

I proclaim my skepticism of their contention that the government is hiding alien spacecraft and bodies, or that I'm suppressing information about those US Navy videos of UAPs. Holocaust deniers think that I'm Jewish (I'm not) and that I'm being paid off by the Zionist lobby (whoever they are). After my *Scientific American* column on 9/11 conspiracies,[1] I was deluged with more mail than I've ever received for any of my monthly columns over an 18-year run (I suspect it was a coordinated effort). Here are a few letter excerpts that serve as a window into the mind of the conspiracist. One person stated, "The broadcast and print media are almost totally controlled by the Zionist criminals who are behind the evil undertakings of our government. They operate through blackmail, and bribery, and have taken complete control of this government and foreign policy to further their expansion in the middle east."

Sadly, he wasn't the only one to identify Zionists as conspirators: "Please, accept my cancellation for *Scientific American* as your 9–11 report is neither scientific nor American but religious and Zionist. SHAME, SHAME, SHAME— another quisling to the Israeli overlords." And this one as well: "Your whitewash on the 9–11 does not work. Your Zionist front guys are treating your readership as fools. I have been a life long subscriber of your magazine and I have all the issues since 1971. I will cancel my subscription due to your treasonous servility to the foreign power [Israel]." Another correspondent fingered the magazine and me as part of the conspiracy:

> I'm deeply shocked *Scientific American* could so obviously discredit its reputation, with such nonsense. Why not run stories about little green men on the moon? I mean, you've gone this low, why not go further? Don't be surprised if the scientific community starts laughing at you, and sales dry up. You can't publish crap like this AND keep your reputa-

tion. Mere pawns for the military-industrial complex—that's what you are.

One fellow determined that President George W. Bush knew about the attacks ahead of time, as evidenced by his continuing to read a book about goats out loud to a classroom of children during the attacks:

> With a supposedly unknown number of airplanes flying over the country and crashing into buildings, President Bush's presence at Booker Elementary School announced in the media three days before, and an airport just four miles away, how did the United States Secret Service know for a fact that Bush was safe where he sat reading about goats? How did they know they did not need to throw him into that bomb-proof limo and drive off in any direction to foil a possible inbound? How did they know Bush was not a target? And the only possible answer is that they already knew what the targets were.

A different interlocutor pleaded with me:

> Please, PLEASE, don't become a shill of the NWO [New World Order] and debunk the legitimate theories about the truth of 9–11. It has got to be clear to any intelligent, thinking person that the official explanation of 9–11 . . . is also only a theory and that with a great many, huge holes in it. When the government declared they knew it was Bin Laden, the world asked, "How do you know?" The government said, "Trust us, we have the proof." Then the government attacked Afghanistan. Then, by sheer luck and chance, the Osama confession tape was found. WELL, there you go, he did do it. The trouble is, that tape has easily been demonstrated to be fake.

Undaunted, and powered by conspiratorial paranoia, one site, called World for 9–11 Truth, dedicated an entire section to refuting me. Another told me to "wipe the smile off your smug gob right now Michael Shermer." One correspondent growled, "Explain WTC 7 to me Mr. Shermer. It is still the 47-story elephant in the living room."

I have in my files hundreds more such letters, but the gist of this chapter, and this book in general, is that once conspiracy theorists get a particular explanation for an event into their heads, it is very difficult to change minds, regardless of the facts. Nevertheless, it can be done. It begins with learning how to have difficult conversations with anyone about anything, skills that I have honed over decades of talking to people whose views do not perfectly align with my own, as well as in understanding how to reason and think, and how to teach other people to do so.[2]

• - - • - - •

What follows are some tools I've developed over the years on how to talk to anyone who holds opinions different from your own on important topics, especially if those concepts are emotionally salient, which most conspiracy theories are.

1. *Keep emotions out of the exchange.* Negative emotions are especially destructive. If you feel your blood boiling, or if the other person is noticeably heating up, take a break.

2. *Discuss ideas, don't attack people.* Ideally, rational conversations should be focused on ideas, not on the people espousing them. Attacking individuals, instead of their beliefs, is a logical fallacy, known as "ad hominem." In recent years, as opinions have become ever more polarized, a new fallacy (of an old practice) has been named "ad Hitlerum." The moment you equate someone's beliefs with something Hitler or the Nazis believed, or you call someone a Nazi outright, the conversation is over.

3. *Show respect and assume best intentions.* Just as you want to be treated with respect and be given the benefit of the doubt as to motives behind your ideas, so, too, do others.

In conversations with people with whom we disagree, the tendency is to try to catch them out on some triviality and assume the worst about what they are trying to convey. Try doing the opposite, by assuming they're good people with good intents and, at worst, are simply wrong, not immoral or evil.

4. *Acknowledge that you understand why someone might maintain an opinion you don't hold.* This shows respect and an assumption of best intentions on your part. It also signals to the other person that you're listening to what's being presented. For example, in debates on gun control, I'll say, "I grew up with guns and so I totally get why you want fewer regulations on them." Or, "I was once a global warming skeptic, so I can see why you are as well, but over time I accepted the science once I looked at it carefully." Or, "I used to be in favor of capital punishment because it seemed only just that if you take a life you should give up your own, but then I found out that too many inmates on death row were wrongly convicted and subsequently freed after DNA evidence exonerated them." Admissions like these signal that changing your mind is not only acceptable, but can also be a virtue.

5. *Call on someone to articulate their position in more detail.* For example, if they say, "I'm against Obamacare," ask them what Obamacare is, exactly. You will often find them dumbstruck. People's positions on such issues are often held for politically tribal reasons, not for empirical, rational ones. The same applies to other hot-button issues—like immigration, foreign aid, critical race theory, or transgender issues—which few people understand in any detail but on which nearly everyone has a strong opinion. If they say they're against the North American Free Trade Agreement (NAFTA), ask them what it is in the trade agreement that they are opposed to. You're likely to find that they have no idea what's actually in NAFTA, and that their opposition

to it is more of a political truth claim than an empirical one.

6. *Try arguing the other side of an issue.* This will enhance your understanding of the opposition, as well as strengthen your own position. For example, most of my students are political liberals and, as such, are pro-choice on the abortion issue. I ask them to articulate the best arguments on the pro-life side. Most of them can't do it, because they don't know those arguments. As John Stuart Mill said:, "He who knows only his own side of the case knows little of that."[3] You may have to do this privately, but it's a good exercise in rationality. Even if you don't change your mind, it can buttress your own stance.

7. *Practice active listening.* Listen to others in a way that enables you to comprehend what they are saying. Convey—through both your words and your actions—that you are really hearing what they say, and make sure they are aware of this. Don't stare, but often look at their faces, especially into their eyes, instead of looking away or down at your feet. Nod attentively when they are speaking. This also shows respect, which we all want, so perhaps they will actively listen to you in turn.

8. *"Steel-man" the other person's position* (i.e., articulate their argument as well as they do). Repeat, in your own words, what you think the other person is saying. For example, begin with "I want to be sure I understand what you're telling me . . ." and then use your own words to restate their argument. I don't mean to perfectly mirror their stance with a word-for-word repetition. Reiterate *in your words* what you think they said. In most conversations, we tend to "straw-man" the other person's beliefs and opinions—that is, we mischaracterize them in a way that is easy to refute—so by "steel-manning" the other person's position, you gain a deeper understanding of it. Again, this shows respect.

9. *Channel your inner Socrates.* The ancient Greek philosopher Socrates once said, "The unexamined life is not worth living." The way Socrates examined life was through questioning—today it's called the Socratic method. The point of asking questions like a philosopher is to bring out the best in both conversational partners and, along the way, discover what is true. In *How to Have Impossible Conversations*, Peter Boghossian and James Lindsay outlined many tools for engaging with others with whom we disagree. On the Socratic method, they provide a number of suggestions for the types of questions you can ask your interlocutor:[4]

- *Questions about clarity.* "Are you sure about that?" "How do you know that's true?" "Why do you say that?" "How does this relate to our discussion?"
- *Questions about sources and assumptions.* "What's your source for that fact?" "What could we assume instead?" "Is it really that black and white, or is it possible that there are shades of grey in between?"
- *Questions that probe reasons and evidence.* "What evidence do you have for that belief?" "What percentage of certainty would you place on that belief?" "Is that all the relevant evidence, or just a selection in support of your belief?"
- *Questions about viewpoints and perspectives.* "What would be an alternative to X?" "What is another way to look at X?"
- *Questions that probe implications and consequences.* "What are you implying?" "What are the consequences of that assumption?"

10. *Identify flawed or dishonest arguments.* Nothing can trip up a conversation faster than when it's sidetracked because of some flawed or dishonest argument made on the part of one or both people in a conversation. Someone's

intentions or motivations obviously matter, but focusing on the problems with that person's argument, rather than their inner state of mind, can keep the conversation on track. Examples provided by Boghossian and Lindsay in their book include the following (steel-manned in my own words):[5]

- *Questioning the motives of the other person.* Conversations should be about ideas, not intentions, so you want to try to stay focused on the topic under discussion, not on why you or the other person is making a certain argument.
- *Questioning the authority of the other person.* Saying "you're not qualified to comment on that" is unfair, because, presumably, you are not having a conversation about resumés, accomplishments, and titles. Rather, you should be conversing about ideas, so stay focused on what is under discussion, not on what titles or qualifications the other person has.
- *Claiming membership in a group to gain authority.* This is a type of authority boasting, implying that only someone who is a member of X is qualified to speak about X. Again, conversations should focus on ideas, not on one's affiliation with a particular group or on which groups are the most qualified. The latter, in itself, is a form of stereotyping or prejudice. This is an especially sensitive topic when we're talking about assemblages based on race, gender, religion, or political party, making this an even bigger problem for smooth conversations.
- *Changing the subject.* Watch out for this one, because it can become tricky to spot. Suppose you're having a lively discussion about whether global warming is real and human caused, and all of a sudden you're talking about socialism and government regulation.

Those are not the same issues! The first has to do with a fact about the world—either temperatures on the planet are rising, and that warming is human caused, or it is not—while the second deals with what to do about it.

- *Separating people from ideas.* For example, say "that opinion" instead of "your opinion," or "that statement" instead of "your statement." Use collaborative language, like "we" and "us." Instead of asking "How do you know that?" ask "How do we know that?" Acknowledge the other person's opinion before you offer your own or try to refute theirs. Say "I hear you" or "I understand" or "I see where you're coming from" or "I can see why you think that." And, if it is a friend you are talking to, unbundle friendships from opinions.

11. *Determine how confident your conversational partner is in their beliefs.* Boghossian and Lindsay suggested asking, "On a scale from 1 to 10, how confident are you that X is true?" Or, "As a percentage where 100 percent is absolutely certainty, how positive are you that X is true?"[6] What this strategy does is provide some idea of the other person's confidence in what's being said, given that most beliefs fall somewhat short of being 100 percent true. It also moves the conversation into a more analytical and less emotional direction.

12. *Be willing to change your mind and suggest to your conversational partner that it's also okay if they change their opinion.* For example, you might say something like, "You know, you make some really good points that make me wonder if I should change my mind." Or, "I think I might be wrong." Or even, "You're right! You've convinced me!" This might embolden the other person and lead to hubris about their beliefs, but it might also give them permission to

alter their opinion, or at least listen to you more thought-fully and open-mindedly. I've shifted my stance on a number of positions on hot-button issues, such as gun control, capital punishment, and even climate change. Admitting as much does two things. First, it demonstrates to your interlocutor that you could change your mind when confronted with irrefutable facts contrary to your current position. Second, it is a form of social proof, indicating that not only is it acceptable to change one's mind in the teeth of contradictory evidence, but also that this is a virtue to be admired—as in the quip variously attributed to Daniel Patrick Moynihan, John Maynard Keynes, and others: "When the facts change, I change my mind. What do you do, sir?"[7]

13. *Try to show how changing facts does not necessarily mean changing worldviews.* If someone is deeply rooted in a belief—so strongly that it practically defines them and what they stand for—there is little chance you can get them to abandon that belief through reason alone. Remember the power of the myside bias and try to avoid it by doing an end run around that worldview. For example, in speaking with Christians who are uncertain about what to believe regarding the theory of evolution, I don't give them a choice between accepting Darwin or accepting Jesus, because that's a no-brainer: the evolutionary sage loses every time. Darwin offers a scientific explanation for the diversity of life; Jesus offers eternal life. Instead, I point them to Francis Collins's book, *The Language of God*, because he is one of the clearest expositors of evolution who is writing today, while at the same time being an Evangelical Christian (who also happens to be the director of the National Institutes of Health and headed the Human Genome Project).[8] His faith puts him squarely in the tribe of Christians, making it more acceptable for them to acknowledge the science supporting evolutionary theory without having to give up a component of their self-identity. Remember this when

talking to conspiracy theorists, because of one facet of proxy conspiracism—where a particular conspiracy theory stands in for a larger truth. Trying to refute the underlying concept will feel like an attack on the believer's self-identity.

• - - • - - •

Given how contentious conspiracy theories have become in recent years, a final word on talking with conspiracists, especially family members or those whom you know personally and consider to be friends, comes from Thomas Jefferson, the third president of the United States and author of the Declaration of Independence, among his many accomplishments. He is a model of rational conversation, having corresponded with thousands of people throughout his long career and engaged with the greatest minds of his time during the founding of our country. When asked how he managed to maintain friendships with people who were often his political foes, Jefferson responded, "I never considered a difference of opinion in politics, in religion, in philosophy, as a cause for withdrawing from a friend."[9]

That wasn't an easy path to follow when Jefferson was conversing with people about the most contentious topics involved in the creation of a nation. Nonetheless, doing so is the key to navigating argumentative conversations with conspiracists. The principle here is to separate friendships from opinions. That is, tell yourself ahead of time that no matter where the conversation goes, no matter what opinions or positions the other person stakes out, those who are your friends will still remain your friends. Friendships are not about agreement, but about mutual respect, mutual interests, kindness, honesty, empathy, and trust. On the other hand, opinions about ideas are just that—opinions, not insults to you if you don't agree. The axiom here is, "Let people be wrong." Nonetheless, they don't think they're wrong, or else they wouldn't be saying what they do, and that's the point.

Words are all we have to express our thoughts, so they must be chosen carefully and delivered strategically. Given the emotional valence (usually negative) that conspiracy theories project, this principle especially applies when talking with conspiracists, more than to most others.

CHAPTER 13

How to Rebuild Trust in Truth

Reason, Rationality, and Empiricism
in Reality-Based Communities

As we move into the third decade of the twenty-first century, polls consistently show a lack of trust in traditional institutions and authorities to give us the truth we need to safely navigate our personal and public lives. For example, a September 2020 Pew poll of 9,100 registered US voters reported that for years, "public trust in the federal government has hovered at near-record lows," reaching back through both the George W. Bush and Barack Obama administrations and continuing through the Donald Trump administration, with only 20 percent of the respondents saying they trust the government in Washington, DC, to "do the right thing" most of the time.[1] An explanation for this lack of trust may be found in an October 2020 *Newsweek* poll of 3,100 registered US voters, where a majority of them believed lying has become acceptable in American politics.[2]

The focus and directionality of the trust problem is highly politicized. On the Right, conservatives accuse Hollywood, academia, science, and, especially, mainstream media of a liberal bias that distorts reality and bends the truth on a number of important issues, such as climate change, vaccines, COVID-19, immigrants, abortion, religion, and even sex and gender.[3] On the Left, liberals accuse politicians, religious leaders, pundits, and talk radio and television hosts of a conservative bias so egregious that the normal political dissembling and spin-doctoring of the facts has now slid into outright unabashed mendacity.[4] The effect has been a shift in the norms for who and what is trusted in public discourse, with pundits and social scientists tracking back the decline in truth telling, and the rot it brings, to the confidence we have in both our public and private lives.[5]

It is tempting to finger former president Donald Trump as the culprit, inasmuch as he has taken the practice to Brobdingnagian levels—as I noted previously, the *Washington Post* registered over 30,000 provably false or misleading statements Trump made during his time in office.[6] But he's not the only one. President Joe Biden has been caught in a number of misstatements and exaggerations, and he even admitted to plagiarism in law school, where his stated academic accomplishments were also embellished.[7] As politicians from both parties engage in the old-time art of spin-doctoring the truth in speeches, real time fact-checking has emerged as a new form of journalism, to combat this illiberalism of untruth. Fact-checkers at OpenSecrets.org, Snopes.com, FactCheck.org, and PolitiFact.com routinely publish the errors, distortions, and lies by politicians and other public figures, with PolitiFact cheekily ranking statements as "True," "Mostly True," "Half True," "Mostly False," and "Pants on Fire." Mainstream media like CNN now have fulltime fact-checkers on the air, to unpack the list of lies du jour. Legacy media sources themselves—on both the Left (e.g., MSNBC) and the Right (e.g., Fox News)—have been called out in real time for obvious misreporting, distortions, and outright fabrication of facts well beyond the expected errors that normally creep into any journalistic first draft of history.[8]

People are so hungry for the truth from sources they can trust that there is now a market demand for fact-checking. As PolitiFact's editor, Angie Holan, explained, "Journalists regularly tell me their media organizations have started highlighting fact-checking in their reporting because so many people click on fact-checking stories after a debate or high-profile news event."[9] Before we wring our hands in despair over living in a post-truth, alternative facts world where the truth has never been so distorted, however, it is helpful to remind ourselves that politicians have always prevaricated and lied. The following are but a few examples, traveling back in time:

- Barack Obama lied about the US surveillance program and how deep and extensive it was, which included not only the surveiling of American citizens, but also that of foreign leaders, like German chancellor Angela Merkle.[10]
- George W. Bush lied about the reasons for invading Iraq, insisting that there was evidence Saddam Hussein had weapons of mass destruction when there never was any proof, either before or after the invasion.[11]
- Bill Clinton lied about his relationship with a White House intern, which ultimately got him impeached, and in general he dissembled so much that Christopher Hitchens wrote a book titled No One Left to Lie To.[12]
- Ronald Reagan lied about Iran-Contra and the secret exchange of arms for hostages, later claiming that his memory failed him.[13]
- Richard Nixon lied about the Watergate break-in and, before his impeachment trial in Congress began, resigned from the presidency before his term was up.[14]

- Lyndon Johnson lied about the Gulf of Tonkin incident, in which a US Navy ship was allegedly attacked by the North Vietnamese, so he could escalate the Vietnam War.[15]
- John F. Kennedy lied about how he really resolved the Cuban Missile Crisis—by promising to remove our missiles from Turkey if the Soviets would remove theirs from Cuba.[16]
- Dwight D. Eisenhower lied about U-2 spy plane flights over Russia, which caused him considerable grief when one of them was shot down and its pilot was captured.[17]
- Harry Truman lied about Hiroshima being a military base, so he could justify the utter annihilation of a city with one bomb.[18]
- Franklin Roosevelt lied about preparations for war against Hitler, in order to quell the protests of the "America First" movement before the attack on Pearl Harbor.[19]
- Abraham Lincoln lied about his secret peace negotiations with the Confederacy, which he hoped would bring about a quicker end to the Civil War.[20]
- Thomas Jefferson lied about the true motive for the Lewis and Clark expedition, saying that it was purely exploratory and scientific, when it instead was "for the purpose of extending the external commerce of the United States."[21]

And so on, back to the founding of the Republic and before.

Trump remains worse—by orders of magnitude—but he didn't invent the practice. An October 2020 Gallup poll found that only 40 percent of Americans thought Trump was trustworthy, but Biden logged in at merely 52 percent—not exactly Honest Abe levels.[22] Lies require a receptive audience to carry them forward, as well as a culture to nourish them. As Edward R. Morrow, the august CBS reporter, said in 1954 about Senator Joseph McCarthy, "He didn't create this situation of fear; he merely exploited it, and rather successfully. Cassius was right. 'The fault, dear Brutus, is not in our stars, but in ourselves.'"[23] Over six decades later, we can apply that observation to Trump and his false conspiracy theories by noting that he didn't create the situation of fear in the country, but, rather, exploited what was already percolating in the media and the overall culture, especially in online communities. This climate of distrust has been building for some time. So what can we do about it? Continuing with the tools of reason and communication I discussed previously, here are some suggestions on ways in which we can to help restore trust in each other and in our institutions.

1. *Reinforce norms of truth telling and honesty.* Telling the truth and being honest are virtues, and the more people respect them as such, the less likely they are to violate them. My late friend and colleague Christopher Hitchens, an indefatigable investigative journalist and tireless defender of reason, liked to quote John O'Sullivan, his *National Review* editor, on this aspect of truth seeking: "If you hear the Pope saying he believes in God you think, 'Well the Pope's doing his job again today.' If you hear the Pope saying he's really begun to doubt the existence of God, you begin to think, 'He might be on to something.'"[24] It's a poignant observation, because we expect people to think a certain way, especially if it's their job to do so. When their minds operate in some other direction, which goes against the grain of expectations, it not only surprises us, it grabs our attention and makes us wonder if maybe we should give this latter mode of perception a little more credence. Elevating such a concept to a virtuous principle of rationality would go a long way toward reinforcing such norms.

2. *Practice active open-mindedness.* Psychologist Gordon Pennycook and his colleagues measured this behavior through a survey in which people indicated whether they agreed or disagreed with the following statements (the more open-minded answer is given in parentheses):[25]

> Beliefs should always be revised in response to new information or evidence. (Agree)
> People should always take into consideration evidence that goes against their beliefs. (Agree)
> I believe that loyalty to one's ideals and principles is more important than "open-mindedness." (Disagree)
> No one can talk me out of something I know is right. (Disagree)
> Certain beliefs are just too important to abandon, no matter how good a case can be made against them. (Disagree)

In another paper, Pennycook and his coauthor reported that additional studies showed there was a correlation between active open-mindedness and skepticism of conspiracy theories (along with paranormal and supernatural beliefs), as well as higher trust in scientific institutions and consensus science, such as climate change and vaccines.[26] The principle here is that open-mindedness leads to a more objective assessment of evidence, especially when it contradicts beliefs.

3. *Valorize norms of reason and rationality.* Just as we should treat honesty and truth-seeking as virtues, we should elevate the norm of rationality to its rightful place in the human pantheon of virtues to cultivate. While Steven Pinker, in his book *Rationality*, acknowledged that "we can no more impose values from the top down than we can dictate any cultural change that depends on millions of individual choices, like tattooing or slang," the following is how he thought it could happen:

But norms can change over time, like the decline of ethnic slurs, littering, and wife jokes, as reflexes of tacit approval and disapproval proliferate through social networks. And so we can each do our part in smiling or frowning on rational and irrational habits. It would be nice to see people earn brownie points for acknowledging uncertainty in their beliefs, questioning the dogmas of their political sect, and changing their minds when the facts change, rather than for being steadfast warriors for the dogmas of their clique. Conversely, it could be a mortifying faux pas to overinterpret anecdotes, confuse correlation with causation, or commit an informal fallacy like guilt by association or the argument from authority.[27]

In addition to practicing active open-mindedness and being willing to change our minds when the evidence changes, Pinker proposed that we should pressure institutions to develop those norms that lead to truth-seeking rather than territory-defending, including—and especially—academia, with its "stifling left-wing monoculture, with its punishment of students and professors who challenge reigning dogmas on gender, race, culture, genetics, colonialism, and sexual identity and orientation."[28] Pinker noted how "universities have turned themselves into laughingstocks for their assaults on common sense (as when a professor was recently suspended for mentioning the Chinese pause-word *ne ga* because it reminded some students of the racial slur)." The media has also morphed into partisan politics, where one can toggle between, say, Fox News and MSNBC and note the same story being spun so radically far to the Right or the Left that one has to wonder how they can possibly be talking about the same subject.

4. *Avoid group polarization and echo chambers by talking to people with different opinions.* In a series of experiments, Cass Sunstein and his colleagues explored how irrational

beliefs can be reinforced in echo chambers of like-minded people. These were summarized in *Going to Extremes: How Like Minds Unite and Divide* and were applied to conspiracy theories, which are often fueled by group polarization, in Sunstein and Adrian Vermeule's widely read article, "Conspiracy Theories: Causes and Cures."[29] The participants were divided into two groups, liberals and conservatives, and tasked with discussing three issues: climate change, affirmative action, and civil unions for same-sex couples. Their opinions were recorded at three stages: (1) at the beginning, privately and anonymously; (2) in the middle, after discussing the issues with each other until they reached a group verdict on the topic; and (3) after the discussion, privately and anonymously. The findings confirmed the group polarization hypothesis, or what we now call the *echo-chamber effect*:

> On all three issues, both liberals and conservatives became more unified and more extreme after talking only to one another—not merely in their public verdicts but also in their private, anonymous views. Group discussions made conservatives more skeptical of climate change and more hostile to affirmative action and same-sex unions, while liberals showed the opposite pattern. Before discussion, both groups showed far more diversity than they did afterward, and the individuals in the liberal groups were not so very far apart from those in conservative groups. After discussion, the two sets of groups became much more divided.[30]

The implications are clear enough: you should make it a point to talk to people with opinions on hot-button issues that differ from your own; read opinion-page editorials by authors with whom you disagree; and, on social media, follow people, groups, media sources, and institutions that are not perfectly aligned with your own beliefs and ideologies.

5. *Develop a scout mindset.* Julia Galef, the cofounder of the Center for Applied Rationality, had first-hand experience in running workshops to teach people how to use the tools of rationality—probability, logic, and, especially, ways to avoid cognitive biases—only to discover that this wasn't enough. Learning about cognitive biases does no more to improve your judgment than reading about exercise improves your fitness. Instead, she argued, we need to cultivate an attitude of truth-seeking, through what she calls the "scout mindset," in contrast to the "soldier mindset."[31] The soldier mindset leads us to defend our beliefs against outside threats; seek out and find evidence to support our beliefs, while ignoring or rationalizing away counterevidence; and resist admitting we're wrong, because that feels like defeat. The scout mindset, by contrast, seeks to discover what is true through evidence and move toward conclusions that lead to a more accurate map of reality—in Galef's words, "the motivation to see things as they are, not as you wish they were."

The differences in the norms of reasoning between these two mindsets are striking. In order to win the battle of beliefs, soldiers rationalize, deny, deceive and self-deceive, and engage in motivated reasoning and wishful thinking. "We talk about our beliefs as if they're military positions, or even fortresses, built to resist attack," Galef noted. "Beliefs can be *deep-rooted, well-grounded, built on fact, and backed up* by arguments. They *rest on solid foundations.* We might hold a *firm* conviction or a *strong* opinion, be *secure* in our convictions or have an *unshakeable* faith in something." This soldier mindset prompts us to defend ideas against people who might poke holes in our logic, shoot down our perceptions, or confront us with a knock-down argument, all of which may result in our beliefs being undermined, weakened, or even destroyed, so we become entrenched in them, lest we surrender to the opposing position.

If you *are* right, this approach can be effective. If there really is a nefarious conspiracy afoot and you've uncovered it, then channeling your "inner soldier" to destroy it can seem like a potent strategy. But the problem is that none of us are omniscient, and almost all reasoning and decision making happen under uncertainty, so a soldier mindset can easily lead to error. Attacking a conspiracy theory that doesn't exist can harm a great many people, including the reputation of the alleged conspiracist. In seeking truth—that is, an accurate map of reality—we should engage in more open-minded discovery, objectivity, and intellectual honesty, in which "I was wrong" and "I changed my mind" are virtues instead of vices. We should reject statements like "Changing your mind is a sign of weakness" or "It is important to persevere in your beliefs, even when evidence is brought to bear against them." Instead, we should agree with the following precepts: "People should take into consideration evidence that goes against their beliefs," and "It is more useful to pay attention to those who disagree with you than pay attention to those who agree." We should be Bayesian reasoners, revising our estimations of the probability of something being true after gaining new information about it.

6. *Employ a technique rebuttal strategy, rather than a topic rebuttal strategy, when dealing with conspiracists.* Although it is difficult to get people to change their minds about beliefs they hold for deeply moral or self-identity reasons, see if you can zero in on the particular conspiracy claim under consideration. Instead of trying to rebut it point by point—which is extremely difficult, unless you know as much about the conspiracy theory as the conspiracist does, something that is unlikely for most of us for the majority of conspiracy theories (myself included)—concentrate on the techniques of the conspiracist. In a 2019 study on "Effective Strategies for Rebutting Science Denialism in Public Discus-

sions," Phillip Schmid and Cornelia Betsch used climate change and vaccine denial as examples they presented to 1,773 participants in the United States and Germany.[32] The authors employed four different strategies: no response, topic rebuttal, technique rebuttal, and both forms of rebuttal. For example, if you engage conspiracists who don't trust vaccines and are suspicious of government agencies or the corporations dispensing them, you can ignore them (give no response), rebut their topic claims (cite studies that show vaccines are safe and effective), or identify and rebut one or more of the five techniques employed by all science deniers: (1) cherry-picking the data; (2) inferring conspiracy theories behind the claim; (3) quoting fake experts; (4) using illogical reasoning (after-the-fact reasoning, ad hominem arguments, misleading or irrelevant conclusions); and (5) requiring impossible standards for scientific reasoning (argue that no medical treatment is 100 percent safe or effective). The researchers found that ignoring misinformation only encouraged deniers to continue down the path of their beliefs, while technique rebuttal and topic rebuttal were equally effective if you had at your fingertips all the minutia of the claim under consideration—which is unlikely, even for those of us well-steeped in conspiracy theories.

Recall the chapter on JFK assassination conspiracy theories, which barely scratched the surface of what is out there. One would need to practically memorize Vincent Bugliosi's 1600-page book on the subject in preparation for rebuttals. In How to Talk to a Science Denier, philosopher of science Lee McIntyre agreed that "this is great news for those who wish to fight back against science deniers," but it is no panacea.[33] "Once people had been exposed to scientific misinformation, it had some lingering effect. The best possible thing is for people not to be exposed to any misinformation at all. The worst possible thing is for misinformation to be shared and not challenged in any way." The middle ground of countering misinformation with either topic rebuttal (if you have the right information) or technique rebuttal (if you know their strategies) is encouraging. Nonetheless, as McIntyre concluded, "Since we live in a world in which scientific misinformation is ubiquitous, it should come as no surprise that further work remains."

7. *Reinforce the foundations of the constitution of knowledge, the reality-based community, and justified true belief.* In *The Constitution of Knowledge: A Defense of Truth*, journalist and civil rights activist Jonathan Rauch outlined and defended the epistemic operating system of Enlightenment liberalism's social rules for attaining reliable knowledge when people cannot agree on what is true.[34] This reality-based community included the following:

- Scholars, scientists, and researchers, who "gather evidence, form hypotheses, survey the existing literature, engage in critical exchange, conduct peer review, publish findings, compare and replicate findings, credit and cite others' work, populate conferences, edit journals and books, develop methodologies, set and enforce research standards, and train other people to do all of those things."
- Journalists, who "gather facts, cultivate sources, organize investigations, sift documents, triangulate viewpoints, develop stories, check stories, edit stories, decide to publish or not publish stories, decide whether to follow or debunk stories published elsewhere, evaluate mistakes and publish corrections, and train other people to do all of those things."
- Government agencies, that "gather intelligence, perform research, compile statistics, and develop regulations." These include intelligence communities, consisting of people "who develop specialties

and expertise, cultivate sources, collect and assess information, weight their confidence in their assessments, evaluate competing assessments, publish their assessments for their clients, conduct postmortem reviews to understand their errors, and train others to do all of those things."

- Lawyers, judges, and legal scholars, comprising the world of law and jurisprudence, "who develop specialties and expertise, gather facts, survey case law and precedent, build cases and claims, cite evidence in support of their claims, argue with other professionals, render and justify judgments, publish judgments, hold themselves and each other accountable through layers of appeal, build and respect a cumulating body of precedent, set and enforce professional standards, and train others to do all of those things."

Of course, anyone in any profession can engage in these practices, because they all point to the same goal: establishing justified true belief and reliable knowledge when uncertainty is present and people disagree on what is true, which is most of the time. Although those committed to reality-based communities differ in the details of what, exactly, should be done to determine justified true belief and reliable knowledge, Rauch suggested 10 features, held in common, to establish the *constitution of knowledge*, or the social rules for turning disagreement into knowledge.[35]

1. *Fallibilism*: "the ethos that any of us might be wrong."

2. *Objectivity*: a commitment to the proposition that there is a reality, which we can know through reason and empiricism.

3. *Disconfirmation*: reality-based individuals, who "understand that their claims will and must be challenged; they anticipate those challenges and respond; they subject their

scholarship to peer review and replication, their journalism to editing and fact-checking, their legal briefs to adversarial lawyers, their intelligence to red-team review."

4. *Accountability*: reality-based community members, who recognize that "being wrong is undesirable, but it is also inevitable," so we need to hold everyone accountable for their mistakes.

5. *Pluralism*: the acceptance of and insistence on viewpoint diversity, along with the "maximum freedom to propose, to critique, to challenge, to defend" any and all ideas.

6. *Civility*: reality-based community members, who "develop and follow elaborate protocols which encourage them to argue calmly and depersonalize their rhetoric—protocols which it is in their interest to observe."

7. *Professionalism*: a belief that "earned credentials count. To develop a track record and reputation, you need to study and practice for years, often decades. . . . As such, you will be accountable to other professionals, and you will share with them a sense of integrity: a deeply instilled understanding that there are right and wrong ways to do things."

8. *No bullshitting*: a complete rejection of behaving "without any sincere regard for truth." Liars acknowledge truth when they try to conceal or deny it, whereas bullshitters don't care what reality is or to what extent they accurately express what it is.

The general idea behind the constitution of knowledge is that there is a reality we can know, but the path to it is convoluted, and uncertainties abound. The people on the journey to reality don't always concur on what it is or how to get there, so we need an agreed-upon set of rules and guidelines to consult when disagreements arise, which they inevitably will. To that end, the constitution of knowledge resembles the US Constitution, inasmuch as they are both social technologies in public decision making and conflict adjudication.

The storming of the US Capitol on January 6, 2021—the event with which I began this book—was a direct assault on the US Constitution. Through the "rigged election" conspiracy theory, it was also an express attack on the constitution of knowledge and the reality-based community therein. That leaders of the attacking mob's own party— from Vice President Mike Pence to Attorney General Bill Barr—denounced the conspiracy theory as a big lie mattered little to those who participated or cheered them on from the sidelines (or in a nearby facility, watching it unfold on television, as President Trump did). Facts were tossed aside, the truth was stomped on, and we are still reeling from the effects of rejecting that reality.

9. *Make a commitment to scientific naturalism and Enlightenment humanism:* most of the moral progress that unfolded over the centuries—the abolition of slavery, torture, cruel and unusual punishment, capital punishment, corporeal punishment, witch crazes, inquisitions, pogroms, and violence in general, along with the recognition of and legal foundation for civil rights, women's rights, LGBTQ rights, children's rights, worker's rights, and even animal rights— was ultimately the result of the application of reason and science to understanding causality and solving problems, in order to increase the survival and flourishing of more people in more places.[36] *Scientific naturalism* is the principle that the world is governed by the laws of nature and forces that can be understood, and that all phenomena are a part of nature and can be explained by elemental causes, including human cognitive, moral, and social phenomena. In the centuries following the Scientific Revolution, the gradual but systematic displacement of religious dogmatism, authority, and supernaturalism by scientific naturalism, particularly its application toward explaining the human world, led to the widespread adoption of *Enlightenment humanism*, a cosmopolitan worldview that places

supreme value on science and reason, eschews the supernatural entirely, and relies exclusively on nature and nature's laws—including the fundamental characteristics of humans and the laws and forces that govern us and our societies—for a complete understanding of the cosmos and everything in it, from particles to people.[37]

Scientific naturalism and Enlightenment humanism made the modern world.[38] Never again need we be the intellectual slaves of those who would bind our minds with the chains of dogma and authority. In its stead, we use reason and science as the arbiters of truth and knowledge. The following tenets are how I summed up the past several centuries in a short speech at the 2012 Reason Rally, before a crowd of over 20,000 humanists and science enthusiasts on the Mall in Washington, DC:[39]

- Instead of divining truth through the authority of an ancient holy book or philosophical treatise, people began to explore aspects of nature for themselves.
- Instead of looking at hand-drawn and -painted illustrations in botanical books, scholars went out into nature, to observe what was actually growing out of the ground.
- Instead of relying on the woodcuts of dissected cadavers in old medical texts, physicians opened bodies themselves, to see what was there with their own eyes.
- Instead of human sacrifices to assuage the angry weather gods, naturalists made measurements of temperature, barometric pressure, and winds, to create the meteorological sciences.
- Instead of enslaving people because they were a lesser species, we expanded our knowledge to include all humans as members of the species, through the evolutionary sciences.

- Instead of treating women as inferiors because a holy book says it is a man's right to do so, we discovered natural rights, dictating that all people should be treated equally, through the moral sciences.
- Instead of a supernatural belief in the divine right of kings, people employed a more down-to-earth credence in the legal rights of democracy, and this gave us political progress.
- Instead of a tiny handful of elites holding most of the political power by keeping their citizens illiterate and unenlightened, through science, literacy, and education, people could see for themselves the power and corruption that held them down, so they began to throw off their chains of bondage and demand their natural rights.

The constitutions of nations ought to be grounded in the constitution of humanity, which science and reason are best equipped to understand. That is the heart and core of scientific naturalism and Enlightenment humanism.

10. *Accentuate norms of free speech and open dialog, as well as attenuate censorious behavior that silences or cancels people who disagree with you:* avoidance of a dangerous norm on many college campuses today, where hate speech is the equivalent of physical violence, so it can only be countered with censorship or violence. This is wrong. Hate speech can only be countered with free speech. In his 1859 classic work, *On Liberty*, John Stuart Mill said, "If all mankind minus one, were of one opinion, and only one person were of the contrary opinion, mankind would be no more justified in silencing that one person, than he, if he had the power, would be justified in silencing mankind."[40] The great dissident Rosa Luxemburg put it even more succinctly: "The freedom of speech is meaningless unless it means the freedom of the person who thinks differently."[41] In *Giving*

the Devil His Due, I made an impassioned case for free speech fundamentalism, providing a list of reasons why we should defend free speech against censorship and why we should listen to others, including and especially those with whom we disagree:[42]

Who decides which speech is acceptable and which is unacceptable? You? Me? The majority? The language police?

What criteria are used to censor certain kinds of speech? Ideas that I disagree with? Thoughts that differ from your thoughts? Anything that the majority determines is unacceptable?

We might be completely right, but we could still learn something new in hearing what someone else has to say.

We might be partially right and partially wrong, so by listening to other viewpoints, we might stand corrected and thus refine and improve our beliefs.

We might be completely wrong, so hearing criticism or counterpoint gives us the opportunity to change our minds and improve our thinking. No one is infallible.

Whether right or wrong, by listening to the opinions of others, we have the opportunity to develop stronger arguments and build better facts to buttress our positions.

Freedom of inquiry is the basis for all human progress, because of human fallibility. We are all wrong some of the time (and, for many of us, most of the time), so the only way to know for sure is to talk to and listen to others.

My freedom to speak and dissent is inextricably tied to your freedom to do likewise. If I censor you, why shouldn't you censor me? If you silence me, why shouldn't I silence you?

• - - • - - •

After reading this book, if you object to any of my arguments, disagree with any of my conclusions, or dissent
from my point of view, the norms and customs of free
speech and open inquiry are what allow you to do so. Nonetheless, the volume is at least a start to reestablish trust in
the institutions we depend on for determining the truth
about the world. It remains not just the domain of conspiracy theorists, but instead belongs to anyone who is
curious and desires to understand the truth. Call it the *truth-
based community*, one to which we should all belong.[43]

What People Believe About Conspiracy Theories and Why

Results of the Skeptic Research Center Survey

In seeking to understand what people believe about conspiracy theories and why they believe them, over the spring and summer of 2021, my organization—the Skeptic Research Center—in conjunction with my social scientist colleagues Anondah Saide and Kevin McCaffree, employed the online survey company Qualtrics to poll 3,139 randomly selected Americans on their attitudes about and belief in 29 different conspiracy theories.[1]

Of those 3,139 survey takers, 53.14% were females and 46.86% were males. Education levels (graph C.30) ranged from a high school diploma or equivalent (20.58%), some college or an associate's degree (27.14%), a bachelor's degree (31.32%), and a graduate or professional degree (20.96%). Their incomes (graph C.31) ranged from $0 to $24,999 (17.9%), $25,000 to $49,999 (24.56%,) $50,000 to $74,999

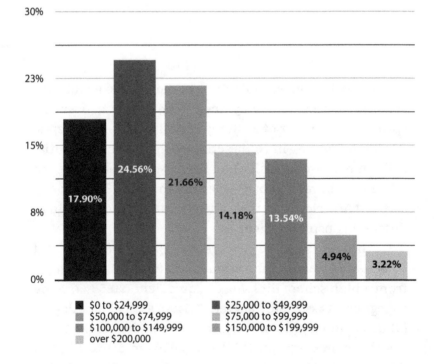

Education

High School Diploma 20.58%
Some College or an Associate's Degree 27.14%
Bachelor's Degree 31.32%
Graduate or Professional Degree 20.96%

Legend:
- High School Diploma
- Some College or an Associate's Degree
- Bachelor's Degree
- Graduate or Professional Degree

Income

$0 to $24,999 17.90%
$25,000 to $49,999 24.56%
$50,000 to $74,999 21.66%
$75,000 to $99,999 14.18%
$100,000 to $149,999 13.54%
$150,000 to $199,999 4.94%
over $200,000 3.22%

Legend:
- $0 to $24,999
- $25,000 to $49,999
- $50,000 to $74,999
- $75,000 to $99,999
- $100,000 to $149,999
- $150,000 to $199,999
- over $200,000

(21.66%), $75,000 to $99,999 (14.18%), $100,000 to $149,999 (13.54%), $150,000 to $199,999 (4.94%), and over $200,000 (3.22%), all fairly close to national averages.[2]

For each of the 29 conspiracy theories we offered survey takers a seven-point scale: slightly agree, moderately agree, strongly agree, uncertain, slightly disagree, moderately disagree, and strongly disagree. We mixed up the order of the conspiracy theories, to avoid any preference or clustering effects in respondents' answers, but the results presented here are grouped according to conspiracy type (see chapter 1). For ease of analysis, I have added a short label to tag a particular statement to a popular conspiracy theory, although such labels were not included in our survey. In the bar graphs accompanying each theory, I combined the three intensity options (slightly, moderately, and strongly) into aggregate percentages of agreement and disagreement for each conspiracy, as well as indicated the percentage for those who were uncertain. Researchers interested in seeing the raw data may request this information.[3]

Within the percentages of people likely to agree or disagree (or remain uncertain) for each of the 29 conspiracy theories, we were curious to know more about them, so we also collected demographic data—specifically the sex, race, income, education, and political affiliation of those in our sample—to assess how such factors influenced or affected belief or disbelief in a number of the more prominent conspiracy theories, including (in my conspiracy labels): QAnon, Deep State, JFK assassination, 9/11 inside job, Obama Birtherism, Israel/Jews, secret societies, Epstein murder, global warming hoax, UFOs, COVID-19 Chinese lab, COVID vaccine surveillance chips, and COVID vaccine magnetic reaction (our made-up conspiracy theory).

The results of a factor analysis we conducted on the conspiracy theories enabled us to form a bottom-up typology, organized around statistical similarities in agreement or disagreement across conspiracies. This typology holds together and accounts for the variance in beliefs in relation to the two overarching types of conspiracy theories presented in part I of this book, paranoid conspiracy theories and realistic conspiracy theories, along with the three predominant factors at work that explain why people believe conspiracy theories: proxy conspiracism, tribal conspiracism, and constructive conspiracism.

The results for these are presented as odds ratios, a statistic that quantifies the strength of the association between two variables—in this case agreement or disagreement with a particular conspiracy theory—and how that association may be influenced by sex, race, income, education, or political affiliation. For example, we computed the odds of someone agreeing with a particular conspiracy theory if they are female or male, Black/Hispanic or white, Republican or Democrat, lower or higher income earners, and better or less educated. Some of our variables are binary, such as sex (male or female), race (Black/Hispanic or white), or political affiliation (Republican or Democrat; independents were very low in number in our sample and we found no particularly interesting effects for them). For example, we can say that someone is X times more likely to agree or disagree with a conspiracy theory if they are Y (e.g., Republicans are 2.5 times more likely to agree with the Deep State conspiracy theory than are Democrats). Other variables, like income and education, were continuous. For example, we can say that someone is X times more likely to agree or disagree with a conspiracy theory for each unit of Y (e.g., for each increase in education—from high school only, to some college, to a bachelor's degree, to a graduate degree—people were 1.3 times less likely to agree with the QAnon conspiracy theory). All reported effects were statistically significant, at least at the $p < 0.05$ level of significance, and often at the $p < 0.01$ or $p < 0.001$ level.

With this in mind, below are the rates of agreement, disagreement, and uncertainty about the 29 conspiracy theories in our survey, along with the factors that were most influential in the participants' beliefs about some (but not all) of them. Where there is no discussion after the bar graphs we did not compute odds ratios.

Government/Political Conspiracy Theories

QAnon

The government, media, and financial worlds in the United States are controlled by a group of Satan-worshipping pedophiles who run a global child sex-trafficking operation.

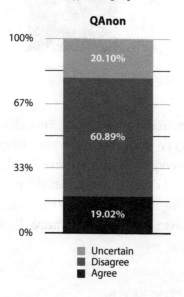

There were no differences according to sex or income. Blacks and Hispanics were 1.6 times more likely to agree than whites. Each level of educational attainment decreased the odds of someone agreeing with this statement by about 30%. Republicans were 1.4 times more likely to agree than Democrats.

Deep State

The actions of the US government are not determined by elected officials, but by an unelected secret group of business and cultural elites known as the Deep State.

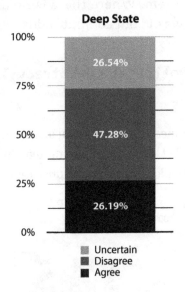

There was no income difference. Females were about 35% less likely to agree with the statement than males. Blacks and Hispanics were 1.5 times more likely to agree than whites. Each level of educational attainment decreased the odds of someone agreeing with this statement by about 20%. Republicans were 2.5 times more likely to agree than Democrats.

Rigged Election 2016

The 2016 presidential election of Donald Trump was fraudulent, because it was tampered with by high-ranking politicians and computer programmers in Russia.

Rigged Election 2016

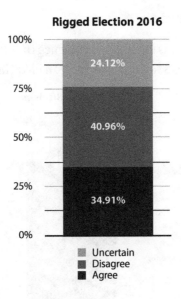

Rigged Election 2020

The 2020 presidential election of Joe Biden was fraudulent, because it was tampered with by high-ranking politicians, voting machine programmers, and poll workers.

Rigged Election 2020

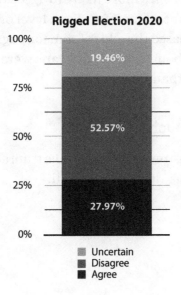

Obama Birtherism

The government has suppressed evidence that Barack Obama was not born on US soil and was thus an illegitimate president.

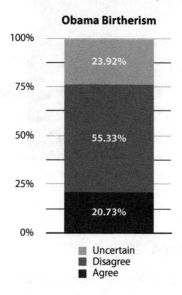

There were no sex or income differences. Blacks and Hispanics were 1.1 times more likely to agree than whites (but barely significant, at $p < 0.04$). Each level of educational attainment decreased the odds of someone agreeing with this statement by about 20%. Republicans were 6.3 times more likely to agree than Democrats.

9/11 Inside Job

The Bush administration has hidden the truth about their role in bringing down the Twin Towers on 9/11.

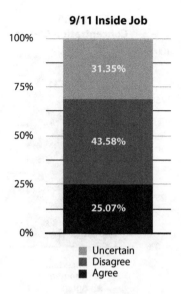

9/11 Inside Job

There were no sex or income differences. Blacks and Hispanics were 1.8 times more likely to agree than whites. Each level of educational attainment decreased the odds of someone agreeing with this statement by about 30%. Democrats were 1.4 times more likely to agree than Republicans.

FEMA Concentration Camps

FEMA (Federal Emergency Management Agency) is secretly building concentration camps in the United States that will be used as holding cells for citizens and political prisoners.

**FEMA
Concentration Camps**

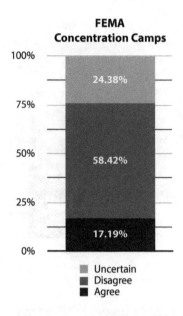

Moon Landing Faked

NASA and the American government are hiding the truth that the moon landing in 1969 was faked.

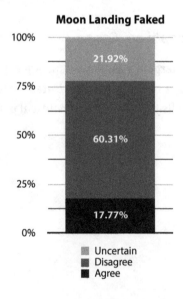

Global Warming Hoax

Global warming is a hoax developed by liberal elites and careerist scientists who are hoping to appeal to political popularity.

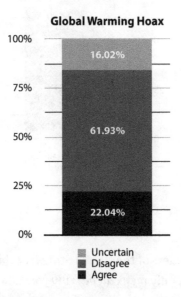

There was no income difference. Men were 1.4 times more likely to agree than women. Blacks and Hispanics were 1.2 times more likely to agree than whites. Each level of educational attainment decreased the odds of someone agreeing with this statement by about 10%, so this factor only barely affected the outcome ($p < 0.03$). Republicans were 4.4 times more likely to agree than Democrats.

Woke Race

The way the founders of the United States set things up ensures that, even today, only whites can be truly free and successful.

Woke Race

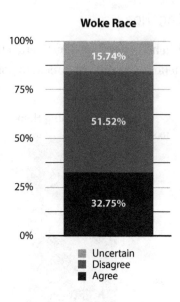

Woke Gender

The way the founders of the United States set things up ensures that, even today, only men can be truly free and successful.

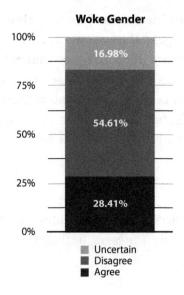

Reptilian Aliens

Reptilian aliens occupy positions of significant power and influence in the US government, as well as in the media.

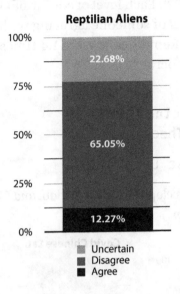

UFOs

The US government is hiding the truth about alien visitations to Earth.

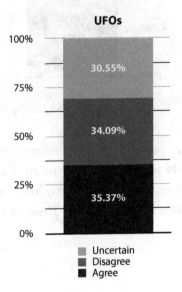

There was no sex difference. Blacks and Hispanics were 1.4 times more likely to agree than whites. Each level of increase in income just barely decreased the odds of belief, by only 10% ($p < 0.02$). Each level of educational attainment decreased the odds of someone agreeing with this statement by about 30%. Republicans were 1.4 times more likely to agree than Democrats.

Medical / Vaccine / COVID-19 Conspiracy Theories

COVID Chinese Lab

COVID-19 was developed in a Chinese lab, and Chinese officials have covered it up.

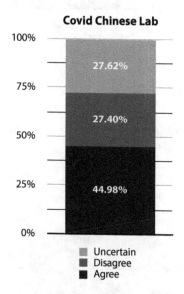

There were no race or income differences. Men were 1.3 times more likely to agree than women. Each level of educational attainment decreased the odds of someone agreeing with this statement by about 10%, so this factor only barely affected the outcome ($p < 0.03$). Republicans were 7.0 times more likely to agree than Democrats.

COVID Vaccine Surveillance Chips

The COVID-19 vaccine contains tiny computer chips, to help make government surveillance of people easier.

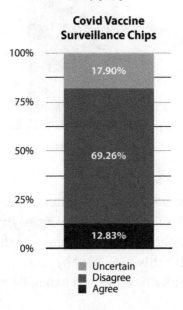

There was no income difference. Men were 1.3 times more likely to agree than women. Blacks and Hispanics were 1.5 times more likely to agree than whites. Each level of educational attainment decreased the odds of someone agreeing with this statement by about 30%. Republicans were 1.4 times more likely to agree than Democrats.

COVID Vaccine Magnetic Reactions (made-up conspiracy theory)

Political and medical elites are hiding the truth about how the COVID-19 vaccines cause magnetic reactions.

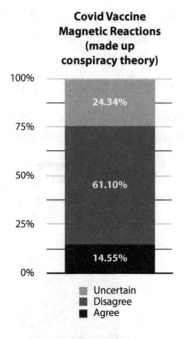

Covid Vaccine Magnetic Reactions (made up conspiracy theory)

There were no sex or income differences. Blacks and Hispanics were 1.6 times more likely to agree than whites. Each level of educational attainment decreased the odds of someone agreeing with this statement by about 30%. Republicans were 1.5 times more likely to agree than Democrats.

Vaccines Cause Autism

Political and medical elites are hiding the truth about the harmful role of vaccines in causing autism in children.

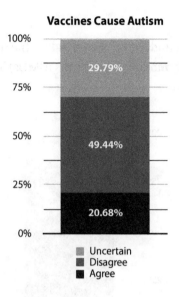

Chemtrails

The US government and major corporations have been involved in releasing toxic poisons through the chemtrails generated by commercial airliners.

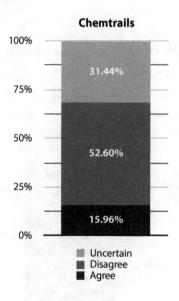

GMOs

Governments around the world are hiding the truth about the role of genetically modified organisms (GMOs) in rising rates of cancer and autism.

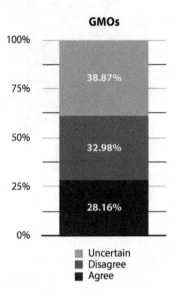

5G COVID

5G cell-phone towers reduce our immune functioning and increase our risk of COVID-19 infection.

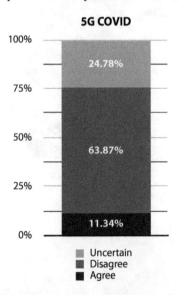

5G Dakota Crash (made up conspiracy theory)

High-ranking officials in the US Air Force are hiding important information regarding the role of 5G technologies in the Dakota crash.

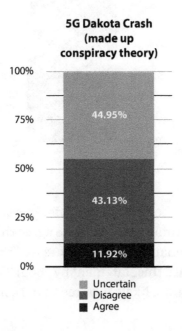

Suspicious Deaths Conspiracy Theories

JFK Assassination

Individuals within the US government have hidden the truth about who was really responsible for the assassination of John F. Kennedy.

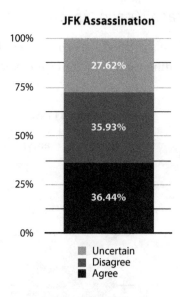

There were no sex or income differences. Blacks and Hispanics were 1.6 times more likely to agree than whites. Each level of educational attainment decreased the odds of someone agreeing with this statement by about 20%. Republicans were 1.3 times more likely to agree than Democrats.

Princess Diana Murder

Powerful people are hiding evidence that Princess Diana was murdered.

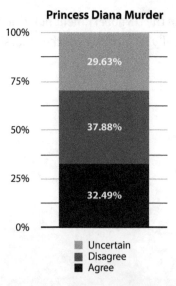

Epstein Murder

High-ranking officials, powerful politicians, and noted celebrities are hiding information about the murder of Jeffrey Epstein, to cover up illegal or immoral sexual activity.

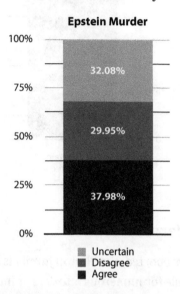

There was no income difference. Women were 1.4 times more likely to agree than men. Blacks and Hispanics were 1.3 times more likely to agree than whites. Each level of educational attainment decreased the odds of someone agreeing with this statement by about 10%, so this factor only barely affected the outcome ($p = 0.05$). Republicans were 2.8 times more likely to agree than Democrats.

Sandy Hook False Flag

The Sandy Hook school shooting was staged as a false-flag operation, so progressive liberals could further promote gun control laws or even overturn the Second Amendment.

Sandy Hook False Flag

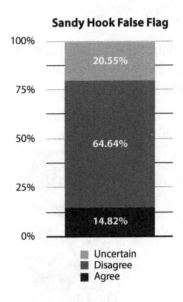

Clinton Murders

Though it goes unreported, the Clinton family is known to be directly responsible for numerous murders of important political figures.

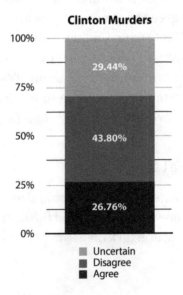

Secret Organization Conspiracy Theories

Secret Societies

Global and national politics are controlled by the world's richest individuals and secret societies, such as the Illuminati, the Rothschild family, the Rockefeller family, and British royals, who advocate a New World Order.

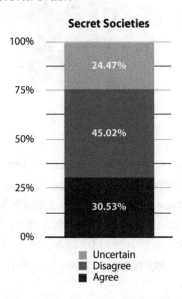

There was no sex difference. Blacks and Hispanics were 1.5 times more likely to agree than whites. Each higher level of income just barely decreased the odds of belief, by only 10% ($p < 0.03$). Each level of educational attainment decreased the odds of someone agreeing with this statement by about 20%. Republicans were 1.5 times more likely to agree than Democrats.

Israel/Jews

Israel/Jews secretly control most of the decision-making processes across key US institutions, including government and media.

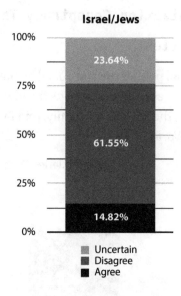

Israel/Jews

There was no income difference. Men were 1.4 times more likely to agree than women. Blacks and Hispanics were 1.7 times more likely to agree than whites. Each level of educational attainment decreased the odds of someone agreeing with this statement by about 30%. Democrats were 1.3 times more likely to agree than Republicans.

Smart Phone Spying

Political and business elites are regularly using iPhones and other popular consumer electronics to spy on us without our consent.

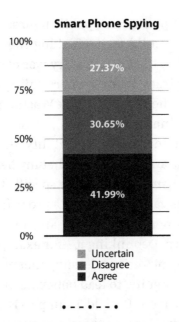

These results are enlightening and, at times, discouraging. Over 60% of our survey takers disagreed that "the government, media, and financial worlds in the United States are controlled by Satan-worshipping pedophiles who run a global child sex-trafficking operation" (QAnon), which seems encouraging, but almost one in five think it's possible, which is puzzling. Some insight may be found in the fact that Republicans were 1.4 times more likely to agree with this conspiracy theory than Democrats; Blacks and Hispanics 1.6 times more likely to agree than whites; and, for each level of educational attainment, there was a 30% decrease in the likelihood of agreement with this statement. While these odds ratios are statistically significant (at better than the standard $p < 0.05$, or a 95% confidence level), that anyone could believe this conspiracy theory on any level almost beggars belief. What are these survey takers thinking?

One possibility is that people are equating Jeffrey Epstein's predilection for nubile teenage girls and his affiliation with prominent politicians, public figures, financiers, and celebrities with a child sex-trafficking ring, as well as that, in popular media, the Epstein story was conflated with the Pizzagate conspiracy theory, where this type of operation was ongoing in the basement of a Washington, DC, pizzeria, with prominent names (e.g., Hillary Clinton, Tom Hanks) added to increase its credibility. Alternatively, and more likely, this an example of what my belief model calls proxy conspiracism, in which the specific QAnon conspiracy theory (in its various forms) is a proxy for a broader distrust of government, the media, and financial worlds in the United States. Debunking it—for example, going to the Comet Ping Pong pizzeria and seeing that no such operation exists—was never going to lead believers in this conspiracy to flip their vote from Donald Trump to Hillary Clinton in the 2016 election. Nor was there any possibility they were going to vote for Hillary, because of tribal loyalty to the Republican Party.

Additional findings in our study affirm the proxy conspiracism hypothesis. For example, over a quarter of those in our survey agreed on some level that there is a "secret group of business and cultural elites known as the Deep State" determining the actions of the US government. Moreover, this represents another form of proxy conspiracism, which also taps into tribal conspiracism and constructive conspiracism, inasmuch as Republicans were 2.5 times more likely to agree with the Deep State conspiracy theory than Democrats, and Blacks and Hispanics were 1.5 times more likely to agree than whites. Given that Republicans tend to be suspicious of big government agencies, and that, historically, Blacks and Hispanics have had far more negative interactions with the government than whites, there is an understandable form of reasoning behind believing that powerful elites conspire to gain an immoral or illegal advantage over others. (The very definition of a conspiracy, from chapter 1, is "two or more people, or a group, plotting or acting in secret to gain an advantage or harm others immorally or illegally.")

Such conspiracies, in various forms, sometimes have historically been real, as well as imagined. Thus we should not be surprised that even absurd ones, like QAnon, are able to get a toehold on the cliff face of popular culture. We can't know for certain, since we can't get into the minds of survey takers (or the people who stormed the Capitol building on January 6, 2021, or anyone else, for that matter), so such conjectures are necessarily provisional. Nonetheless, although what is being proposed here is on a level of absurdity that is hard to fathom, I suggest that using proxy, tribal, and constructive conspiratorial beliefs as an explanation is entirely reasonable. I can imagine such a conspiracist thinking, "I don't know if the Pizzagate conspiracy theory is true, but it's the sort of thing Democrats would do!"

The above two conspiracy theories—QAnon and the Deep State—when combined, are also proxies for the corrosion of public trust in our elected officials, in our representative democracy, and in authorities of all kinds. Additional evidence for this hypothesis may be seen in our study's findings that over a third (35%) of our respondents believed that the 2016 election was fraudulent, "because it was tampered with by high-ranking politicians and computer programmers in Russia," and over a quarter (28%) believed the 2020 election was "tampered with by high-ranking politicians, voting machine programmers, and poll workers." Related political conspiracy theories also found robust agreement in our survey takers. One in four (25%) believed that 9/11 was an inside job by the George W. Bush administration, and just over one in five (21%) still think Barack Obama was not born on US soil. Nearly a quarter (22%) of those in our survey said they thought it possible that the entire scientific theory of global warming was "a hoax developed by liberal elites and careerist scientists who are hoping to appeal to political popularity."

So eroded is trust in truth, as affirmed by august institutions in science and government, that over one in six participants (17%) in our survey thought it possible that the 1969 moon landing was faked and that "FEMA (Federal Emergency Management Agency) is secretly building concentration camps in the United States that will be used as holding cells for citizens and political prisoners." Seriously? Concentration camps? In America? I've been hearing about these camps for decades (this conspiracy theory dates back to the 1990s, under the Clinton administration). When believers are pressed for evidence of said camps, I'm usually given aerial photographs or telephoto shots of large fenced-off areas in Texas or Wyoming that turn out to be farms and ranches, or an actual forced labor camp in North Korea.[4] We shouldn't be surprised at such beliefs, given that over a third (35%) of the participants in our survey said they believed that UFOs represent "alien visitations to Earth," as well as that the US government knows about it and is keeping it a secret. Moreover, one in eight (12%) of our survey takers said they agreed that "reptilian aliens occupy positions of significant power and influence in the US government, as well as in the media." While I know some people who are of the opinion that most politicians are metaphorical reptiles, thinking only with their lizard brains, some people take this conspiracy theory literally. Astonishing.

Given that our society is presently undergoing a cultural shift, pushed along by the #metoo movement, the #BLM movement, the antiracism movement, critical race theory, and the like, culminating in protests and riots in mid-2020 after the brutal murder of George Floyd by Derek Chauvin—itself just one of many police killings captured on cell-phone videos—we should not be surprised at the findings of the two questions we labeled "woke race" and "woke gender." For the former, a third (33%) of our survey takers said they agreed that "the way the founders of the United States set things up ensures that, even today, only whites can be truly free and successful," while over a quarter (28%) said they agreed that "the way the founders of the United States set things up ensures that, even today, only men can be truly free and successful." Calling these "conspiracy theories" may sound incongruous—inasmuch as such repressions have been taking place for some time—but many people believe that the problems underlying discrimination against minorities and women are "systemic" and "baked into" our society, such that there is a ongoing "conspiracy" of sorts, even if its perpetrators are neither racist nor misogynist. Historically, such beliefs were not uncommon in the bad old days of the pre–civil rights period, in which Jim Crow racism and the 1960s culture of misogyny portrayed in the Mad Men TV series were pervasive. Thus, these findings affirm all three of my conspiracisms: proxy, tribal, and constructive.

All three forms of conspiracism can also be found in our questions on COVID-19 and vaccines. Nearly half of our survey takers (45%) thought it possible that the virus was "developed in a Chinese lab, and Chinese officials have covered it up," which may very well turn out to be true on some level (intentional or unintentional, as medical research or as bioweapon gain-of-function research), which fuels conspiracism about vaccines. For example, one in eight participants in our survey agreed it was possible that COVID-19 vaccines contained "tiny computer chips, to help make government surveillance of people easier," and even more (15%) agreed with our entirely made-up statement that "political and medical elites are hiding the truth about how the COVID-19 vaccines cause magnetic reactions." These conspiracy theories are probably influenced by the older anti-vaxxer claim (thoroughly debunked) that vaccines cause autism, with which one in five (21%) of our survey takers agreed. The simultaneous rollout of 5G cell-phone towers and the spread of COVID-19 naturally fueled conspiracisms, leading nearly one in eight (11%) respondents to agree with our statement that "5G cell-phone towers reduce our immune functioning and increase our risk of COVID-19 infection." Even more absurdly, one in seven of our survey takers (15%) agreed with our fake magnetic reactions conspiracy theory—for which Republicans were 1.5 times more likely to agree than Democrats, Blacks and Hispanics were 1.6 times more likely to agree than whites, and, with each unit decrease in education, the odds of agreeing with the conspiracy went up by about 40%. (As it turns out, after we concocted the magnetic reactions conspiracy theory, videos appeared online in which people claimed that the COVID-19 vaccine made them magnetic, thereby affirming the axiom that life imitates art.)

My tripartite model of conspiracism belief—proxy, tribal, and constructive—is further reinforced by the correlations between specific conspiracy theories. For example, in what we called "suspicious deaths" conspiracy theories, there are strong correlations between the particular theories. For example, the JFK assassination conspiracy theory is moderately correlated with the Princess Diana murder theory and strongly correlated with the Jeffrey Epstein murder theory. In turn, the Princess Diana murder theory is only moderately correlated with the Jeffrey Epstein murder theory, but strongly correlated with the JFK assassination theory. Not surprisingly, the Jeffrey Epstein murder theory was strongly correlated with the Princess Diana murder theory, yet only moderately correlated with the JFK assassination theory.

Perhaps revealingly, we also found comparable rates of belief between the JFK assassination (36%), Princess Diana murder (32%), and Epstein murder (38%) conspiracy theories, although rates of belief were lower for the Clinton murders (27%) and Sandy Hook false flag (15%) theories. Our survey takers' 36% agreement on the JFK assassination theory was well below national averages, which have been in the 50%–60% range over the past half century (see chapter 10). While our survey's overall percentage of people who believed Jeffrey Epstein was murdered does not stand out, it is noteworthy that Republicans were 2.8 times more likely to agree than Democrats, fitting the M.O. of the alleged contention that Epstein was supplying underage sex partners to prominent Democrats.

Finally, it should surprise no one that COVID and vaccine conspiracy theories are highly correlated with each other. For example, the vaccines cause autism theory was either moderately or significantly correlated with the COVID Chinese lab theory, the COVID vaccine surveillance chips theory, and even our made-up COVID vaccine magnetic reactions theory. In turn, the COVID Chinese lab theory was moderately correlated with the COVID vaccine surveillance chips theory and the phony COVID vaccine magnetic reactions theory. Unsurprisingly, the COVID vaccine surveillance chips theory was very strongly correlated with the COVID magnetic reactions theory.

Tangential to the 5G and vaccine surveillance chip conspiracy theories was our measure of how many people agreed with our statement that "political and business elites are regularly using iPhones and other popular consumer electronics to spy on us without our consent" (42%), which we added because so many people who expressed fears that the COVID-19 vaccines might be used for tracking people seemed not to realize that such tracking is already being done by big tech and social media companies (and, indirectly, by the government) through our cell phones. Out of the 7.9 billion people alive today, no less than 5.27 billion (67%) have a mobile device. "They" know where you are;

when you are there; what and who you like; where you shop; what you read and listen to; your food, drink, and porn preferences; what (and who) else you might like in the future; and much more. In China, they know when you are sleeping, they know when you're awake, and they especially know if you've been bad or good.

Talk about constructive conspiracism!

• - - • - - •

With so much data available from our survey takers regarding their attitudes and beliefs about conspiracy theories, we were curious to know if there were any statistical similarities among the many conspiracy theories we asked about (for this we employed what is called a Kaiser-Meyer-Olkin, or KMO, test), as well as searching for different sources of similarity between groups of conspiracy theories (for this we conducted a factor analysis, to look for shared underlying, unmeasured sources of variation across the many conspiracy questions). Let me explain these methods in a little more detail.

A KMO test assesses how appropriate it would be to search for some underlying source of shared variation among a group of survey questions or items. The calculation effectively estimates the strength of partial correlations within the set (i.e., correlations between each conspiracy question, holding constant the correlations between all other questions). Thus a KMO test ensures not only that questions or items reveal bivariate correlations with each other (i.e., they are answered in similar ways by survey takers), but also that partial correlations are small (i.e., the other conspiracies in our set also account for a substantial amount of the variation in agreement or disagreement between any two questions). A KMO value above 0.8 is the conventional standard for ensuring that each question in the set is related (positively or negatively) with the others. Also, knowing scores on the other questions helps predict the strength of any one correlation. In other words, a KMO test tells us that answers for each question are similar to the answers given for every other question, and that the similarity between any two questions can be substantially accounted for by knowing the scores on all other questions. Our goal here was to establish that our conspiracy theories clustered individually with one another, while also holding together as a group. Our KMO values exceeded the conventional standard, indicating that there was indeed something that these conspiracies had in common.

To determine the commonalities, we employed a factor analysis. Given that our conspiracies seemed to share some family resemblance, we wanted to know which conspiracies in particular were most similar to one another (in terms of rates of agreement). Given the above explanation of a KMO test, if responses to questions are similar, and if this similarity helps predict responses to other questions, it is reasonable to ask how many "sources" or "factors" of similarity there might be in any set of questions or items in the survey. So, having established with KMO tests that each of our questions or items might plausibly be tapping into some broad generic dimension (which we might call *conspiratorialism*), we then sought to determine, within this generic dimension, if there were unique sources of differences (or factors) or emergent patterns in the correlations between the variables.

Using these techniques, we found three general factors that corresponded to my earlier distinction between paranoid conspiracy theories and realistic conspiracy theories, plus a third factor corresponding to what we called wokeness conspiracy theories, which were related to the two questions we asked about race and gender. Below are the preliminary results of how these conspiracy theories clustered, according to the factors.

1. Conspiracy questions comprising Factor 1 (paranoid conspiracy theories)

QAnon
Sandy Hook false flag
FEMA concentration camps
Israel/Jews
reptilian aliens
5G COVID
COVID vaccine surveillance chips
COVID vaccine magnetic reactions (made up conspiracy
  theory)
9/11 inside job
moon landing faked
Deep State
secret societies
UFOs
Princess Diana murder
chemtrails

2. Conspiracy questions comprising Factor 2 (realistic conspiracy theories)

smart phone spying
Epstein murder
Clinton murders
global warming hoax
2020 election rigged
2016 election rigged
Obama Birtherism
woke race
woke gender
COVID-19 Chinese lab
GMOs
vaccines and autism
5G COVID-19

3. *Conspiracy questions comprising Factor 3 (wokeness conspiracy theories)*

woke race
woke gender

Exploring the correlates of Factor 1 (paranoid conspiracy theories) in our factor analysis, we found the following:

- *Age* was moderately to strongly negative correlated with Factor 1 (significant at $p < 0.05$). That is, as people got older, they were less likely to agree with these paranoid conspiracy theories.
- *Sex* was only weakly negative correlated (not statistically significant).
- *Race* was positively correlated with Factor 1 (significant at $p < 0.05$). That is, Black/Hispanic race was positively correlated with these paranoid conspiracy theories.
- *Income* was slightly negatively correlated with Factor 1 (significant at $p < 0.05$). That is, the more money people made, the less likely they were to agree with these paranoid conspiracy theories.
- *Education* was negatively correlated with Factor 1 (significant at $p < 0.05$). That is, the more education people had, the less likely they were to agree with these paranoid conspiracy theories.
- *Political affiliation* was positively correlated with Factor 1 (significant at $p < 0.05$). That is, Republicans were slightly more likely to agree with these paranoid conspiracy theories.

Exploring the correlates of Factor 2 (realistic conspiracy theories) in our factor analysis, we found the following:

- *Age* was not correlated with Factor 2.
- *Sex* was weakly positively correlated with Factor 2 (statistically significant at $p < 0.05$). That is, females

were slightly more likely to believe these realistic conspiracy theories.

- *Race* was slightly positively correlated with Factor 2 (significant at $p < 0.05$). That is, Black/Hispanic race was positively correlated with these realistic conspiracy theories.
- *Income* was slightly negatively correlated with Factor 2 (significant at $p < 0.05$). That is, the more money people made, the less likely they were to agree with these realistic conspiracy theories.
- *Education* was slightly negatively correlated with Factor 2 (significant at $p < 0.05$). That is, the more education people had, the less likely they were to agree with these realistic conspiracy theories.
- *Political affiliation* was positively correlated with Factor 2 (significant at $p < 0.05$). That is, Republicans were slightly more likely to agree with these realistic conspiracy theories.

Exploring the correlates of Factor 3 (woke conspiracy theories) in our factor analysis, we found the following:

- *Age* was moderately negatively correlated with Factor 3 (significant at $p < 0.05$). That is, younger people were more likely to agree with these woke conspiracy theories.
- *Sex* was positively correlated with Factor 3 (significant at $p < 0.05$). That is, females were more likely to agree with these woke conspiracy theories.
- *Race* was moderately positively correlated with Factor 3 (significant at $p < 0.05$). That is, Black/Hispanic race was positively correlated with these woke conspiracy theories.
- *Income* was slightly negatively correlated with Factor 3 (significant at $p < 0.05$). That is, the more money

people made, the less likely they were to agree with these woke conspiracy theories.

- *Education* was negatively correlated with Factor 3 (significant at $p < 0.05$). That is, the more education people had, the less likely they were to agree with these woke conspiracy theories.
- *Political affiliation* was strongly positively correlated with Factor 3 (significant at $p < 0.05$). That is, Republicans were far less likely to agree with these woke conspiracy theories.

The point of this analysis is that to understand *what* people believe about conspiracy theories and *why* they believe them, we need to search for underlying commonalities, such as how they cluster in the three domains of paranoid conspiracy theories, realistic conspiracy theories, and woke conspiracy theories, which we have demonstrated above. Moreover, in many of these conspiracy theories, we have seen how the elements in my tripartite model of proxy conspiracism, tribal conspiracism, and constructive conspiracism overlap and reinforce each other in further confirming beliefs, both in individual conspiracy theories, and in a deeper conspiracism about how the world works and who we should trust.

• Acknowledgments

This book is published by a highly respected university press, and I am grateful for the critical feedback provided by its peer reviewers, as I believe their suggestions, comments, and criticisms greatly strengthened the quality of the volume. My literary philosophy is that all writers need editing and, à la Karl Popper, all conjectures need refutations.* None of us is omniscient, and we are all subject to the motivated reasoning, driven by a suite of cognitive biases, that often distort our perceptions to fit preconceived concepts. So, no matter what belief system is in place—religious, political, economic, social, or conspiratorial—it shapes how we interpret information that comes through our senses and motivate us to reason our way into finding the world to be precisely the way we wish it to be.† Thus we depend on others to identify and correct our errors and help us steer closer to truth.

As such, I would like to acknowledge the insights of one of the peer reviewers, who identified himself as Jan-Willem van Prooijen, a leading researcher of conspiracy theories and why people believe them, along with the team at Johns Hopkins University Press who worked on the book, such as Ezra Rodriguez and Juliana McCarthy, and especially Laura Davulis, whose careful reading and editing of the manuscript elevated the work to a higher standard, and Kathleen Capels, whose precise copyediting improved it beyond measure. The manuscript itself started

* Karl R. Popper, *Conjectures and Refutations* (London: Routledge & Kegan Paul, 1963).
† For a full analysis of this problem, what I call "belief-dependent realism," see Michael Shermer, *The Believing Brain: From Ghosts and Gods to Politics and Conspiracies—How We Construct Beliefs and Reinforce Them as Truths* (New York: Henry Holt, 2011).

as a book proposal of loose and unconnected ideas that my agent, Christopher Rogers, helped shape into a coherent set of arguments and narrative.

Since we all build on the work of others, allow me to acknowledge those on whose shoulders I stood. The friendship, generosity, and, especially, the ideas of Steven Pinker were central to the development of this book, as well as the following friends and colleagues who were gracious enough to appear on my podcast and talk through—for hours—many of the ideas that are central to my thinking about beliefs and truths in general, and conspiracy beliefs in particular.* They are listed in alphabetical order: Ayaan Hirsi Ali, David Barash, Peter Boghossian, Howard Bloom, Paul Bloom, David Buss, Robert Cialdini, Nicholas Christakis, Deepak Chopra, Matthew Cobb, Antonio Damasio, Richard Dawkins, Daniel Dennett, Jared Diamond, Andrew Doyle, Ann Druyan, Bobby Duffy, Kevin Dutton, Chris Edwards, Bart Ehrman, Niall Ferguson, Angus Fletcher, Robert Frank, Benjamin Friedman, Julia Galef, Michael Gordin, Alexander Green, Brian Greene, Jonathan Haidt, Jeff Hawkins, Joseph Henrich, Donald Hoffman, Bruce Hood, Daniel Kahneman, Scott Barry Kaufman, Brian Keating, Christof Koch, Mel Konner, Maria Konnikova, Anthony Kronman, Greg Lukianoff, John Mackey, Lee McIntyre, John McWhorter, Hugo Mercier, Geoff Miller, Leonard Mlodinow, Mark Moffett, Douglas Murray, Tom Nichols, Richard Nisbett, Andy Norman, Naomi Oreskes, Robert Pennock, Jordan Peterson, John Petrocelli, Helen Pluckrose, Donald Prothero, Nichola Raihani, Jonathan Rauch, Matt Ridley, Stuart Ritchie, Mike Rothschild, Dave Rubin, Gad Saad, Amber Scorah, Nancy Segal, Martin Sherwin, Debra Soh, Katherine Stewart, Cass Sunstein, James Traub, Neil deGrasse Tyson, Bari Weiss, Craig Whitlock, David Sloan Wilson, and Phil Zimbardo.

I would also like to acknowledge my thirty-year partnership with Pat Linse at the helm of the Skeptics Society and *Skeptic* magazine. Pat sadly passed away as I was finishing the book. She

---

* *The Michael Shermer Show*, https://www.skeptic.com/michael -shermer-show/.

will be sorely missed, both personally and professionally. This volume, in no small measure, owes a debt of gratitude to her superlative powers of creativity and cognition, and I have dedicated it to her. I would also like to acknowledge the Skeptics Society office manager, Nickole McCullough, and her administrative assistant, Priscilla Loquellano; our webmeister (and so much more), William Bull; the producer and engineer of my podcast, Alexander Pietrus-Rajman; my colleagues in researching why people believe conspiracy theories, Anondah Saide and Kevin McCaffree; and the editor and illustrator of *Junior Skeptic* magazine (and so much more), Daniel Loxton.

Finally, I am grateful in ways inexpressible by words for the love of my wife, Jennifer, my son, Vincent, and my daughter, Devin.

Notes

Apologia

1. Author and literary agent John Brockman popularized the term in his 1995 book, *The Third Culture*, a collection of essays by Third Culture authors.

2. Charles Percy Snow, *The Two Cultures* (Cambridge: Cambridge University Press, reprint edition 2001; originally published 1969).

3. E. O. Wilson, *Consilience: The Unity of Knowledge* (New York: Knopf, 1998).

4. Jared Diamond, *Guns, Germs, and Steel: The Fate of Human Societies* (New York: W. W. Norton, 1997).

5. Richard Dawkins, *The Selfish Gene* (Oxford: Oxford University Press, 1976).

6. Steven Pinker, *The Better Angels of Our Nature: Why Violence Has Declined* (New York: Viking, 2011).

7. Charles Darwin to Henry Fawcett, 18 September 1861, letter no. 133 in Francis Darwin (ed.), *More Letters of Charles Darwin*, vol. 1 (New York: D. Appleton, 1903), 194–196.

8. Michael Shermer, "Colorful Pebbles & Darwin's Dictum," *Scientific American* 284, no. 4 (April 2001), 38.

Prologue. The Conspiracy Effect

Epigraph: Joe M, "Q—the Plan to Save the World (remastered)," documentary video, 2019, https://bit.ly/3oVioLQ/.

1. Mike Rothschild, *The Storm Is Upon Us: How QAnon Became a Movement, Cult, and Conspiracy Theory of Everything* (Brooklyn: Melville House, 2021), xiii.

2. Mike Rothschild, personal correspondence, August 13, 2021.

3. Lauren Leatherby, Arielle Ray, Anjali Singhvi, Christiaan Triebert, Derek Watkins, and Haley Willis, "How a Presidential Rally Turned Into a Capitol Rampage." *New York Times*, January 12, 2021, https://nyti.ms/3v19PAP/.

4. Quoted in Daniel Loxton, "QAnon Is Just a Warmed Over Witch Panic—and It's Also Very Dangerous." *Skeptic* 24, no. 4 (2020), https://bit.ly/32ziIW9/.

5. Tucker Higgins, "Man Who Carried Confederate Flag to Capitol During Jan. 6 Riot Indicted," CNBC, April 8, 2021, https://cnb.cx/2QaEnB5/.

6. Matthias Schwartz, "A Trail of 'Bread Crumbs,' Leading Conspiracy Theorists into the Wilderness," *New York Times Magazine*, September 11, 2018.

7. Mike Rothschild, personal correspondence, August 13, 2021.

8. Kevin Roose, "What Is QAnon, the Viral Pro-Trump Conspiracy Theory?," *New York Times*, March 4, 2021, https://nyti.ms/2RBxrgJ/.

9. Michael E. Miller, "The Pizzagate Gunman Is Out of Prison: Conspiracy Theories Are Out of Control," *Seattle Times*, February 16, 2021, https://bit.ly/3ssMQN8/.

10. Daniel Funke, "What Rep. Marjorie Taylor Greene Has Said About Conspiracy Theories," *Tampa Bay Times*, February 3, 2021, https://bit.ly/3dpb32T/.

11. William Saletan, "Republicans Still Sympathize with the Insurrection: They Identify with the People Who Stormed the Capitol," *Slate*, April 15, 2021, https://bit.ly/3uV8jA3/.

12. Ballotpedia, "Election Results 2020: Control of the U.S. House," February 8, 2021, https://bit.ly/3zYHcHx/.

13. Quoted in David Gilbert, "How QAnon Is Tearing Families Apart," Vice News, March 31, 2021, https://bit.ly/2QwFkn4/.

14. David Gilbert, "I'm a Parkland Shooting Survivor: QAnon Convinced My Dad It Was All a Hoax," Vice News, July 26, 2021, https://bit.ly/3ze2UWq/.

15. Laura J. Nelson, "California's Yoga, Wellness, and Spirituality Community Has a QAnon Problem," *Los Angeles Times*, June 23, 2021, https://lat.ms/3gTQnS9/.

16. Julie Carrie Wong, 2020. "Facebook Restricts More Than 10,000 QAnon and US Militia Groups." *Guardian* (Manchester), August 19, 2021, https://bit.ly/3cOU60T/.

17. PRRI staff, "Understanding QAnon's Connection to American Politics, Religion, and Media Consumption," Public Religion Research Institute, May 27, 2021, https://bit.ly/2TAQDMH/.

18. Donald J. Trump, "Donald Trump's Statement On Saturday Night Live and Late Night Losers," *Free Press* (Tampa), June 22, 2021, https://bit.ly/3d8weFz/.

19. Kyle Mantyla, "Mike Lindell Promises 'Donald Trump Will Be in Office by This Fall, for Sure,'" Right-Wing Watch, June 22, 2021, https://bit.ly/3gUHzKC/.

20. Saletan, "Republicans Still Sympathize."

21. Daniel A. Cox, "After the Ballots Are Counted: Conspiracies, Political Violence, and American Exceptionalism; Findings from the January 2021 American Perspectives Survey," American Survey Center, February 11, 2021, https://bit.ly/3e7keE1/.

22. Zeke Miller, Jill Colvin, and Amanda Seitz, "Trump Praises QAnon Conspiracists, Appreciates Support," AP News, August 19, 2020, https://bit.ly/3dmpQv5/.

23. Vincent Bugliosi, *Outrage: The Five Reasons Why O.J. Simpson Got Away with Murder* (New York: W. W. Norton, 1996); Jeffrey Toobin, *The Run of His Life: The People v. O.J. Simpson* (New York: Random House, 1996); Christopher A. Darden, *In Contempt* (New York: HarperCollins, 1996); Marcia Clark, *Without a Doubt* ([Los Angeles]: Graymalkin Media, 2016).

24. This thesis is fleshed out in a 2016 ESPN documentary series, *O.J.: Made in America*, directed by Ezra Edelman (https://es.pn /3e7muew/), which provides a detailed and lengthy analysis of the relationship of the L.A.P.D. and the African American community in Los Angeles since the 1950s. See also "The O.J. Verdict," directed by Ofra Bikel, in the PBS *Frontline* series, particularly the evaluation of the prosecution's case and how they responded to the planted-evidence conspiracy theory defense, in the article "Evaluating the Prosecution's Case," PBS, https://to.pbs.org/3spBuJV/.

25. Sam Smith, "America's Extremist Center," *Progressive Review*, July 1995, https://bit.ly/3nF9ine/.

26. Geoffrey Miller, *Virtue Signaling: Essays on Darwinian Politics and Free Speech* (n.p.: Cambrian Moon, 2019).

27. Drew Harwell, "Lonely, Angry, Eager to Make History: Online Mobs Are Likely to Remain a Dangerous Reality," *Washington Post*, February 17, 2021, https://wapo.st/3uZbQgW/.

28. Russell Hardin, "The Crippled Epistemology of Extremism," in Albert Breton, Gianluigi Galeotti, Pierre Salmon, and Ronald Wintrobe (eds.), *Political Rationality and Extremism* (Cambridge: Cambridge University Press, 2002), 3–22.

29. Michael Shermer, *Why People Believe Weird Things: Pseudoscience, Superstition, and Other Confusions of Our Time* (New York: St. Martin's Griffin, revised and expanded edition, 2002; originally published New York: W. H. Freeman, 1997).

30. The title of my Chapman University First-Year Foundations course is "Skepticism 101: How to Think Like a Scientist." Most of the lectures for that course—recorded during the 2020 pandemic— are available at https://www.skeptic.com/skepticism-101/.

31. Quoted in Jeffrey Goldberg, "Why Obama Fears for Our Democracy," *Atlantic*, November 15, 2020, https://bit.ly/3gfzJwv/.

32. Hannah Arendt, *The Origins of Totalitarianism*, new edition (San Diego: Harcourt Brace Jovanovich, 1994; originally published New York: Harcourt, Brace, 1951), 474.

Chapter 1. Conspiracies and Conspiracy Theories

1. Recounted in Michael Shermer, "Conspiracy Contradictions," [alternate title: "Why People Believe Conspiracy Theories"], *Scientific American* 307, no. 3 (September 1, 2012), 91, https://bit.ly /3mWRu4R/.

2. Andy Blicq, director, "Conspiracy Rising," documentary TV episode, *Doc Zone* series, CBC, 2012, description at https://bit.ly/3easSSh/, trailer at https://bit.ly/3dsAuAA/. For a critical review, see Adrian Mack, "CBC: Conspiracy Theorists Are Mentally Ill and Not to Be Trusted," October 20, 2011, Straight, https://bit.ly/3eejHQD/.

3. For example, see "Alex Jones and Tim Dillon," *The Joe Rogan Experience* #1555, video, YouTube, October 27, 2020, https://bit.ly/3dqIB0d/.

4. For example, see a discussion of the JFK assassination conspiracy theories by Joe Rogan and Michael Shermer, "Who Really Killed Kennedy?," *The Joe Rogan Experience* #1222, video, YouTube, January 10, 2019, https://bit.ly/3stK8qA/.

5. Leanne Naramore, "Sandy Hook Families Are Suing Alex Jones: This Is What He Said About the Shooting," *MediaMatters*, April 17, 2018, https://bit.ly/35vNalk/.

6. Tom Dreisbach, "Alex Jones Still Sells Supplements on Amazon Despite Bans from Other Platforms," NPR, March 24, 2021, https://n.pr/3x47J4T/.

7. For example, see Matthew R. X. Dentith, *The Philosophy of Conspiracy Theories* (London: Palgrave Macmillan, 2014); Michael Butter, *Plots, Designs, and Schemes: American Conspiracy Theories from the Puritans to the Present* (Berlin: Walter de Gruyter, 2014); Cass R. Sunstein, *Conspiracy Theories and Other Dangerous Ideas* (New York: Simon and Schuster, 2014); J. Eric Oliver and Thomas J. Wood. *Enchanted America: How Intuition and Reason Divide Our Politics* (Chicago: University of Chicago Press, 2018).

8. Joseph Uscinski and Joseph Parent, *American Conspiracy Theories* (Oxford: Oxford University Press, 2014), 1–2.

9. Jan-Willem van Prooijen and Mark Van Vugt, "Conspiracy Theories: Evolved Functions and Psychological Mechanisms," *Perspectives on Psychological Science* 13, no. 6 (2018), 770–788.

10. Mike Rothschild, personal correspondence, August 13, 2021.

11. Jesse Walker, *The United States of Paranoia: A Conspiracy Theory* (New York: Harper Perennial, 2013), 16–17.

12. Michael Barkun, *A Culture of Conspiracy: Apocalyptic Visions in Contemporary America*, 2nd edition (Berkeley: University of California Press, 2013), 6–8.

13. Brian Dunning, *Conspiracies Declassified* (New York: Adams Media, 2018), 9–10.

14. The latter version is Jonathan Vankin and John Whalen, *The 80 Greatest Conspiracies of All Time* (New York: Citadel, 2004).

15. Gary Allen and Larry Abraham, *None Dare Call It Conspiracy* (Seal Beach, CA: Concord Press, 1971).

16. Rob Brotherton, *Suspicious Minds: Why We Believe Conspiracy Theories* (New York: Bloomsbury Sigma, 2016), 80.

17. Richard Hofstadter, *The Paranoid Style in American Politics and Other Essays*, reprint edition (New York: Vintage Books, 2008; originally published 1964), 3–40.

18. Quoted in Anna Merlan, *Republic of Lies: American Conspiracy Theorists and Their Surprising Rise to Power* (New York: Metropolitan Books, 2019), 14.

19. Uscinski and Parent, *American Conspiracy Theories*, 56–70.

20. Uscinski and Parent, *American Conspiracy Theories*, 56–70.

21. Summarized in detail in Joseph Uscinski (ed.), *Conspiracy Theories and the People Who Believe Them* (New York: Oxford University Press, 2019), 1–32.

22. Uscinski, *Conspiracy Theories*, 337.

23. Christopher Bader, Joseph Baker, Edward Day, and Ann Gordon, *Fear Itself: The Causes and Consequences of Fear in America* (New York: New York University Press, 2020).

24. The Voice of Wilkinson, "What Aren't They Telling Us? Chapman University Survey of American Fears," October 11, 2016, https://bit.ly/3amYnY9/.

25. Abdullah Azzam, *The Defense of the Muslim Lands—the Most Important of Individual Obligations*, trans. by Brothers in Ribatt (Amman, Jordan: al-Risalah al-Hadithah Library, 1987; originally published in Arabic 1979).

26. Jan-Willem van Prooijen, *The Psychology of Conspiracy Theories* (London: Routledge, 2018), 67–68.

27. van Prooijen, *Psychology of Conspiracy Theories*, 75.

28. van Prooijen, *Psychology of Conspiracy Theories*, 105.

29. Craig Whitlock and the *Washington Post*, *The Afghanistan Papers: A Secret History of the War* (New York: Simon & Schuster, 2021).

30. Kathryn S. Olmsted, *Real Enemies: Conspiracy Theories and American Democracy, World War I to 9/11*, 2nd edition (New York: Oxford University Press, 2019), 1–12.

Chapter 2. A Brief History of Conspiracy Theories and Conspiracists

1. Rhiannon Hoyle, Rachel Pannett, Adrien Taylor, and Rob Taylor, "Terror Attacks at New Zealand Mosques Leave 50 People Dead," *Wall Street Journal*, March 15, 2019, https://on.wsj.com/3almlD5/.

2. Norimitsu Onishi, "The Man Behind a Toxic Slogan Promoting White Supremacy," *New York Times*, September 20, 2019, https://nyti.ms/2Q9WVBu/.

3. Nellie Bowles, "'Replacement Theory': A Racist, Sexist Doctrine Spreads in Far-Right Circles," *New York Times*, May 17, 2019, https://nyti.ms/3mYq6U1/.

4. Brenton Harrison Tarrant, "The Great Replacement: Towards a New Society," 74-page manifesto, https://bit.ly/3sse7iT/.

5. See also Kathy Gilsinan, "How White-Supremacist Violence Echoes Other Forms of Terrorism," *Atlantic*, March 15, 2019, https://bit.ly/3tFQvsg/.

5. Ben Kiernan, *Blood and Soil: A World History of Genocide and Extermination from Sparta to Darfur* (New Haven, CT: Yale University Press, 2009).

7. "David Lane," Southern Poverty Law Center, https://bit.ly /3ssUtDh/.

8. George Michael, "David Lane and the Fourteen Words," *Totalitarian Movements and Political Religions* 10, no. 1 (July 9, 2009), 43–61, https://bit.ly/3x6NSlo/.

9. Brian Palmer, "White Supremacists by the Numbers: What's Up with 14 and 88?," *Slate*, October 29, 2008, https://bit.ly/32ox37v/.

10. Quoted in Barry Balleck, *Modern American Extremism and Domestic Terrorism: An Encyclopedia of Extremists and Extremist Groups* (Santa Barbara, CA: ABC-CLIO, 2018), 4.

11. Richard J. Evans, *The Coming of the Third Reich* (New York: Penguin, 2003), 150.

12. Stephen Eric Bonner, *A Rumor About the Jews: Reflections on Antisemitism and the Protocols of the Learned Elders of Zion* (New York: Oxford University Press, 2000).

13. Henry Ford, *The International Jew: The World's Foremost Problem*, 4 vols., available online at https://bit.ly/3e6Syzc/.

14. Jonathan R. Logsdon, "Power, Ignorance, and Anti-Semitism: Henry Ford and His War on Jews." *Independent Studies* (Hanover College History Department), 1999, https://bit.ly /3tuhGXc/.

15. Andrew McKenzie-McHarg, "Conspiracy Theory: The Nineteenth-Century Prehistory of a Twentieth-Century Concept," in Joseph Uscinski (ed.), *Conspiracy Theories and the People Who Believe Them* (New York: Oxford University Press, 2019), 62–81.

16. Quoted in "The Assassin," *Boston Journal*, July 5, 1881, 4.

17. "The Assassin," *Boston Journal*.

18. "'The Conspiracy Theory,'" *St. Louis Globe-Democrat*, November 21, 1881, issue 185.

19. Lance deHaven-Smith, *Conspiracy Theory in America* (Austin: University of Texas Press, 2013), 25–27.

20. Katharina Thalmann, *The Stigmatization of Conspiracy Theory Since the 1950s* (London: Routledge, 2019), 8.

21. Thalmann, *Stigmatization of Conspiracy Theory*, 186.

22. Mick West, *Escaping the Rabbit Hole: How to Debunk Conspiracy Theories Using Facts, Logic, and Respect* (New York: Skyhorse, 2018).

23. West, *Escaping the Rabbit Hole*, 3.

24. West, *Escaping the Rabbit Hole*, 5–7.

25. West, *Escaping the Rabbit Hole*, 8–9.

26. Joseph Uscinski and Joseph Parent, *American Conspiracy Theories* (Oxford: Oxford University Press, 2014), 5.

27. I unpack both of these observations in two of my *Scientific American* columns. See Michael Shermer, "The Left's War on Science," *Scientific American* 308, no. 2 (February 1, 2013), 88; Michael Shermer, "For the Love of Science," *Scientific American* 318, no. 1 (January 1, 2018), 77.

28. Uscinski and Parent, *American Conspiracy Theories*, 16–18.

29. Uscinski and Parent, *American Conspiracy Theories*, 83.

30. Joshua Hart and Molly Graether, "Something's Going On Here: Psychological Predictors of Belief in Conspiracy Theories," *Journal of Individual Differences* 39, no. 4 (2018), 229–237, https://bit.ly/3vlm4ND/.

31. Arthur Bloch, *Murphy's Law, Book Two: More Reasons Why Things Go Wrong!* (Los Angeles: Price/Stern/Sloan, 1980), 52.

32. Jennifer A. Whitson and Adam D. Galinsky, "Lacking Control Increases Illusory Pattern Perception," *Science* 322, no. 5898 (October 1, 2008), 115–117.

33. Jan-Willem van Prooijen and Karen M. Douglas, "Conspiracy Theories as Part of History: The Role of Societal Crisis Situations," *Memory Studies* 10, no. 3 (2017), 323–333.

34. Robert Thomson, Naoya Ito, Hinako Suda, Fangyu Lin, Yafei Liu, Ryo Hayasaka, Ryuzo Isochi, and Zian Wang, "Trusting Tweets: The Fukushima Disaster and Information Source Credibility on Twitter," in Leon Rothkrantz, Jozef Ristvej, and Zeno Franco (eds.), *ISCRAM 2012 Conference Proceedings Book of Papers: Proceedings of the 9th International Information Systems for Crisis Response and Management Conference* (Vancouver: Simon Fraser University, 2012).

35. Whitson and Galinsky, "Lacking Control."

36. Jennifer Whitson, personal correspondence, December 10, 2009.

37. Whitson and Galinsky, "Lacking Control."

38. Ana Stojanov and Jamin Halberstadt, "Does Lack of Control Lead to Conspiracy Beliefs? A Meta-Analysis," *European Journal of Social Psychology* 50, no. 5 (2020), 955–968.

39. Jan-Willem van Prooijen, personal correspondence, June 22, 2021.

40. Daniel Sullivan, Mark J. Landau, and Zachary K. Rothschild, "An Existential Function of Enemyship: Evidence That

People Attribute Influence to Personal and Political Enemies to Compensate for Threats to Control," *Journal of Personality and Social Psychology* 98, no. 3 (2010), 434–449.

41. Mark J. Landau, Aaron C. Kay, and Jennifer A. Whitson, "Compensatory Control and the Appeal of a Structured World," *Psychological Bulletin* 141, no. 3 (2015), 694–722.

42. Jan-Willem van Prooijen, *The Psychology of Conspiracy Theories* (London: Routledge, 2018), 52–53.

43. van Prooijen, *Psychology of Conspiracy Theories*, 54–55.

44. C. L. Park, "Making Sense of the Meaning Literature: An Integrative Review of Meaning Making and Its Effects on Adjustment to Stressful Life Events," *Psychological Bulletin* 136, no. 2 (2010), 257–301; Marvin Zuckerman, *Behavioral Expressions and Biosocial Bases of Sensation Seeking* (Cambridge: Cambridge University Press, 1994); M. Zuckerman, S. Eysenck, and H. J. Eysenck, "Sensation Seeking in England and America: Cross-Cultural, Age, and Sex Comparisons," *Journal of Consulting and Clinical Psychology* 46, no. 1 (February 1978), 139–149.

45. Jan-Willem van Prooijen, Joline Ligthart, Sabine Rosema, and Yang Xu, "The Entertainment Value of Conspiracy Theories," *British Journal of Psychology*, July 14, 2021.

46. Campbell Robertson, Christopher Mele, and Sabrina Tavernise, "11 Killed in Synagogue Massacre; Suspect Charged with 29 Counts," *New York Times*, October 27, 2018, https://nyti.ms /3dtTRcc/.

Chapter 3. Proxy and Tribal Conspiracism

1. Glenn Kessler, Salvador Rizzo, and Meg Kelly, "Trump's False or Misleading Claims Total 30,573 Over 4 Years," Fact Checkers, *Washington Post*, January 20, 2021.

2. Michael Shermer, *The Believing Brain: From Ghosts and Gods to Politics and Conspiracies—How We Construct Beliefs and Reinforce Them as Truths* (New York: Henry Holt, 2011), 5–7.

3. I patterned this process of belief-dependent realism after the philosophy of science called "model-dependent realism" by Stephen Hawking and Leonard Mlodinow, who asserted that because no one model is adequate to explain reality, we are free to use different models for different aspects of the world. Model-dependent realism "is based on the idea that our brains interpret the input from our sensory organs by making a model of the world. When such a model is successful at explaining events, we tend to attribute to it, and to the elements and concepts that constitute it, the quality of reality or absolute truth. But there may be different ways in which one could model the same physical situation, with each employing different fundamental elements

and concepts. If two such physical theories or models accurately predict the same events, one cannot be said to be more real than the other; rather, we are free to use whichever model is most convenient." Stephen Hawking and Leonard Mlodinow, *The Grand Design* (New York: Bantam Books, 2010), 7.

4. Steven Pinker, *Rationality: What It Is, Why It Seems Scarce, Why It Matters* (New York: Viking, 2021).

5. Pinker, *Rationality*, 300.

6. Daniel Loxton, personal correspondence, December 7, 2020.

7. Pinker, *Rationality*.

8. Daniel Loxton, "The Fringe Is Mainstream: Why Weird Beliefs Are a Normal, Central, Almost Universal Aspect of Human Affairs," *Skeptic* 26, no. 2 (2021), 37–43.

9. Leon Festinger, Henry W. Riecken, and Stanley Schachter, *When Prophecy Fails: A Social and Psychological Study* (New York: HarperCollins, 1964), 174.

10. Festinger, Riecken, and Schachter, *When Prophecy Fails*, 3.

11. See my discussion of end-of-the-world prophecies and how believers respond to them in Michael Shermer, *How We Believe: The Search for God in an Age of Science* (New York: Henry Holt, 2000), 191–213.

12. Two of Leon Festinger's students documented thousands of experiments demonstrating how people spin-doctor facts to fit preconceived beliefs, in order to reduce dissonance. See Carol Tavris and Elliott Aronson, *Mistakes Were Made (but Not by Me)* (New York: Mariner Books, 2007).

13. Julian Nundy and David Graves, "Diana Crash Caused by Chauffeur, Says Report," *Daily Telegraph* (London), September 4, 1999, https://bit.ly/2TKyuw0/. See also Gordon Rayner, "Diana Jury Blames Paparazzi and Henri Paul for Her 'Unlawful Killing,'" *Daily Telegraph* (London), April 7, 2008, https://www.telegraph.co.uk/news/uknews/1584160/Diana-jury-blames-paparazzi-and-Henri-Paul-for-her-unlawful-killing.html.

14. In 2019, the number of drunk driving–related auto deaths in the United States alone was 10,142. See National Highway Traffic Safety Administration, "Drunk Driving," NHTSA, https://bit.ly/3A9N9I2/.

15. There are many conspiracy-oriented books related to the death of Princess Diana. Some examples are Dylan Howard and Colin McLaren, *Diana: Case Solved; The Definitive Account the Proves What Really Happened* (London: Skyhorse, 2019); Noel Botham, *The Murder of Princess Diana: The Truth Behind the Assassination of the People's Princess* (London: John Blake, 2018); John Morgan, *How They Murdered Princess Diana: The Shocking Truth* ([United States]: John Morgan, 2014); Jon King and John Beveridge, *Princess Diana:*

The Hidden Evidence; How MI6 and the CIA Were Involved in the Death of Princess Diana (New York: S.P.I. Books, 2009).

16. Michael J. Wood, Karen M. Douglas, and Robbie M. Sutton, "Dead and Alive: Beliefs in Contradictory Conspiracy Theories," *Social Psychological and Personality Science* 3, no. 6 (January 25, 2012), 767–773, https://bit.ly/32qMBYw/. A full text PDF of the article is available at https://bit.ly/3x2oP34/.

17. Robbie M. Sutton and Karen M. Douglas, "Examining the Monological Nature of Conspiracy Theories," in Jan Willem van Prooijen and Paul A. J. van Lange (eds.), *Power, Politics, and Paranoia: Why People Are Suspicious of Their Leaders.* (Cambridge: Cambridge University Press, 2014), 254–272.

18. Karen M. Douglas, Robbie M. Sutton, and Aleksandra Cichocka, "The Psychology of Conspiracy Theories," *Current Directions in Psychological Science* 26, no. 6 (December 7, 2017), 538–542, https://bit.ly/3v5qoeV/. A full text PDF is available at https://bit.ly/3glRjz4/.

19. Pascal Wagner-Egger, Sylvain Delouvée, Nicolas Gauvrit, and Sebastian Dieguez, "Creationism and Conspiracism Share a Common Teleological Bias," *Current Biology* 28, no. 16 (August 20, 2018), R867–R868, https://bit.ly/2QyvGRd/.

20. Stephan Lewandowsky, Klaus Oberauer, and Gilles Gignac, "NASA Fakes the Moon Landing—therefore (Climate) Science Is a Hoax: An Anatomy of the Motivated Rejection of Science," *Psychological Science* 24, no. 5 (2013), 622–633.

21. Bonnie Sherman and Ziva Kunda, "Motivated Evaluation of Scientific Evidence," paper presented at the annual meeting of the American Psychological Society, Arlington, VA, 1989.

22. Deanna Kuhn, "Children and Adults as Intuitive Scientists," *Psychological Review* 96, no. 4 (1989), 674–689.

23. Deanna Kuhn, Michael Weinstock, and Robin Flaton, "How Well Do Jurors Reason? Competence Dimensions of Individual Variation in a Juror Reasoning Task," *Psychological Science* 5, no. 5 (1994), 289–296.

24. Arthur Goldwag, *Cults, Conspiracies, and Secret Societies* (New York: Vintage, 2009), xxxi.

25. Baruch Fischhoff, "For Those Condemned to Study the Past: Heuristics and Biases in Hindsight," in Daniel Kahneman, Paul Slovic, and Amos Tversky, *Judgment Under Uncertainty: Heuristics and Biases* (Cambridge: Cambridge University Press, 1982), 335–351.

26. Presidential Commission on the Space Shuttle Challenger Accident, "Report to the President," June 6, 1986, https://go.nasa.gov/3xqvvrc/.

27. "Report of the Columbia Accident Investigation Board, Volume 1," August 26, 2003, https://go.nasa.gov/2TOwxhY/.

28. John C. Zimmerman, "Pearl Harbor Revisionism: Robert Stinnett's Day of Deceit," *Intelligence and National Security* 17, no. 2 (2002), 127–146.

29. Michael Powell, "The Disbelievers," *Washington Post*, September 8, 2006.

30. Roberta Wohlstetter, *Pearl Harbor: Warning and Decision* (Stanford, CA: Stanford University Press, 1962), 3. See also Roland H. Worth Jr., *Pearl Harbor: Selected Testimonies, Fully Indexed, from the Congressional Hearings (1945–1946) and Prior Investigations of the Events Leading Up to the Attack* (Jefferson, NC: McFarland, 2013).

31. The Bin Laden memo even has its own Wikipedia entry, "Bin Laden Determined to Strike in US," at https://bit.ly/3cQefni/.

32. Paul Thompson, *The Terror Timeline* (New York: HarperCollins, 2004), 100.

33. *The 9/11 Commission Report: Final Report of the National Commission on Terrorist Attacks Upon the United States* (Washington, DC: US Government Printing Office, 2004).

34. Grant N. Marshall, Camille B. Wortman, Ross R. Vickers, Jeffrey W. Kusulas, and Linda K. Hervig, "The Five-Factor Model of Personality as a Framework for Personality-Health Research," *Journal of Personality and Social Psychology* 67, no. 2 (1994), 278–286; Jerome Tobacyk and Gary Milford, "Belief in Paranormal Phenomena: Assessment Instrument Development and Implications for Personality Functioning," *Journal of Personality and Social Psychology* 44, no. 5 (1983), 1029–1037.

35. Tobacyk and Milford, "Belief in Paranormal Phenomena."

36. Quotation in Dez Vylenz, director, *The Mindscape of Alan Moore*, documentary film, Shadowsnake Films, 2003.

37. Wood, Douglas, and Sutton, "Dead and Alive."

38. Adam Enders and Steven M. Smallpage, "Who Are Conspiracy Theorists? A Comprehensive Approach to Explaining Conspiracy Beliefs," *Social Science Quarterly* 100, no. 6 (2019), 2017–2032.

39. Wood, Douglas, and Sutton, "Dead and Alive."

40. Errol Morris, director, *Wormwood*, docudrama TV miniseries, Netflix, 2017, https://bit.ly/3q9vK7F/.

41. Rob Brotherton, *Suspicious Minds: Why We Believe Conspiracy Theories* (New York: Bloomsbury Sigma, 2016), 80.

42. Lisa D. Butler, Cheryl Koopman, and Philip G. Zimbardo, "The Psychological Impact of Viewing the Film 'JFK': Emotions, Beliefs, and Political Behavioral Intentions," *Political Psychology* 16, no. 2 (1995), 237–257.

43. Brotherton, *Suspicious Minds*, 57.

44. Brotherton, *Suspicious Minds*, 58.

45. Keith E. Stanovich, *The Bias that Divides Us: The Science and Politics of Myside Thinking.* (Cambridge, MA: MIT Press 2021).

46. Stanovich, *Bias that Divides Us*, 1.

47. Michael Shermer, *Why People Believe Weird Things: Pseudoscience, Superstition, and Other Confusions of Our Time* (New York: St. Martin's Griffin, revised and expanded edition, 2002; originally published New York: W. H. Freeman, 1997).

48. Stanovich, *Bias that Divides Us*, 3–4.

Chapter 4. Constructive Conspiracism

1. Robert S. Mueller III, *Report on the Investigation into Russian Interference in the 2016 Presidential Election* (Washington, DC: US Department of Justice, March 2019), https://bit.ly/3x8GOVJ/.

2. Joseph Uscinski, "The 5 Most Dangerous Conspiracy Theories of 2016," Politico, August 22, 2016, https://politi.co/3e6BJEo/.

3. Adriana Cohen, "James Comey Should Be Worried About His Own Conspiracy Theory Track Record," *Boston Herald*, June 2, 2019, https://bit.ly/3gDYHW9/.

4. James Ridgeway, "After Bush-Gore: Lawsuits, Conspiracy Theories, and an Isolated Left," *Village Voice*, November 7, 2000, https://bit.ly/2RAHCSL/.

5. Jake Tapper and Avery Miller, "Conspiracy Theories Abound After Bush Victory," ABC News, November 9, 2004, https://abcn.ws/3mZFmjI/.

6. Asawin Suebsaeng and Dave Gilson, "Chart: Almost Every Obama Conspiracy Theory Ever," *Mother Jones*, November 2, 2012, https://bit.ly/3x4y2If/.

7. Avery Anapol, "Obama: If I Watched Fox News 'I Wouldn't Vote for Me,'" *The Hill*, December 1, 2017, https://bit.ly/3ebPPo8/.

8. Jan-Willem van Prooijen, personal correspondence, May 17, 2021.

9. Jared Diamond, "That Daily Shower Can Be a Killer," *New York Times*, January 28, 2013, https://nyti.ms/3duLAVv/.

10. Steven Pinker, *Rationality: What It Is, Why It Seems Scarce, Why It Matters* (New York: Viking, 2021), 307–308.

11. Napoleon Chagnon, *Yanomamö*, 5th edition (Fort Worth, TX: Harcourt, Brace, 1997), 194.

12. Interview with Kenneth Good, December 5, 2000, in Michael Shermer, "Spin-Doctoring Science: Science as a Candle in the Darkness of the Anthropology Wars," *Science Friction: Where the Known Meets the Unknown* (New York: Henry Holt, 2004), 69–90.

13. Pinker, *Rationality*, 307–308.

14. Lawrence Kelly, *Warless Societies and the Origins of War* (Ann Arbor: University of Michigan Press, 2000), 4.

15. Jan-Willem van Prooijen and Mark Van Vugt. "Conspiracy Theories: Evolved Functions and Psychological Mechanisms," *Perspectives on Psychological Science* 13, no. 6 (2018), 770–788.

16. Roy F. Baumeister, Ellen Bratslavsky, Catrin Finkenauer, and Kathleen D. Vohs, "Bad Is Stronger Than Good," *Review of General Psychology* 5, no. 4 (2001), 323–370.

17. Thomas Gilovich and Gary Belsky, *Why Smart People Make Big Money Mistakes and How to Correct Them: Lessons from the New Science of Behavioral Economics* (New York: Fireside, 2000).

18. Curry Kirkpatrick, "Cool Warmup for Jimbo," *Sports Illustrated*, April 28, 1975.

19. Opening scene of *The Armstrong Lie*, directed by Alex Gibney, documentary film, Sony Pictures Classics, 2013.

20. Roy F. Baumeister and Kenneth J. Cairns, "Repression and Self-Presentation: When Audiences Interfere with Self-Deceptive Strategies," *Journal of Personality and Social Psychology* 62, no. 5 (1992), 851–862.

21. John M. Atthowe, "Types of Conflict and Their Resolution: A Reinterpretation," *Journal of Experimental Psychology* 59, no. 1 (1960), 1–9; Sharon L. Manne, Kathryn L. Taylor, James Dougherty, and Nancy Kemeny, "Supportive and Negative Responses in the Partner Relationship: Their Association with Psychological Adjustment Among Individuals with Cancer," *Journal of Behavioral Medicine* 20, no. 2 (1997), 101–125.

22. Myron Rothbart and Bernadette Park, "On the Confirmability and Disconfirmability of Trait Concepts," *Journal of Personality and Social Psychology* 50, no. 1 (1986), 131–142.

23. James P. David, Peter J. Green, René Martin, and Jerry Suls, "Differential Roles of Neuroticism, Extraversion, and Event Desirability for Mood in Daily Life: An Integrative Model of Top-Down and Bottom-Up Influences," *Journal of Personality and Social Psychology* 73, no. 1 (1997), 149–159.

24. Kennon M. Sheldon, Richard Ryan, and Harry T. Reis, "What Makes for a Good Day? Competence and Autonomy in the Day and in the Person," *Personality and Social Psychology Bulletin* 22, no. 12 (1996), 1270–1279.

25. C. Cahill, S. P. Llewelyn, and C. Pearson, "Long-Term Effects of Sexual Abuse Which Occurred in Childhood: A Review," *British Journal of Clinical Psychology* 30, no. 2 (1991), 117–130.

26. Dwight R. Riskey and Michael H. Birnbaum, "Compensatory Effects in Moral Judgment: Two Rights Don't Make Up for a Wrong," *Journal of Experimental Psychology* 103, no. 1 (1974), 171–173.

27. J. Czapinski, "Negativity Bias in Psychology: An Analysis of Polish Publications," *Polish Psychological Bulletin* 16 (1985), 27–44.

28. Baumeister, Bratslavsky, Finkenauer, and Vohs, "Bad Is Stronger."

29. Paul Rozin and Edward B. Royzman, "Negativity Bias, Negativity Dominance, and Contagion," *Personality and Social Psychology Review* 5, no. 4 (2001), 296–320.

30. Paul Rozin, Leslie Gruss, and Geoffrey Berk, "The Reversal of Innate Aversions: Attempts to Induce a Preference for Chili Peppers in Rats," *Journal of Comparative and Physiological Psychology* 93, no. 6 (1979), 1001–1014.

31. Paul Rozin, L. Berman, and Edward B. Royzman, "Positivity and Negativity Bias in Language: Evidence from 17 Languages," unpublished manuscript, 2001.

32. Nico H. Frijda, *The Emotions* (Cambridge: Cambridge University Press, 1986).

33. The Anna Karenina principle was made prominent in Diamond, *Guns, Germs, and Steel*.

34. H. N. C. Stevenson, "Status Evaluation in the Hindu Caste System," *Journal of the Royal Anthropological Institute of Great Britain and Ireland* 84, no. 1–2 (1954), 45–65.

35. Paul Rozin and James W. Kalat, "Specific Hungers and Poison Avoidance as Adaptive Specializations of Learning," *Psychological Review* 78, no. 6 (1971), 459–486.

36. Steven Pinker, *Enlightenment Now: The Case for Reason, Science, Humanism, and Progress* (New York: Penguin, 2018) 16–19. See also Steven Pinker, "The Psychology of Pessimism," *Cato's Letter* 15, no. 1 (Winter 2015), 1–6, http://bit.ly/2eQEnhJ/; Steven Pinker, "The Second Law of Thermodynamics," in the annual question, "2017: What Scientific Term or Concept Ought to Be More Widely Known?," *Edge*, http://bit.ly/2hr7P2J/.

37. Michael Shermer, *Giving the Devil His Due: Reflections of a Scientific Humanist* (Cambridge: Cambridge University Press, 2020), 103–109.

38. Michael Shermer, *The Believing Brain: From Ghosts and Gods to Politics and Conspiracies—How We Construct Beliefs and Reinforce Them as Truths* (New York: Henry Holt, 2011), 59–86.

39. van Prooijen and Van Vugt, "Conspiracy Theories."

40. Martie G. Haselton and David M. Buss, "Error Management Theory: A New Perspective on Biases in Cross-Sex Mind Reading," *Journal of Personality and Social Psychology* 78, no. 1 (2000), 81–91. See also Steven L. Neuberg, Douglas T. Kenrick, and Mark Schaller, "Human Threat Management Systems: Self-Protection and Disease Avoidance," *Neuroscience and Biobehavioral Reviews* 35, no. 4 (2011), 1042–1051.

41. van Prooijen and Van Vugt, "Conspiracy Theories." See also John Tooby and Leda Cosmides, "Groups in Mind: The Coalitional Roots of War and Morality," in Henrik Høgh-Olesen (ed.), *Human*

Morality and Sociality: Evolutionary and Comparative Perspectives (New York: Palgrave MacMillan, 2010), 191–234.

42. David P. Schmitt and June J. Pilcher, "Evaluating Evidence of Psychological Adaptation: How Do We Know One When We See One?," *Psychological Science*, 15, no. 10 (2004), 643–649.

43. van Prooijen and Van Vugt, "Conspiracy Theories."

44. Bruce M. Hood, *Supersense: Why We Believe in the Unbelievable* (New York: HarperCollins, 2009), 213.

45. Hood, *Supersense*, 183.

46. Peter Brugger and Christine Mohr, "Out of the Body, but Not Out of the Mind," *Cortex* 45, no. 2 (2009), 137–140.

47. Peter Brugger and Christine Mohr, "The Paranormal Mind: How the Study of Anomalous Experiences and Beliefs May Inform Cognitive Neuroscience," *Cortex* 44, no. 10 (2008), 1291–1298.

48. Joshua Hart and Molly Graether, "Something's Going On Here: Psychological Predictors of Belief in Conspiracy Theories," *Journal of Individual Differences* 39, no. 4 (2018), 229–237, https://bit .ly/3vlm4ND/.

49. Roland Imhoff and Pia Lamberty, "How Paranoid Are Conspiracy Believers? Toward a More Fine-Grained Understanding of the Connect and Disconnect Between Paranoias and Belief in Conspiracy Theories," *European Journal of Social Psychology* 48, no. 7 (2018), 909–926.

50. Abraham Rabinovich, *The Yom Kippur War: The Epic Encounter That Transformed the Middle East* (New York: Schocken Books, 2004).

51. David Stahel, *Operation Barbarossa and Germany's Defeat in the East*, Cambridge Military Histories Series (Cambridge: Cambridge University Press, 2011).

52. Robert B. Stinnett, *Day of Deceit: The Truth About FDR and Pearl Harbor* (New York: Free Press, 1999).

53. James M. Naughton, "Nixon Says a President Can Order Illegal Actions Against Dissidents," *New York Times*, May 19, 1977, https://nyti.ms/32klbXn/.

54. George Orwell, "In Front of Your Nose," *Tribune* (London), March 22, 1946.

Chapter 5. A Case Study in Conspiracism

1. Isabella Grullón Paz and Michael Levenson, "11 Arrested in Armed Roadside Standoff in Massachusetts," *New York Times*, July 3, 2021, https://nyti.ms/2UXSnAe/.

2. Rise of the Moors, http://www.riseofthemoors.org/.

3. *United States of America v. Miles J. Julison*, case no. 3:11-cr-00378-SI, 2015, July 29, 2013, https://casetext.com/case /united-states-v-julison/.

4. FBI's Counterterrorism Analysis Section, "Domestic Terrorism: Sovereign Citizens a Growing Domestic Threat to Law Enforcement," Federal Bureau of Investigation, September 1, 2011, https://bit.ly/3n0yClr/.

5. "Sovereign Citizens Movement," Southern Poverty Law Center, https://bit.ly/3ajt3K4/.

6. *United States v. Julison.*

7. Peter Knight (ed.), *Conspiracy Theories in American History: An Encyclopedia*, vol. 1 (Santa Barbara, CA: ABC-CLIO, 2003).

8. Gary Felicetti and John Luce, "The Posse Comitatus Act: Setting the Record Straight on 124 Years of Mischief and Misunderstanding Before Any More Damage Is Done," *Military Law Review* 175 (2003), 86–184.

9. Quoted in Thomas Milan Konda, *Conspiracies of Conspiracies: How Delusions Have Overrun America* (Chicago: University of Chicago Press, 2019).

10. Dan Harris, "Deadly Arkansas Shooting by 'Sovereigns' Jerry and Joe Kane Who Shun U.S. Law," ABC News, July 1, 2010, https://abcn.ws/2P0nA3b/.

11. Documents provided by the attorneys for Miles Julison, now in the author's archives.

12. All of these factors are discussed and documented in Michael Shermer, *The Believing Brain: From Ghosts and Gods to Politics and Conspiracies—How We Construct Beliefs and Reinforce Them as Truths* (New York: Henry Holt, 2011).

13. I first presented the belief engine construct in Michael Shermer, *How We Believe: The Search for God in an Age of Science* (New York: W. H. Freeman, 2000).

14. Robert B. Cialdini, *Influence: The Psychology of Persuasion*, new and expanded edition (New York: Harper Business, 2021).

15. Stanley Milgram, *Obedience to Authority: An Experimental View* (New York: Harper & Row, 1969).

16. See my replication of Milgram's experiment for a two-part *Dateline NBC* special, "What Were You Thinking?," in 2010, recounted in detail in Michael Shermer, *The Moral Arc: How Science and Reason Lead Humanity Toward Truth, Justice, and Freedom* (New York: Henry Holt, 2015). The videos are available online at https://bit.ly/3xqfGAO/.

17. Robert B. Cialdini, "Harnessing the Science of Persuasion," *Harvard Business Review* 79, no. 9 (2001), 72–79; Robert B. Cialdini, Wilhelmina Wosinska, Daniel W. Baret, Jonathan Butner, and Malgorzata Gornik-Durose, "Compliance with a Request in Two Cultures: The Differential Influence of Social Proof and Commitment/Consistency on Collectivists and Individualists," *Personality and Social Psychology Bulletin* 25, no. 10 (1999): 1242–1253.

18. Brian Collisson and Jennifer Lee Howell, "The Liking-Similarity Effect: Perceptions of Similarity as a Function of Liking," *Journal of Social Psychology* 154, no. 5 (2014), 384–400.

19. Mark A. Adams, "Reinforcement Theory and Behavior Analysis," *Behavioral Development Bulletin* 9, no. 1 (2000), 3–6. See also Douglas J. Navarick, *Principles of Learning: From Laboratory to Field* (New York: Addison-Wesley, 1979).

20. Raymond Nickerson, "Confirmation Bias: A Ubiquitous Phenomenon in Many Guises," *Review of General Psychology* 2, no. 2 (1998), 175–220.

21. Mark Snyder, "Seek and Ye Shall Find: Testing Hypotheses About Other People," in Edward Tory Higgins, C. Peter Herman, and Mark P. Zanna (eds.), *Social Cognition: The Ontario Symposium on Personality and Social Psychology* (Hillsdale, NJ: Erlbaum, 1981), 277–303.

22. Daniel Kahneman, *Thinking: Fast and Slow* (New York: Farrar, Straus & Giroux, 2011), 113.

23. Kahneman, *Thinking*, 255.

24. Michael Shermer, *Why People Believe Weird Things: Pseudoscience, Superstition, and Other Confusions of Our Time* (New York: St. Martin's Griffin, revised and expanded edition, 2002; originally published New York: W. H. Freeman, 1997), 279.

25. Philip Tetlock, *Expert Political Judgment: How Good Is It? How Can We Know?* (Princeton, NJ: Princeton University Press, 2005).

26. Koen A. Dijkstra and Ying-yi Hong, "The Feeling of Throwing Good Money After Bad: The Role of Affective Reaction in the Sunk-Cost Fallacy," *PLoS One* 14, no. 1 (January 8, 2019), e0209900; Hal R. Arkes and Catherine Blumer, "The Psychology of Sunk Cost," *Organizational Behavior and Human Decision Processes* 35, no. 1 (1985), 124–140.

27. Daniel Kahneman, Jack Knetsch, and Richard Thaler, "Experimental Tests of the Endowment Effect and the Coase Theorem," *Journal of Political Economy* 98, no. 6 (December 1990), 1325–1348.

Chapter 6. The Conspiracy Detection Kit

1. Mick West, *Escaping the Rabbit Hole: How to Debunk Conspiracy Theories Using Facts, Logic, and Respect* (New York: Skyhorse, 2018).

2. Gerald Posner, *Pharma: Greed, Lies, and the Poisoning of America* (New York: Simon & Schuster, 2020). See also Patrick Radden Keefe, *Empire of Pain: The Secret History of the Sackler Dynasty* (New York: Doubleday, 2021).

3. Tapio Schneider, "How We Know Global Warming Is Real: The Science Behind Human-Induced Climate Change," *Skeptic* 14,

no. 1 (2008), 31–37, https://bit.ly/3x8khsz/. See also Donald Pro-thero, "How We Know Global Warming Is Real and Human Caused," Skeptics Society Forum, February 8, 2021, https://bit.ly /3qWmc2m/.

4. Paul Sabin, *The Bet: Paul Ehrlich, Sulian Simon, and Our Gamble Over Earth's Future* (New Haven, CT: Yale University Press, 2013).

5. Daniel Loxton, "Understanding Flat Earthers," *Skeptic* 24, no. 4 (2019), 10–23.

6. Milton Rokeach, *The Three Christs of Ypsilanti* (New York: New York Review Books, 2011; originally published New York: Knopf, 1964).

7. Jon Henley, "US Invented Air Attack on Pentagon, Claims French Book," *Guardian* (Manchester), April 1, 2002.

8. West, *Escaping the Rabbit Hole*.

9. Karl Popper, *The Logic of Scientific Discovery* (London: Hutchin-son, 1959; originally published New York: Basic Books, 1954).

10. Popper, *Logic of Scientific Discovery*, 18.

11. Carl Sagan, *The Demon-Haunted World: Science as a Candle in the Dark* (New York: Random House, 1996), 201–218.

12. Brian S. Everitt, *The Cambridge Dictionary of Statistics* (Cambridge: Cambridge University Press, 1998).

13. David Hume, *An Enquiry Concerning Human Understanding* (New York: Oxford University Press, 1999; originally published London: printed for A. Miller, 1748).

14. Carl Sagan, "Encyclopaedia Galactica," episode 12, *Cosmos*, documentary series, PBS, 1980.

15. Thomas Bayes, "An Essay Toward Solving a Problem in the Doctrine of Chances," *Philosophical Transactions of the Royal Society of London* 53 (1764), 370–418. See also *Stanford Encyclopedia of Philosophy* online, under "Bayes' Theorem," https://stanford.io /2S0lqlO/.

16. For example, see Joseph E. Uscinski (ed.), *Conspiracy Theo-ries and the People Who Believe Them* (Oxford: Oxford University Press, 2019), 347–394.

17. Leonard Mlodinow, *The Drunkard's Walk: How Randomness Rules Our Lives* (New York: Pantheon, 2007).

18. Gary Smith, *Standard Deviations: Flawed Assumptions, Tortured Data, and Other Ways to Lie with Statistics* (New York: Abrams, 2014).

19. Ben Cohen, "Spotify Made Its Shuffle Feature Less Random So That It Would Actually Feel More Random to Listeners—here's Why." *Business Insider*, March 16, 2020, https://bit.ly/3xjxSvS/.

20. Mlodinow, *The Drunkard's Walk*.

21. Epigram in Jesse Walker, *The United States of Paranoia: A Conspiracy Theory* (New York: Harper Perennial, 2013), vii.

22. David Aaronovitch, *Voodoo Histories: The Role of the Conspiracy Theory in Shaping Modern History* (New York: Riverhead, 2010), 356.

Chapter 7. Truthers and Birthers

1. I recounted this episode in Michael Shermer, "Paranoia Strikes Deep," *Scientific American* 301, no. 3 (September 1, 2009), 30–31, https://bit.ly/3tywEv5/.

2. These claims by 9/11 Truthers, and many more, were outlined and debunked by *Popular Mechanics* in one of the best analyses of the subject to date, now expanded into book form. See David Dunbar, Brad Reagan, and James B. Meigs, *Debunking 9/11 Myths: Why Conspiracy Theories Can't Stand Up to the Facts* (New York: Hearst Books, 2011).

3. Thierry Meyssan, *L'Effroyable imposture* (Chatou, France: Carnot, 2002).

4. Jim Marrs, *Inside Job: Unmasking the 9/11 Conspiracies* (San Rafael, CA: Origin Press, 2004); David Ray Griffin, *The New Pearl Harbor: Disturbing Questions about the Bush Administration and 9/11* (n.p.: Interlink, 2004); David Ray Griffin and Elizabeth Woodworth, *9/11 Unmasked: An International Review Panel Investigation* (Northampton, MA: Olive Branch Press / Interlink, 2018); George Humphrey, *9/11: The Great Illusion; End Game of the Illuminati; Our Choice: Fear or Love?* (n.p.: Common Sense, 2002).

5. Thierry Meyssan, *Before Our Very Eyes, Fake Wars, and Big Lies: From 9/11 to Donald Trump* (n.p.: Progressive Press, 2019).

6. The text string "9/11 truth organizations" in a search window will take you to these and additional organizations.

7. Mark Fenster, *Conspiracy Theories: Secrecy and Power in American Culture* (Minneapolis: University of Minnesota Press, 2008), 242.

8. 9-11 Research, "An Attempt to Uncover the Truth About September 11th, 2001," https://911research.wtc7.net. This organization carries a disclaimer: "9-11 Research does not promote incivility, junk science, or 'no-jetliner' claims—to distance themselves from even more fringier elements in this community."

9. Thomas W. Eagar and Christopher Musso, "Why Did the World Trade Center Collapse? Science, Engineering and Speculation," *Journal of the Minerals, Metals & Materials Society* 53, no. 12 (2001), 8–11.

10. Phil Molé, "9/11 Conspiracy Theories: The 9/11 Truth Movement in Perspective," *Skeptic* 12, no. 4 (2011), https://bit.ly/3gpfg6R/.

11. You can read Brent Blanchard's entire analysis at his website, www.implosionworld.com.

12. "The fall of Building 7 with all of the characteristics of a controlled demolition is the focus of the ongoing campaign called *Remember Building 7*," WTC7 website, https://wtc7.net.

13. Chris Mohr, "9/11 and the Science of Controlled Demolitions," eSkeptic, September 7, 2011, https://www.skeptic.com/eskeptic/11-09-07/.

14. Dylan Avery, director, Loose Change 9/11: An American Coup, documentary film, Microcinema International, 2009, https://loosechange911.com.

15. This type of argument is very common in pseudoscience and fringe science. For example, if anything remains unexplained by the theory of evolution, then creationism must be true. Or, if I can't figure out how the pyramids were built, then they can't have been built by the ancient Egyptians.

16. Quoted in Popular Mechanics Editors, "Myths About the 9/11 Pentagon Attack: Debunked," Popular Mechanics, September 7, 2021, https://bit.ly/3wlUAU0/.

17. Brian Keith Dalton, director, "You Can't Handle the Truther," video, YouTube, 2013, https://bit.ly/2TP5WRZ/.

18. "Remarks by the President on Teaching American History and Civic Education," White House archives, September 17, 2002, https://bit.ly/3jwJfgv/.

19. Popular Mechanics Editors, "Debunking the 9/11 Myths: The Airplanes," September 10, 2021, https://bit.ly/3oPIpfy/.

20. Neal J. Roese and Kathleen D. Vohs, "Hindsight Bias," Perspectives on Psychological Science 7, no. 5 (2012), 411–426.

21. Roese and Vohs, "Hindsight Bias."

22. Quoted in David Mikkelson, "Were Stocks of Airlines Shorted Just Before 9/11?," Snopes, October 3, 2001, https://bit.ly/3tJFJkM/.

23. Quoted in Beata Safrany, "9/11 Conspiracy Theories," Hungarian Journal of English and American Studies 19, no. 2 (2013), 11–30.

24. Amos Tversky and Daniel Kahneman, "Extensional versus Intuitive Reasoning: The Conjunction Fallacy in Probability Judgment," Psychological Review 90, no. 4 (1983), 293–315.

25. Vincent Bugliosi, Reclaiming History: The Assassination of President John F. Kennedy (New York: W. W. Norton, 2007), xliii.

26. Jonathan Kay, Among the Truthers: A Journey Through America's Growing Conspiracist Underground (New York: Harper-Collins, 2011), 312.

27. During Obama's eight years in office, various conspiracists made these exact accusations against the president.

28. Josh Clinton and Carrie Roush, "Poll: Persistent Partisan Divide Over 'Birther' Question," NBC News, August 10, 2016, https://nbcnews.to/3czLlrB/.

29. Kyle Dropp and Brendan Nyhan, "It Lives: Birtherism Is Diminished but Far from Dead," New York Times, September 23, 2016, https://nyti.ms/2TjXEBq/. See also Kaleigh Rogers, "The

Birther Myth Stuck Around for Years: The Election Fraud Myth Might Too," *FiveThirtyEight*, November 23, 2020, https://53eig.ht /3vfGWR1/; "Half of 'Birthers' Call It 'Suspicion': A Third Approve of Obama Anyway," ABC News/*Washington Post* Poll: Birthers, May 7, 2010, https://abcn.ws/3cy5HS4/.

30. Quoted in B. J. Reyes, "Certified," (Honolulu) *Star-Bulletin* [now *Star-Advertiser*], October 31, 2008, https://bit.ly/30NdnNt/.

31. Lisa Marie Segarra, "Watch John McCain Strongly Defend Barack Obama During the 2008 Campaign," *Time*, originally published July 20, 2017, updated August 25, 2018. A video of the exchange is available at https://bit.ly/3jZW2qi/.

32. Quoted in Robert Farley, "Obama's Birth Certificate: Final Chapter; This Time We Mean It!," *PolitiFact*, July 1, 2009, https:// bit.ly/3wjcd6O/.

33. PolitiFact ended up publishing three rebuttals to the Birther claims. See Amy Hollyfield, "Obama's Birth Certificate: Final Chapter," *PolitiFact*, originally published June 27, 2008, then updated March 2011, https://bit.ly/3grHJsF/; Farley, "Obama's Birth Certificate.

34. For a chronological summary of events surrounding the development of the Birther movement, see Martha M. Hamilton, *PolitiFact*, April 27, 2011, https://bit.ly/3CCJXP4/.

35. *Economist*/YouGov Poll, conducted December 3–5, 2017, https://bit.ly/32vbt18/.

36. Ashley Jardina and Michael Traugott, "The Genesis of the Birther Rumor: Partisanship, Racial Attitudes, and Political Knowledge," *Journal of Race, Ethnicity, and Politics* 4, no. 1 (2018), 60–80, https://bit.ly/3strbV7/.

Chapter 8. JFK Blown Away

1. *The Warren Commission Report: The Official Report on the Assassination of President John F. Kennedy*, PDF, September 27, 1964, GPO: US Government Bookstore, https://bit.ly/3gocb8w/.

2. US House of Representatives, *Report of the Select Committee on Assassinations*, March 1979, JFK Assassination Records, National Archives, https://bit.ly/3mZFi3r/; Gerald Posner, *Case Closed: Lee Harvey Oswald and the Assassination of JFK* (New York: Random House, 1993); Vincent Bugliosi, *Reclaiming History: The Assassination of President John F. Kennedy* (New York: W. W. Norton, 2007). For a new and definitive debunking of JFK conspiracy theories, see Michel Jacques Gagné, *Thinking Critically About the Kennedy Assassination: Debunking the Myths and Conspiracy Theories* (New York: Routledge, 2022).

3. Michel Gagné, personal correspondence, September 23, 2021.

4. Quoted in a *Playboy* interview with Jim Garrison, October 1967, John F. Kennedy assassination media collection, UMass Dartmouth ArchivesSpace, https://bit.ly/3oL0QlC/. Note that published materials may be accessed in person only.

5. "Papers of Jim Garrison," JFK Assassination Records, National Archives, https://bit.ly/2P1e6Vo/.

6. US House of Representatives, *Select Committee on Assassinations*.

7. Markus Schmidt, "Sabato: Audio Analysis Debunks Theory of Fourth Shot at JFK," *Richmond Times-Dispatch*, October 16, 2013, https://bit.ly/3dx7R5m/.

8. Bugliosi, *Reclaiming History*, xxiv.

9. Rushmore DeNooyer, director, "Cold Case JFK," documentary, *Nova* series, PBS, November 13, 2013.

10. Todd Kwait and Rob Stegman, directors, *Truth Is the Only Client: The Official Investigation of the Murder of John F. Kennedy*, documentary film, BlueStar Media, Ezzie Films, 2019.

11. Dana Blanton, "Poll: Most Believe 'Cover-Up' of JFK Assassination Facts," Fox News Poll, originally published June 18, 2004, updated November 23, 2015, https://fxn.ws/3sxEmEo/.

12. CBS News.com Staff, "CBS Poll: JFK Conspiracy Lives," CBS News, November 20, 1998, https://cbsn.ws/3dx9Kis/.

13. Gary Langer, "Poll: Lingering Suspicion Over JFK Assassination." ABC News, November 16, 2003, https://abcn.ws/3goWtds/.

14. Art Swift, "Majority in U.S. Still Believe JFK Killed in a Conspiracy: Mafia, Federal Government Top List of Potential Conspirators," Gallup News, November 15, 2013, https://bit.ly/3eiSnki/.

15. The Voice of Wilkinson, "What Aren't They Telling Us? Chapman University Survey of American Fears," October 11, 2016, https://bit.ly/3amYnY9/.

16. Full results of the Skeptic Research Center study on conspiracy theory beliefs, along with beliefs in the paranormal and supernatural, will be published in the coming years in professional journals, with preliminary reports to be published sooner in *Skeptic* magazine. For more information, see Skeptic Research Center, https://www.skeptic.com/research-center/.

17. Bugliosi, *Reclaiming History*, xxv.

18. Oliver Stone, director, JFK, film, Warner Bros., 1991, https://imdb.to/2QGTtOD/. The filmscript is available at https://sfy.ru/?script=jfk/.

19. The scene was so well known that it was even reenacted in an episode of the NBC comedy series *Seinfeld*, in a convoluted set-up in which Kramer gets hit in the head by the expectorate of professional baseball player Keith Hernandez at a Yankees game,

causing Kramer's head to snap "back and to the left." Included in the scene was Jerry Seinfeld's nemesis, Newman, played by Wayne Knight, who also stared in Oliver Stone's film JFK.

20. David Reitzes, "JFK Conspiracy Theories at 50: How the Skeptics Got It Wrong and Why It Matters," *Skeptic* 18, no. 3 (2013), 36–51, https://bit.ly/3apHqfL/.

21. William Cran and Ben Loeterman, producers, "Who Was Lee Harvey Oswald?," episode 4, *Frontline* series, PBS, November 19, 2013, https://to.pbs.org/32seYWb/.

22. All the facts presented here come from Posner, *Case Closed*, and Cran and Loeterman, "Who Was Lee Harvey Oswald?"

23. Delroy L. Paulhus and Kevin M. Williams, "The Dark Triad of Personality: Narcissism, Machiavellianism, and Psychopathy," *Journal of Research in Personality* 36, no. 6 (2002), 556–563.

24. Bugliosi, *Reclaiming History*, 1116.

25. Elizabeth Loftus and John C. Palmer, "Reconstruction of Automobile Destruction: An Example of the Interaction Between Language and Memory," *Journal of Verbal Learning and Verbal Behavior* 13, no. 5 (1974), 585–589.

26. Maryanne Garry, Charles G. Manning, Elizabeth F. Loftus, and Steven J. Sherman, "Imagination Inflation: Imagining a Childhood Event Inflates Confidence That It Occurred," *Psychonomic Bulletin and Review* 3, no. 2 (1996), 208–214.

27. Bugliosi, *Reclaiming History*, 90.

28. Reitzes, "JFK Conspiracy Theories."

29. Errol Morris, "The Umbrella Man," *New York Times*, November 21, 2011, https://nyti.ms/3y5CupA/. See also "Umbrella Man," *The JFK 100*, https://bit.ly/2REA4hS/.

30. Nicholas R. Nailli, "Gunshot-Wound Dynamics Model for John F. Kennedy Assassination," *Heliyon* 4, no. 4 (April 30, 2018), https://bit.ly/3gaA3vM/.

31. Dale K. Myers, "Summary of Conclusions, 2: The Relative Positions of JFK and JBC at Zapruder Frame 223–224," Secrets of a Homicide: JFK Assassination, 2008, https://bit.ly/3tsVj4i/.

32. See Dale K. Myers's animation in a clip from "The Kennedy Assassination: Beyond Conspiracy," ABC News documentary, November 20, 2004, https://bit.ly/3dzIYpD/.

33. A photograph of the bullet appeared in Reitzes, "JFK Conspiracy Theories."

34. There are a number of enhanced versions of the Zapruder film online that are slowed down, so you can clearly see the head shot. For example, see "John F. Kennedy Assassination—Zapruder Film (Improved Quality)," video, YouTube, 2013, https://bit.ly/3xiaCPR/.

35. Michael Shermer, *The Believing Brain: From Ghosts and Gods to Politics and Conspiracies—how We Construct Beliefs and Reinforce Them as Truths* (New York: Henry Holt, 2011), 59–86.

36. John McAdams, *JFK Assassination Logic: How to Think About Claims of Conspiracy* (Washington, DC: Potomac Books, 2011), ix.

37. Bugliosi, *Reclaiming History*, xxv.

38. James Swanson, "Inventing Camelot: How Jackie Kennedy Shaped Her Husband's Legacy," *New York Post*, November 10, 2013, https://bit.ly/3qQsyAa/.

39. Quoted in Scott Bomboy, "What If JFK Had Survived His Assassination?," *Constitution Daily*, November 22, 2015, https://rb .gy/zfnrlp/.

Chapter 9. Real Conspiracies

1. Quoted in Kathryn S. Olmsted, *Real Enemies: Conspiracy Theories and American Democracy, World War I to 9/11*, 2nd edition (New York: Oxford University Press, 2019), epigram.

2. Manuel Eisner, "Killing Kings: Patterns of Regicide in Europe, 600–1800," *British Journal of Criminology* 51, no. 3 (2011) 556–577.

3. Peter Gill, Pavel L. Ivanov, Colin Kimpton, Romelle Piercy, Nicola Benson, Gillian Tully Ian Evett, Erika Hagelberg, and Kevin Sullivan, "Identification of the Remains of the Romanov Family by DNA Analysis," *Nature Genetics* 6, no. 2 (February 1994), 130–135, https://bit.ly/3cyPpbh/. See also Michael D. Coble, "The Identification of the Romanovs: Can We (Finally) Put the Controversies to Rest?," *Investigative Genetics* 2, no. 20 (September 26, 2011), https://bit.ly/3iDFRQi/.

4. Michael D. Coble, Odile M. Loreille, Mark J. Wadhams, Suni M. Edson, Kerry Maynard, Carna E. Meyer; Harald Nieder-stätter, et al., "Mystery Solved: The Identification of the Two Missing Romanov Children Using DNA Analysis," *PLoS One* 4, no. 3 (March 11, 2009), e4838, https://bit.ly/3iPeFOP/.

5. Edward Steers, *The Lincoln Assassination Encyclopedia* (New York: Harper Perennial, 2010).

6. Candice Millard, *Destiny of the Republic: A Tale of Madness, Medicine and the Murder of a President* (New York: Doubleday, 2011).

7. Scott Miller, *The President and the Assassin: McKinley, Terror, and Empire at the Dawn of the American Century* (New York: Random House, 2011).

8. Willard M. Oliver and Nancy E. Marion, *Killing the President: Assassinations, Attempts, and Rumored Attempts on U.S. Commanders-in-Chief* (Santa Barbara, CA: Praeger)<ABC-CLIO published the eBook, not the print book>, 2010).

9. Theodore Roosevelt, speech, delivered at Milwaukee, Wisconsin, October 14, 1912, Theodore Roosevelt Association, https://bit.ly /3l2LpnY/.

10. Quoted in Ewen MacAskill, "The CIA Has a Long History of Helping to Kill Leaders Around the World," *Guardian* (Manchester), May 5, 2017, https://bit.ly/2RRQvrM/.

11. Chairman, Joint Chiefs of Staff, 1962 "Justification for US Military Intervention in Cuba," National Security Archive, March 13, 1962, https://bit.ly/3x7tErZ/.

12. US House of Representatives, *Report of the Select Committee on Assassinations*, March 1979, JFK Assassination Records, National Archives, https://bit.ly/3mZFi3r/.

13. Quoted in James Bamford, *Body of Secrets: Anatomy of the Ultra-Secret National Security Agency* (New York: Doubleday, 2001), 89.

14. Boyd M. Johnson III, "Executive Order 12,333: The Permissibility of an American Assassination of a Foreign Leader," *Cornell International Law Journal* 23, no. 2, article 6 (Spring 1992), 401–435, https://bit.ly/3xgB5w3/.

15. Frank Church, Chairman, US Senate, *Senate Select Committee to Study Governmental Operations with Respect to Intelligence Activities* (The Church Committee), April 29, 1976, https://bit.ly/3dwPpcU/.

16. Gerald R. Ford, "United States Foreign Intelligence Activities," Executive Order No. 11,905, *Weekly Compilation of Presidential Documents* 12, no. 8 (February 23, 1976), https://bit.ly/3pMhl0U/; Executive Order No. 12,333, 3 C.F.R. 200 (1981).

17. Gerald R. Ford, "The President's News Conference," South Bend, Indiana, March 17, 1975, Papers, 361, 363, in "Documents," The American Presidency Project, https://bit.ly/3FxP3hb/.

18. Quoted in Eric L. Chase, "Should We Kill Saddam?," *Newsweek*, February 18. 1991.

19. "War in the Gulf: The President; Transcript of the Comments by Bush on the Air Strikes Against the Iraqis," *New York Times*, January 17, 1991, A14.

20. Church, *Senate Select Committee*.

21. The text of Justice Holmes' opinion in *Schenck v. United States*, 249 U.S. 47, March 3, 1919, is available at https://bit.ly/1NSOD88/.

22. You can see and read the two original fliers in Wikipedia, at https://bit.ly/2BbQWBv/.

23. US Espionage Act, June 15, 1917, firstworldwar.com, https://bit.ly/2G1y2Bi/.

24. Reuters staff, "U.S. Spy Agency Tapped German Chancellery for Decades: WikiLeaks," Reuters, July 9, 2015, https://reut.rs/3x8UiRm/.

25. *Pentagon Papers*, National Archives, https://bit.ly/3xb0rNk/. See also Elizabeth Becker, "Public Lies and Secret Truths," *New York Times*, June 9, 2021, F2–F3, https://nyti.ms/2SxDALT/.

26. Errol Morris, director, *The Fog of War: Eleven Lessons from the Life of Robert S. McNamara*, documentary, Sony Pictures, 2003. A transcript for *The Fog of War* is available at https://bit.ly/2W33w3e/.

27. Errol Morris, director, *The Unknown Known*, documentary, Participant Media, 2013.

28. "Julian Assange: A Timeline of Wikileaks Founder's Case," BBC News, November 19, 2019, https://bbc.in/2RMr7mS/.

29. See Philip Zimbardo, *The Lucifer Effect: Understanding How Good People Turn Evil* (New York: Random House, 2007).

30. "List of Material Published by WikiLeaks," Wikipedia, https://bit.ly/3txnTS1/.

Chapter 10. The Deadliest Conspiracy in History

1. Christopher Clark, *The Sleepwalkers: How Europe Went to War in 1914* (New York: Allen Lane, 2012).

2. Tim Butcher, *The Trigger: Hunting the Assassin Who Brought the World to War* (New York: Grove Press, 2014).

3. Butcher, *The Trigger*.

4. Clark, *The Sleepwalkers*.

5. Butcher, *The Trigger*.

6. Andreas Prochaska, director, *Sarajevo*, TV movie, Netflix, 2014, https://bit.ly/3pMVmH3/.

7. Clark, *The Sleepwalkers*.

8. Clark, *The Sleepwalkers*, 453.

9. Oona A. Hathaway and Scott J. Shapiro, *The Internationalists: How a Radical Plan to Outlaw War Remade the World* (New York: Simon & Schuster, 2017).

10. Hathaway and Shapiro, *The Internationalists*, 43–44.

11. Hathaway and Shapiro, *The Internationalists*, 108.

12. Hathaway and Shapiro, *The Internationalists*, 375.

13. "In Memory of the Vietnam War: 'Waist Deep in the Big Muddy,'" CTD: Country Thang Daily, https://bit.ly/32rXBoo/.

14. Bruce Russett and John Oneal, *Triangulating Peace: Democracy, Interdependence, and International Organizations* (New York: W. W. Norton, 2001).

15. Hathaway and Shapiro, *The Internationalists*, 312–318.

16. Hathaway and Shapiro, *The Internationalists*, 314.

17. "Power and Authority," Lord Acton Quote Archive, Acton Institute, https://bit.ly/3nak57b/.

Chapter 11. Real and Imagined Enemies

1. Kathryn S. Olmsted, *Real Enemies: Conspiracy Theories and American Democracy, World War I to 9/11*, 2nd edition (New York: Oxford University Press, 2019).

2. Olmsted, *Real Enemies*, 4.

3. Olmsted, *Real Enemies*, 152–155.

4. Frank Church, Chairman, US Senate, *Senate Select Committee to Study Governmental Operations with Respect to Intelligence Activities* (The Church Committee), April 29, 1976, https://bit.ly /3dwPpcU/. See also Stephen Kinzer, *Poisoner in Chief: Sidney Gottlieb and the CIA Search for Mind Control* (New York: Henry Holt, 2019).

5. Errol Morris, director, *Wormwood*, docudrama TV miniseries, Netflix, 2011, https://bit.ly/3q9vK7F/.

6. Kathleen Taylor, *Brainwashing: The Science of Thought Control* (Oxford: Oxford University Press, 2004).

7. Olmsted, *Real Enemies*, 178–183.

8. Olmsted, *Real Enemies*, 182.

9. Michael Shermer, "Understanding the Unidentified," Quillette, June 3, 2021, https://bit.ly/2SsBf4I/.

10. Office of the Director of National Intelligence, "Preliminary Assessment: Unidentified Aerial Phenomena," June 25, 2021, https://bit.ly/3haOHTk/.

11. Facts and quotes in this section are from B. D. "Duke" Gildenberg, "A Roswell Requiem," *Skeptic*, 10, no. 1 (2003), 60–73; Donald Prothero and Tim Callahan, *UFOs, Chemtrails, and Aliens: What Science Says* (Bloomington: Indiana University Press, 2017); Karl T. Pflock, *Roswell: Inconvenient Facts and the Will to Believe* (Buffalo, NY: Prometheus Books, 2001).

12. Charles Berlitz and William T. Moore, *The Roswell Incident* (New York: Grosset & Dunlap, 1980); Kevin D. Randle and Donald R. Schmitt, *UFO Crash at Roswell* (New York: Avon Books, 1991); Don Berliner and Stanton T. Friedman, *Crash at Corona: The U.S. Military Retrieval and Cover-Up of a UFO* (New York: Paraview, 2004; originally published New York: Marlowe, 1992)

13. Gildenberg, "A Roswell Requiem."

14. For a good skeptical analysis of Area 51, see Donald Prothero, "Area 51: What Is Really Going On There? UFOs and U-2s, Aliens, and Q-12s," *Skeptic* 22, no. 2 (2017). For a less skeptical but still excellent history of the military base, see Annie Jacobsen, *Area 51: An Uncensored History of America's Top Secret Military Base* (New York: Little, Brown, 2011).

15. Leslie Kean, *UFOs: Generals, Pilots, and Government Officials Go On the Record* (New York: Harmony Books, 2010), 12.

16. For good, scholarly histories of this period, see Thomas C. Leonard, *Illiberal Reformers: Race, Eugenics, and American Economics in the Progressive Era* (Princeton, NJ: Princeton University Press, 2016); Edwin Black, *War Against the Weak: Eugenics and America's Campaign to Create a Master Race* (New York: Four Walls

Eight Windows, 2003); Dan Kevles, *In the Name of Eugenics: Genetics and the Uses of Human Heredity* (New York: Knopf, 1985). Also see Michael Shermer and Alex Grobman, *Denying History: Who Says the Holocaust Never Happened and Why Do They Say It?* (Berkeley: University of California Press, 2000).

17. Black, *War Against the Weak*.

18. James H. Jones, *Bad Blood: The Tuskegee Syphilis Experiment*, new and expanded edition (New York: Free Press, 1993; originally published 1981).

19. Naomi Oreskes and Erik M. Conway, *Merchants of Doubt: How a Handful of Scientists Obscured the Truth on Issues from Tobacco Smoke to Climate Change* (New York: Bloomsbury, 2010).

20. Lisa A. Bero, "Tobacco Industry Manipulation of Research," *Public Health Reports* 120, no. 2 (March–April 2005), 200.

21. Quoted in Oreskes and Conway, *Merchants of Doubt*.

22. Quoted in Oreskes and Conway, *Merchants of Doubt*.

23. Robert Kenner, director, *Food, Inc.*, documentary film, Magnolia Pictures, 2008.

24. Robert Kenner, director, *Merchants of Doubt*, documentary film, Sony Picture Classics, 2014, https://imdb.to/3x91f4y/. See also Oreskes and Conway, *Merchants of Doubt*.

25. Nancy L. Rosenblum and Russell Muirhead, *A Lot of People Are Saying: The New Conspiracism and the Assault on Democracy* (Princeton, NJ: Princeton University Press, 2019).

26. Rosenblum and Muirhead, *A Lot of People*, 3.

27. Deborah A. Prentice and Dale T. Miller, "Pluralistic Ignorance and Alcohol Use on Campus: Some Consequences of Misperceiving the Social Norm," *Journal of Personality and Social Psychology* 64, no. 2 (February 1993), 243–256, https://bit.ly/3txlN4E/.

28. Tracy A. Lambert, Arnold S. Kahn, and Kevin J. Apple, "Pluralistic Ignorance and Hooking Up," *Journal of Sex Research* 40, no. 2 (May 2003), 129–133.

29. Michael W. Macy, Robb Willer, and Ko Kuwabara, "The False Enforcement of Unpopular Norms," *American Journal of Sociology* 115, no. 2 (September 2009), 451–490.

30. Hugo Mercier, *Not Born Yesterday: The Science of Who We Trust and What We Believe* (Princeton, NJ: Princeton University Press, 2020), chapter 10.

31. Steven Pinker, *Rationality: What It Is, Why It Seems Scarce, Why It Matters* (New York: Viking, 2021).

32. Jemima McEvoy, "3 in 10 Republicans Believe Wacky Conspiracy Theory Trump Will Be 'Reinstated' as President This Year, Poll Shows," *Forbes*, June 9, 2021, https://bit.ly/2SugW78/.

33. Macy, Willer, and Kuwabara, "False Enforcement."

Chapter 12. How to Talk to Conspiracy Theorists

1. Michael Shermer, "Fahrenheit 2777," *Scientific American* 292, no. 6 (June 1, 2005), 38, https://bit.ly/3trCRsJ/.

2. The title of my Chapman University First-Year Foundations course is "Skepticism 101: How to Think Like a Scientist."

3. John Stuart Mill, *On Liberty* (New York: Dover, 2002; originally published London: John W. Parker & Son, 1859), text available at https://bit.ly/2xKHu5u/.

4. Peter G. Boghossian and James A. Lindsay, *How to Have Impossible Conversations: A Very Practical Guide* (New York: Life-Long Books, 2019), 43–46.

5. Boghossian and Lindsay, *Impossible Conversations*, 72–77.

6. Boghossian and Lindsay, *Impossible Conversations*, 79.

7. See the Quote Investigator website, https://bit.ly/2QtkKnM/.

8. Francis Collins, *The Language of God: A Scientist Presents Evidence for Belief* (New York: Free Press, 2006).

9. Thomas Jefferson, letter to William Hamilton, April 22, 1800, cited in Boghossian and Lindsay, *Impossible Conversations*, 72.

Chapter 13. How to Rebuild Trust in Truth

1. Pew Poll, "Americans' Views of Government: Low Trust, but Some Positive Performance Ratings," Pew Research Center, September 14, 2020, https://pewrsr.ch/3hgcukG/.

2. Kashmira Gander, "Lying Has Become More Acceptable in American Politics: Poll," *Newsweek*, October 21, 2020, https://bit.ly/3y2ZANS/.

3. Matt Grossmann and David A. Hopkins, "How Information Became Ideological," *Inside Higher Education*, October 11, 2016, https://bit.ly/3w3fXZ6/.

4. James Clayton, "Social Media: Is It Really Biased Against US Republicans?," BBC News, October 27, 2020, https://bbc.in/3hge0TU/.

5. Lee Rainie, Scott Keeter, and Andrew Perrin, "Trust and Distrust in America," Pew Research Center, July 22, 2019, https://pewrsr.ch/3humya7/.

6. Glenn Kessler, Salvador Rizzo, and Meg Kelly, "Trump's False or Misleading Claims Total 30,573 Over 4 Years," Fact Checker, *Washington Post*, January 24, 2021.

7. Glenn Kessler, Adrian Blanco, and Tyler Remmel, "The False and Misleading Claims President Biden Made During His First 100 Days in Office," Fact Checker, *Washington Post*, originally published April 26, 2021, updated April 30, 2021, https://wapo.st/2UD9pDC/; E. J. Dionne Jr., "Biden Admits Plagiarism in School but Says It Was Not 'Malevolent,'" *New York Times*, September 18, 1987, https://nyti.ms/3A7hgd6/.

8. Andrew Sullivan, "When All the Media Narratives Collapse," *The Weekly Dish*, November 12, 2021, https://bit.ly/3FzUMmW/.

9. Angie D. Holan, "All Politicians Lie: Some Lie More Than Others," *New York Times*, December 11, 2015.

10. Jason M. Breslow, "Obama on Mass Government Surveillance, Then and Now," *Frontline* series, PBS, May 13, 2014, https://to.pbs.org/3pPhMaB/.

11. Jonathan Stein and Tim Dickinson, "Lie by Lie: A Timeline of How We Got into Iraq," *Mother Jones*, September/October 2006.

12. Christopher Hitchens, *No One Left to Lie To: The Triangulations of William Jefferson Clinton* (New York: Verso, 1999).

13. Malcolm Byrne, *Iran-Contra: Reagan's Scandal and the Unchecked Abuse of Presidential Power* (Lawrence: University Press of Kansas, 2014); Andrew Glass, "Reagan Explains Secret Sale of Arms to Iran, Nov. 13, 1986," Politico, November 13, 2013, https://politi.co/3iCYyDS/.

14. Michael Dobbs, *King Richard: Nixon and Watergate—an American Tragedy* (New York: Knopf, 2021).

15. Edwin E. Moise, *Tonkin Gulf and the Escalation of the Vietnam War* (Chapel Hill: University of North Carolina Press, 1996).

16. Martin J. Sherwin, *Gambling with Armageddon: Nuclear Roulette from Hiroshima to the Cuban Missile Crisis* (New York: Knopf, 2020).

17. E. Bruce Geelhoed, "Dwight D. Eisenhower, the Spy Plane, and the Summit: A Quarter-Century Retrospective," *Presidential Studies Quarterly* 17, no. 1 (1987), 95–106; "U-2 Spy Plane Incident," Dwight D. Eisenhower Presidential Library, https://bit.ly/35gZ6qQ/.

18. Alex Wellerstein, "A 'Purely Military' Target? Truman's Changing Language About Hiroshima," Restricted Data: The Nuclear Secrecy Blog, January 19, 2018, https://bit.ly/2TqsKas/.

19. Mallary A. Silva, "Conspiracy: Did FDR Deceive the American People in a Push for War?," *Inquiries* 2, no. 1 (2010), https://bit.ly/35cRoOL/.

20. James B. Conroy, *Our One Common Country: Abraham Lincoln and the Hampton Roads Peace Conference of 1865* (Guilford, CT: Lyons, 2014).

21. "Jefferson's Secret Message Regarding the Lewis & Clark Expedition: Primary Documents in American History," Library of Congress, https://bit.ly/3iBMpih/.

22. Lydia Saad, "Gallup Election 2020 Coverage," Gallup Blog, October 29, 2020, https://bit.ly/3vsBB9f/.

23. Edward R. Murrow, "Editorial on Joseph McCarthy," *See it Now*, CBS, March 1954, https://bit.ly/3gFtaSl/.

24. Christopher Hitchens, "On Free Speech," speech, 2006, private video on YouTube at https://bit.ly/1drw1G6/, transcription at https://bit.ly/2vPp4AI/.

25. Gordon Pennycook, James Allan Cheyne, Derek J. Koehler, and Jonathan A. Fugelsang, "On the Belief That Beliefs Should Change According to Evidence: Implications for Conspiratorial, Moral, Paranormal, Political, Religious, and Science Beliefs," *Judgment and Decision Making* 15, no. 4 (July 2020), 476–498.

26. Gordon Pennycook and David G. Rand, "Who Falls for Fake News? The Roles of Bullshit Receptivity, Overclaiming, Familiarity, and Analytic Thinking," *Journal of Personality*, originally published online, March 31, 2019, https://bit.ly/3e64QYC/.

27. Steven Pinker, *Rationality: What It Is, Why It Seems Scarce, Why It Matters* (New York: Viking, 2021).

28. Pinker, *Rationality*. See also the many examples documented by the Heterodox Academy (https://heterodoxacademy.org), the Foundation for Individual Rights in Education (https://www.thefire.org), and Quillette magazine (https://quillette.com).

29. Cass R. Sunstein, *Going to Extremes: How Like Minds Unite and Divide* (New York: Oxford University Press, 2009); Cass R. Sunstein and Adrian Vermeule, "Conspiracy Theories: Causes and Cures," *Journal of Political Philosophy* 17, no. 2 (June 2009), 202–227, reprinted in Cass R. Sunstein, *Conspiracy Theories and Other Dangerous Ideas* (New York: Simon & Schuster, 2014).

30. Sunstein, *Conspiracy Theories*, 20.

31. Julia Galef, *The Scout Mindset: Why Some People See Things Clearly and Others Don't* (New York: Portfolio, 2021).

32. Phillip Schmid and Cornelia Betsch, "Effective Strategies for Rebutting Science Denialism in Public Discussions," *Nature Human Behaviour* 3 (June 24, 2019), 931–939.

33. Lee McIntyre, *How to Talk to a Science Denier: Conversations with Flat Earthers, Climate Deniers, and Others Who Defy Reason* (Cambridge, MA: MIT Press, 2021), 69–70.

34. Jonathan Rauch, *The Constitution of Knowledge: A Defense of Truth* (Washington, DC: Brookings Institution Press, 2021), 100–102.

35. Rauch, *Constitution of Knowledge*, 103–107.

36. Michael Shermer, *The Moral Arc: How Science and Reason Lead Humanity Toward Truth, Justice, and Freedom* (New York: Henry Holt, 2015).

37. I defend this position in Michael Shermer, *Giving the Devil His Due: Reflections of a Scientific Humanist* (Cambridge: Cambridge University Press, 2020).

38. Steven Pinker, *Enlightenment Now: The Case for Reason, Science, Humanism, and Progress* (New York: Viking, 2018).

39. Michael Shermer, "The Moral Arc of Reason," speech, delivered at the Reason Rally, Washington, DC, March 24, 2012. You can read the full text at http://bit.ly/2qQl2RY/. For my essay about the rally and my experiences, see Michael Shermer, "Reason Rally Rocks," March 27, 2012, at http://bit.ly/2qetArg/.

40. John Stuart Mill, *On Liberty* (New York: Dover, 2002; originally published London: John W. Parker & Son, 1859), text available at https://bit.ly/2xKHu5u/.

41. Quotation in Hitchens, "On Free Speech."

42. Shermer, *Giving the Devil*, 7–8.

43. You can literally join a truth-based community in the Skeptics Society, which I direct, and subscribe to its magazine, *Skeptic*, which I edit. Go to www.skeptic.com.

Coda. What People Believe About Conspiracy Theories and Why

1. See Skeptic Research Center, https://www.skeptic.com/research-center/; "Meet the Researchers," Skeptic Research Center, https://www.skeptic.com/research-center/meet-the-researchers/; Qualtrics, https://www.qualtrics.com/lp/survey-platform-2/. We also surveyed the survey participants' attitudes about and belief in the paranormal, the results of which will be reported elsewhere.

2. In terms of national averages, the sex ratio is 50.9% female and 49.1% male, so our sample is within acceptable parameters. Educationally, respondents with a high school or equivalent degree and some college/associate's degree are both within acceptable national ranges, whereas our number of individuals with a bachelor's degree (31%) was a little below the national average of 35%, and our percentage of those having graduate degrees (20%) was higher than the 13% national average. For income, 17.9% of those in our sample were at the bottom level ($0 to $24,999), below the national average of 28.22%; 24.56% were in the $25,000 to $49,999 range, comparable to the national average of 23.25%; 21.66% were in the $50,000 to $74,999 range (national average of 18.27%); in the $75,000 to $99,999 range, our participants came in at 14.18%, compared to the national average of 10.93%; in the $100,000 to $149,999 range, our 13.54% figure was higher than the national average of 9.89%; 4.94% of our survey takers were in the $150,000 to $199,999 range (national average of 3.17%),; and 3.22% of our sample earned over $200,000 (national average of 2.67%). Data on national averages are from the US Census Bureau's 2020 data set, available at https://www.census.gov/data.html.

3. To obtain the Skeptic Research Center's raw survey data, send an email request to research@skeptic.com.

4. Popular Mechanics Editors, "The Evidence: Debunking FEMA Camps Myths," *Popular Mechanics*, December 26, 2014, https://bit.ly/3y3v9GJ/.

About the Author

Dr. Michael Shermer (michaelshermer.com) is the founding publisher and editor-in-chief of *Skeptic* magazine—an international science publication in print, online, and available in every bookstore in North America (skeptic.com). From 1992 through 2015, he hosted the Skeptics Society's Distinguished Science Lecture Series at the California Institute of Technology, which evolved into the "Michael Shermer Show" podcast, in which Dr. Shermer converses with leading scientists, scholars, and intellectuals on a wide range of topics (www.skeptic.com/michael-shermer-show/). For 18 years he was the "Skeptic" monthly columnist for *Scientific American*, penning 214 consecutive monthly essays read by millions. His two TED talks from the main TED stage in 2006 and 2010, viewed over 10 million times, were voted in the top 100 of the more than 2,000 TED talks, for which he was invited to deliver an All-Star TED talk in 2014.

Dr. Shermer received his BA in psychology from Pepperdine University, MA in experimental psychology from California State University, Fullerton, and his PhD in the history of science from Claremont Graduate University. He has taught courses in psychology and the history of science at Glendale College, Occidental College, and Claremont Graduate University. Today he is a Presidential Fellow at Chapman University, where he teaches a critical thinking course titled "Skepticism 101: How to Think Like a Scientist," which is also a full-length audio course for The Teaching Company's Great Courses, under the same title. He is also a *New York Times* bestselling author.

Original Trade Books

Heavens on Earth: The Scientific Search for the Afterlife, Immortality, and Utopia (Henry Holt, 2018)

The Moral Arc: How Science Makes Us Better People (Henry Holt, 2015)

The Believing Brain: From Ghosts and Gods to Politics and Conspiracies—how We Construct Beliefs and Reinforce Them as Truths (Henry Holt, 2011)

The Mind of the Market: Compassionate Apes, Competitive Humans, and Other Tales from Evolutionary Economics (Times Books / Henry Holt, 2008)

Why Darwin Matters: The Case against Intelligent Design (Times Books, 2006)

The Science of Good and Evil: Why People Cheat, Gossip, Care, Share, and Follow the Golden Rule (Times Books, 2004)

How We Believe: The Search for God in an Age of Science (W. H. Freeman, 2000)

Why People Believe Weird Things (W. H. Freeman, 1997; St. Martin's Griffin, revised and expanded edition, 2002)

University Press Books

Giving the Devil His Due: Reflections of a Scientific Humanist (Cambridge University Press, 2020)

Denying History: Who Says the Holocaust Never Happened and Why Do They Say It? (with Alex Grobman, University of California Press, 2000)

In Darwin's Shadow: The Life and Science of Alfred Russel Wallace (Oxford University Press, 2002)

Essay Collections

Skeptic: Viewing the World with a Rational Eye (Henry Holt, 2016)

Science Friction: Where the Known Meets the Unknown (Henry Holt, 2005)

The Borderlands of Science: Where Sense Meets Nonsense (Oxford University Press, 2001)